PLANNING PRIMARY ENGLISH

Kirstie Hewett

PLANNING PRIMARY ENGLISH

HOW TO DESIGN AND TEACH BRILLIANT LESSONS

S Sage

S Sage

1 Oliver's Yard
55 City Road
London EC1Y 1SP

2455 Teller Road
Thousand Oaks
California 91320

Unit No 323-333, Third Floor, F-Block
International Trade Tower
Nehru Place, New Delhi 110 019

8 Marina View Suite 43-053
Asia Square Tower 1
Singapore 018960

Library of Congress Control Number: 2023948209

British Library Cataloguing in Publication data

A catalogue record for this book is available from the British Library

Editor: James Clark
Assistant editor: Esosa Otabor
Production editor: Martin Fox
Marketing manager: Lorna Patkai
Cover design: Sheila Tong
Typeset by: TNQ Tech Pvt. Ltd.
Printed in the UK

ISBN 978-1-5296-2056-6
ISBN 978-1-5296-2055-9 (pbk)

CONTENTS

ABOUT THE AUTHOR

Kirstie Hewett is a school improvement specialist for the University of Chichester Academy Trust and a Senior Lecturer in Initial Teacher Education at the University of Chichester, specialising in the teaching of English across the primary age phase. Prior to this, she spent twenty years working in a number of roles in primary schools, including class teacher, deputy head teacher and SENDCo. She is a Fellow of the Higher Education Academy, Chair of the English Association's Primary and Early Years Committee and supports the editorial board of the UKLA & EA's English 4-11 magazine. She is currently working with teachers from the University of Chichester Academy Trust to develop their professional practice with a specific focus on oracy, and has a particular interest in the use of visual research methods within qualitative and mixed-method research as part of her doctoral studies.

ACKNOWLEDGEMENTS

Thank you to the University of Chichester's wonderful Primary Education community – I am lucky to work with so many generous, passionate and talented staff and student teachers from whom I continue to learn so much.

1

An Introduction to Lesson Planning

Chapter Objectives

This chapter will:

- Consider why lesson planning matters.
- Explore the key elements that make up a typical lesson plan.
- Summarise the thinking of some key researchers.

Introduction

This book offers a starting point for primary school teachers in planning lessons for the English curriculum. It is primarily aimed at initial teacher education students or early career teachers and shows how individual lessons that are underpinned by research into effective teaching, and in particular the effective teaching of English, can be planned for spoken language, reading and writing.

As observed by Coe et al. (2020) and others, teaching is a complex business. It requires the simultaneous orchestration of a number of skills which are underpinned by a deep, secure and flexible knowledge of effective learning and teaching strategies (pedagogy), of the subject and content being taught, and of each individual learner and the context in which they are learning at any given moment in time. Alexander notes that 'each classroom's dynamics, and each of its encounters between teachers and students, is unique' (2020, p. 133). Teaching is therefore unpredictable; a lesson that worked brilliantly once has no guarantee of working brilliantly again (even if it were possible to teach it in exactly the same way as you did before). For many reasons, learners rarely all respond as planned or expected. It is, therefore, extremely difficult to provide a lesson plan with any guarantee that it will indisputably result in an excellent lesson for all learners from all perspectives.

However, a strong lesson plan based on effective pedagogy and strong subject knowledge provides an excellent starting point. When these elements underpin the understanding and design of a lesson, the teacher is best placed to be able to focus on the learners' responses, adapting the learning and teaching to support emerging learning needs.

As Coe et al. state,

> generic principles are useful and important (and supported by evidence), partly because great teachers need to understand the principles of how and why different techniques are effective and when to deploy them. Nevertheless, it is important to remember that most of these elements will look very different in different classrooms, and their relative importance will also vary. (2020, p.15)

Lesson planning requires an investment of time and energy but, as Heathcote notes, it is often one of the 'really joyful and creative aspects of teaching' (2023, p. 48). At its heart, effective lesson planning is an imaginative and inventive process which enables you to think through what the children really need to learn next and design discussions and learning experiences that hook them in and motivate them to keep going with the sometimes messy business of learning so that they can achieve their learning goals. In the context of education, creativity is defined as '...imaginative activity fashioned so as to produce outcomes that are both original and of value' (National Advisory Committee on Creative and Cultural Education, 1999, p. 29). To realise the full potential of the creative element of lesson planning, you will need to adapt the plans in this book so that they become original and of value in the context in which you plan to implement them.

Pedagogy and Repertoire

This book aims to support you in developing an effective pedagogy for teaching primary English. Pollard et al. (2018) conceptualise pedagogy as the skilful interplay between a teacher's knowledge and understanding of teaching, and how they respond to moments in the classroom as the learning unfolds. They suggest that pedagogy is made of three key components:

- Teachers' craft knowledge encompasses the repertoire of approaches, strategies and practices from which they draw to inform their teaching.
- Teaching as an art involves the in-the-moment decisions that teachers make in response as the learning unfolds in a lesson.
- Teaching as a science concerns the teacher's understanding of and engagement with insights from research, reflection and evaluation.

Each of these components has the potential to expand throughout a teacher's professional career as they engage with professional development and in their own evaluations and reflections on their day-to-day teaching. Each chapter aims to develop your understanding of the craft, art and science of teaching primary English, identifying approaches, strategies and practices which are effective in supporting learners, highlighting key principles to inform in-the-moment decisions and drawing on insights gathered from credible research and theory about teaching primary English.

The idea of repertoire is also highlighted by Alexander (2020) who is best known for his work on dialogic talk in the classroom. Dialogic talk is a term used to describe the most effective way in which talk is used by teacher and learners in the classroom to maximise learning. Throughout this book, you will see that teacher and learner talk are at the heart of each lesson, with each chapter exploring what classroom talk could look like in each aspect of the primary English classroom. This enables the planning of key discussions and provides a focus for teachers' formative assessment, some of which will inevitably be unplanned in response to the learning as it unfolds.

This book supports lesson planning by connecting the principles of effective practice in the teaching of primary English with the practical concerns of planning individual lessons. As noted by Alexander (2020), the idea that there is a single formula for effective or 'best practice' is deeply flawed; teaching is far too complex for that. However, illuminating how key theory and research-informed evidence can inform the design of focused and engaging lessons across the primary English curriculum provides a really useful starting point.

Each chapter takes an aspect of the primary English curriculum and connects it to key theories and evidence that underpin effective practice. Some principles relate to such practice more generally, giving suggestions for activities, experiences and sessions which may be shorter than a typical lesson, while others inform the planning of more detailed lessons. In each case, underpinning principles are applied and explained, with clear guidance to show how these can be enacted in the classroom. Each activity, idea or fully developed plan can only be a starting point which must be adapted creatively to best suit a specific context. The accompanying explanations and highlighted principles of effective practice will support student and early career teachers in building their knowledge of effective pedagogy and subject in teaching primary English. After the lesson has taken place, investing time in reflecting on its impact on the learning that actually took place will further develop these crucial aspects of practice.

Introduction to Planning

While good planning does not on its own guarantee good teaching, it is widely recognised as an essential contributor to effective learning and teaching (Hawkins, 2016; Kyriacou, 2018; Wilkinson & Earle, 2022). Good planning is a key element of professional practice which offers teachers and pupils clear direction and purpose; without this, a lesson may well result in frustration for pupils or involve them in completing tasks rather than engaging in meaningful learning (Grigg, 2014).

Many schools plan at three levels: long-term, medium-term and short-term. The purpose of long-term planning is usually to identify the progression of learning for pupils across the school in relation to national requirements. This may well outline themes or topics which allow for cross-curricular learning, but this will depend on the school's approach and beliefs about effective learning. Medium-term planning typically outlines what each year group will learn in a little more depth. Short-term planning provides further detail, usually presenting the learning and teaching to be developed over a week, day or lesson. All three levels of planning can look quite different in different schools, so it is worth talking to your class teacher and/or mentor about how your school has mapped out their curriculum and how teachers use these three levels of planning to underpin the teaching and learning in their classrooms.

Many schools share long- and/or medium-term plans on their websites. Other examples can be found in books which focus on the teaching of primary English such as Bearne and Reedy's *Teaching Primary English: Subject Knowledge and Classroom Practice* (2017) and Clements and Tobin's *Understanding and Teaching Primary English: Theory into Practice* (2021). You might also find it useful to look at some of the sample units of work shared by organisations which focus specifically on the teaching of English such as the Centre for Literacy in Primary Education (CLPE) at https://clpe.org.uk/ and Just Imagine at https://www.takeonebook.org/. Each of the sources suggested is produced by specialists in primary English teaching. They demonstrate how a sequence of learning can be developed effectively over several weeks, connecting speaking, listening, reading and writing. These sources also offer a wealth of ideas for developing your own plans. However, when starting out in teaching, you are typically asked to start by working within a school's existing long- and medium-term level planning to plan and teach individual lessons in the short term, rather than jumping straight into the pressure of planning a full sequence of learning. This book aims to support you in planning these individual lessons across the primary English curriculum.

Producing detailed lesson plans is a significant factor in teacher workload identified by the Department for Education (2016). However, to support you in the development of the crucial skill of short-term planning, most student teachers are required to write lesson plans and are often given additional time and support when on school placements, for example, through a greater proportion of planning, preparation and assessment or non-contact time and through collaboration with other colleagues. Burden and Byrd (2003) identify the goal of lesson planning as to secure pupil learning; therefore, the planning process should help the teacher to design and organise learning and teaching activities which enable that learning to occur.

There are many ingredients in a good lesson, and it can be challenging to balance and manage them effectively. Creating a plan for how you think the lesson should unfold before you come to teach it will allow you to focus on the actual teaching and learning once the lesson is underway. Creating a lesson plan can be a time-consuming business, particularly when it is new to you. In the initial stages of any school experience placement, you are likely to be asked to create a plan for any lesson that you will teach, and going through this process, even if it can feel heavy going at times, will give you invaluable experience, allowing you to internalise the process which will become much more efficient in time. When creating a short-term plan, you may well be asked to use a particular lesson planning proforma by either your initial teacher education provider or your school. The exact layout may differ slightly but there will be a number of similarities which should reflect the components of effective lesson planning discussed in this book.

Lesson plans often require some simple information which relates to the logistics of the lesson such as date, time, number of pupils and year group. There may also be a space to prompt you to write a target for yourself. Effective teaching requires the co-ordination of a complex set of skills, which are impossible to master all at once, so it is often helpful to focus on only one or two skills for yourself per lesson. Suitable targets may well arise from discussions with your school-based mentor or from your reflections on your teaching. When including targets for yourself, ensure that they are expressed positively and are clear and easy to reflect on, for example, 'I will wait for 6–10 seconds after asking an open question to give the children time to process and think of an answer'.

You may also be prompted to consider how your lesson fits within the larger sequences of learning for your pupils; this is really helpful in securing continuity and progression within the curriculum. Identifying prior learning will help you establish how your lesson will build on what the children know and can do. Identifying clear learning objectives for the lessons you are planning will help ensure that lesson time is used purposefully. Considering what learning is likely to happen next will help demonstrate how learning can be developed more fully.

It is helpful to think about how you intend to monitor and assess the learning in advance, linking this explicitly to the learning objective(s) of the lesson, so that you are absolutely clear about what you want the children to know or be able to do and understand exactly how you will be able to check that the learning is on track as it unfolds. You may be expected to identify clear success criteria and to write the key questions and/or tasks which you will use to gauge the impact of the lesson. There may also be space on your lesson plan proforma for you to reflect once the lesson has taken place.

A lesson plan proforma should also allow you plenty of space to outline the lesson itself, noting how you intend to ensure your teaching is responsive to the learners' needs as they unfold in the lesson, and for you to list any resources to be used.

The Key Elements of Effective Lesson Plans

There are three key actions which underpin effective lesson planning (Kyriacou, 2018; Stronge, 2018). These are:

1   Deciding on the learning aim(s) for the lesson.
2   Deciding how to design the learning experiences that will most effectively support pupil progress in relation to the learning objective.
3   Deciding how the pupils' learning will be monitored and evaluated during and after the lesson.

Deciding on the Learning Aim(s) of the Lesson

The first thing you need to do when planning a lesson or learning experience is to ensure that you are clear about what it is you want the children to learn. Deciding on one or more learning aim(s) of the lesson, sometimes referred to as the learning intention(s), objective(s) or focus, is crucial to supporting children to make good progress. Although pupil progress is considered over time rather than in an individual lesson, it is vital that each lesson makes a valuable contribution to the children's progress, maximising the use of precious learning time so that learning develops in a purposeful way enabling pupils to encounter new knowledge and ideas, practise new skills and consolidate their understanding so it is secure.

In the early stages of your training and/or school placement, it is likely that your class teacher will decide on the learning objective for a lesson, probably from the school's long- and medium-term plans, asking you to devise a lesson which enables the pupils to achieve this. Learning typically unfolds through a sequence of lessons, so thinking about what comes before and what comes after is important, even if you are not yet teaching the whole sequence of learning. The learning objective for your lesson should fit well into the sequence of learning overall.

It is important to make sure that the learning objective you choose is clear and focused. This helps both teacher and learners to focus on what really matters in this part of the learning sequence, avoiding unnecessary distractions and reducing the possibility of missing opportunities to develop key knowledge, skills or understanding, thus supporting pupils to make good progress.

When you've chosen the right learning objective(s) that will ensure that both you and your pupils are absolutely clear about what they will learn, you then need to identify exactly what your pupils will need to do to achieve this. This should show you what the success criteria need to be for your lesson and will really help both you and your pupils to monitor their learning.

Research Focus: Shirley Clarke

Shirley Clarke has written extensively on both learning objectives and success criteria, often considering the teaching and learning of writing in particular depth. In terms of learning objectives, she differentiates between two types of skill: closed skills which are either right or wrong (e.g., 'to be able to punctuate direct speech accurately'), and open skills which involve a continuum of achievement and quality (e.g., 'to use adjectives effectively'). Skills are usually based on knowledge; a learner is only able to punctuate direct speech accurately if they first know what is meant by the term 'direct speech'.

Clarke (2014) highlights the importance of identifying learning objectives which are appropriate and clear. Separating a learning objective from the context in which it is to be set in any one lesson enables children to see much more easily that a piece of knowledge or skill can be applied in a number of different contexts. For example, a contextualised learning objective such as 'to write a persuasive leaflet on climate change' does not really help the children to see that the skill of being able to write persuasively can be applied in many different contexts across the curriculum, for example, through letters, leaflets, adverts, written arguments and speeches. Clarke argues that ensuring all lessons have a clear and context-free learning objective allows teachers to design purposeful and relevant learning activities, to give explicit and focused feedback, and enables children to see more easily how their learning can be transferred and applied within different contexts.

Clarke also considers that clearly phrased success criteria provide a framework for formative dialogue between pupils and teachers, enabling them to understand the steps involved in achieving a closed learning objective or the possible ingredients needed to achieve an open learning objective. These are key to supporting both pupils and teachers in identifying where success has been achieved and where pupils might need further support, as well as in discussing strategies for improvement. One example of success criteria which supports pupils to achieve the objective 'to be able to punctuate direct speech accurately' might look something like this:

- Begin a new line each time a different person speaks.
- Use a capital letter at the start of the first word the speaker says each time.
- Put inverted commas around the words the speaker says.
- Make sure any punctuation needed for the end of the speaker's words go inside the inverted commas.

Clarke promotes the use of success criteria which are constructed with the pupils as this can support independence and ownership of learning. You can find a number of strategies for the co-construction of success criteria in her book *Outstanding Formative Assessment: Culture and Practice* (2014).

Activity   Identifying Learning Objectives

The National Curriculum in England: English Programmes of Study for Key Stage 1 and Key Stage 2 specifies what pupils should be taught to do in each year group in Key Stage 1 and Key Stage 2. These are presented as lists of requirements within the different strands of the English curriculum. However, many of these requirements don't specifically use the terms 'knowledge', 'concepts', 'skills' or 'application' and are quite broad, so teachers will need to be able to break them down into smaller parts to teach them effectively.

For example, in Year 1, there is a statutory requirement for reading which states that 'pupils should be taught to respond speedily with the correct sound to graphemes (letters or groups of letters) for all 40+ phonemes, including, where applicable, alternative sounds for graphemes' (DfE, 2013, p. 20).

To achieve this, pupils must know at least one sound to grapheme correspondence for each of the 40+ phonemes, so the teacher needs to break this down into a number of much smaller objectives which will focus on teaching one at a time.

To develop knowledge of all 40+ phonemes, the children will also need to develop the understanding that there is a relationship between each of the sound to symbol correspondences that form the alphabetic code.

The skill of identifying the correct correspondence and articulating the relevant sound accurately will build the automaticity needed for a speedy response, and teachers can assess the children's ability to apply this in a meaningful and purposeful context when they hear the children read words and sentences.

Choose a year group and look at the requirements listed. Try to identify what knowledge, concepts and skills the ability to demonstrate each requirement is built on, and consider what smaller parts it is made from. How might children demonstrate that they have learned these parts securely through relevant and meaningful application tasks?

Designing the Learning Experiences That Support Pupil Progress

The second set of decisions that a teacher must make concerns the design of learning experiences that will most effectively support pupil progress in relation to the learning objective. This will be the biggest part of your plan as you will decide what the teaching and learning will look like, choosing appropriate teaching strategies and designing effective learning opportunities as well as deciding how to sequence the different elements of the lesson so that it unfolds logically. In Chapter 2, we will consider this in more depth specifically within the context of the primary English curriculum building upon the key ideas outlined here that are typically applicable to all lesson plans.

When designing the learning for an individual lesson, it can be very easy to become distracted by what the children might do in the form of tasks and activities. However, it is important to stay focused on the learning objective(s) identified; Slavin et al. (2003) refer to this as intentionality; intentional teachers constantly think about the outcomes they want their children to achieve and how each decision they make moves children towards these outcomes. Once the learning objective has been decided, your lesson plan really centres on what you and your pupils will do in order to achieve it within the time frame of the lesson. It is important to plan your use of time carefully – if the learning objective seems unachievable within the time frame of the lesson, then revisit it and consider whether it could be broken down further.

Hattie suggests that 'any lesson planning must… begin with a deep understanding of what each student already knows and can do' (2012, p. 42), so it is essential to begin any lesson plan with a consideration of the pupils' starting points. Asking yourself what they already know and are able to do will inform your decisions about how to build on this and enable you to connect this lesson to any key prior learning. Of course, it is highly likely that any class of pupils will have a range of different starting points; part of the skill of being a teacher is learning how to harness these in order to establish key connections and provide continuity and progression in learning so that all pupils make good progress. Talk to the class teacher to establish the pupils' starting points. You might also be able to identify these through discussions with pupils and by looking through their written work.

When considering what you as the teacher will do, there are a number of key teaching strategies that you might find useful to consider, for example, modelling, demonstration, explanation and questioning. You will need to plan what the pupils will do through practice activities that will enable them to make progress in acquiring the knowledge, understanding and/or skills that you have identified as learning objective(s), and you could choose to make use of strategies that support collaboration between learners, such as the use of talk partners. Each of these elements must be considered and then sequenced and paced so that they flow logically and keep the learning momentum high. You may choose to plan one longer cycle of learning which starts with some clear instruction from the teacher, followed by an extended period in which pupils will work collaboratively or independently before drawing the learning together, or you may choose to chunk the learning into smaller parts, giving some input followed by pupil practice, reviewing and moving on, perhaps repeating this cycle two or three times (or more!) within a lesson. Your choices will of course be determined by your learning objective(s). It is worth thinking about any routines already in place in the classroom as these can be really effective in creating smooth transitions which support the focus on learning. For example, when teaching phonics or reading fluency, teachers may cup a hand behind their ear to signal to the children that they need to repeat what they heard, or there may be particular resources which the pupils automatically get ready or share round. Of course, you may also want to introduce new routines of your own. We will consider each of these elements in more depth within the context of the different strands of the primary English curriculum in the relevant chapters in this book.

A further lesson planning principle that must be considered is how the lesson can be designed in such a way that all children can be supported to make good progress. As well as coming to your lesson with different levels of prior knowledge and understanding, pupils are likely to progress through the learning at different rates and planning for this in advance will help the lesson to run smoothly. Current thinking in education focuses on adaptive or responsive teaching in which whole-class learning is carefully structured so that potential barriers are anticipated, and effective scaffolding is planned to enable all learners to achieve with teachers providing focused support or challenge at the point of learning (Deunk et al., 2018; Education Endowment Foundation, 2018). An example of this is the use of carefully targeted teaching which breaks down or reinforces knowledge, understanding or skills (Ofsted, 2022), providing additional practice to enable pupils to keep up. This links closely to the use of formative assessment strategies which are discussed a little later in this chapter and which will enable you to check in on the children's learning and intervene, if necessary.

As part of your lesson planning process, you will also want to identify any key vocabulary that will be used in the lesson; if there are keywords that the pupils don't understand then they are likely to find the learning process unnecessarily challenging. Within the primary English curriculum, you may sometimes teach longer sessions which specifically focus on widening children's vocabularies but in all lessons, there will be some keywords which are needed as part of the learning and that you will want to highlight for the pupils.

Another key part of the lesson planning process involves the identification of any resources that are needed to support your teaching and the children's learning. For example, you might want to include the use of props or objects to stimulate thinking or aid verbal or written descriptions, or introduce word mats, dictionaries or word books such as *Descriptosaurus: Supporting Creative Writing for Ages 8–14* (Wilcox, 2017) to support vocabulary use and spelling. To provoke curiosity and conversation, you might make use of key questions or statements for the children to discuss. You may want to make use of large sheets of paper for creating models of writing for or with the children or to support them in writing collaboratively. Adults who are employed by the school, such as teaching assistants, are expensive resources for learning who have the potential to make a significant and positive impact. Therefore, it is important that they have a clear focus and know how best to scaffold pupils' learning in the context of your lesson so ensure that you set aside time to talk to them in advance of the lesson.

Another principle that should underpin your choices concerns children's engagement and motivation. These will be well-supported by the use of authentic and purposeful contexts which are described more fully in Chapter 2, but for now, you will want to begin to consider how to choose teaching strategies that engage your pupils. Tomlinson and McTighe (2019) suggest that this can be partly achieved through the use of a variety of teaching strategies which result in lessons and tasks which are more engaging. You may also wish to consider Keller's (2009) ARCS model of motivation which involves four key elements that support high levels of interest: attention, relevance, confidence and satisfaction (ARCS). Think about how you will capture the children's attention at the start of the lesson, for example, through the use of a great hook such as a stimulating question, a scenario, an object, an image or a film clip. How will you use a range of strategies to maintain this attention throughout the lesson? How will you make sure that the pupils see the point of your lesson, and make use of language and contexts that they can connect to, and that emphasise the relevance of the learning? How will you ensure that the learning is pitched just right so that it is not so hard that it destroys their confidence but is sufficiently challenging to promote high expectations and achievement for all? How will you use formative assessment to check that your pitch is accurate and how will you sequence the learning carefully so that they can achieve? How will you ensure that all pupils feel a sense of achievement at the end of your lesson?

Activity   Reflecting on Your Experiences

When planning lessons, there are many decisions a teacher has to make, and it can be helpful to start with a list of possibilities. Think about the English teaching you have observed or participated in and see how many good ideas you can list under the following headings:

- Lesson starters
- Resources
- Teaching strategies
- Practice tasks
- Ways in which the teacher responded to the children's learning.

You could also talk to your class teacher, mentor, other staff such as support staff and pupils to find out their perceptions to see if you can add more to your list. Use this list as a resource to help you when planning.

Deciding How the Pupils' Learning Will Be Monitored and Evaluated During and After the Lesson

Monitoring and evaluating the lesson is a key part of any lesson. Hattie (2012) suggests that a lesson only ends when teachers seek to gather and analyse the impact of the intended and actual learning on the pupils in relation to the learning objective(s) from their pupils' perspectives. You might plan to achieve this goal through the use of plenaries.

Plenaries

The word plenary really just means a meeting at which all the members of a group are present. Its purpose in a learning context is to bring the class together, typically to reinforce some key learning or to share the learning that has taken place. Beadle (2013) suggests that when plenaries are focused on assessment, consolidating or evaluating learning, or making connections to subsequent learning and the wider world, and give pupils opportunities to articulate what they have learned, they play a vital role in supporting learning. This view is supported by Carroll and Alexander who claim that 'plenaries provide the ultimate opportunity for pupils to recognise their own next steps. … [they are] an essential part of reflective learning for progression' (2016, p. 83).

Plenaries can be planned in advance, with the teacher identifying specific moments where it is likely to be useful to draw everyone together, or unplanned as a response to the unfolding learning. Unplanned plenaries are sometimes referred to as mini plenaries which are defined by Carroll and Alexander as

> reflective pit-stops which should be focused on the learning objective, offering opportunities for pupils to review their learning and make improvements which help to ensure that they are on the track to success, allowing the teacher (and learner) to reflect, adapt and ensure progression. (2016, p. 83)

A mini plenary may take the form of some guided peer or self-review which allows the pupils to reflect on their learning before continuing with their work with renewed focus, understanding or motivation. Ideas for the focus of plenaries and mini plenaries will be considered within the various contexts of the primary English curriculum presented in subsequent chapters.

Another way of deciding how the pupils' learning will be monitored and evaluated during and after the lesson is through the use of formative assessment, also known as assessment for learning or AfL. The purpose of formative assessment is to elicit evidence of learning that is used to inform the next steps of a teacher's planning. Florez and Sammons (2013) note that formative assessment is a key part of effective high-quality planning and is central to effective classroom practice. It has the potential to foster motivation and aims to help learners know how to improve their own learning in relation to the learning objective(s) and success criteria of the lesson.

Effective teachers engage in formative assessment throughout the teaching and learning process, monitoring the learning and identifying any gaps or misconceptions which then inform the teacher's next steps. It can also be used effectively to deepen the knowledge and understanding of pupils who are achieving well within the lesson (Ofsted, 2014). These assessments are not necessarily recorded anywhere as the purpose is to inform the teaching rather than to produce data, but it may be possible to see that effective assessment for learning took place when looking at the trajectory of progress shown in a child's written work or talking to them about their learning. It may also be evident from a teacher's lesson plans or annotations which take account of and are built on the information gathered about their learners in a previous lesson.

To be sure where learners are in their levels of understanding, the teacher needs to plan opportunities to reveal the pupils' thinking so that gaps and misconceptions can be identified, for example, through the use of low-stakes quizzes, questions and focused tasks which demonstrate knowledge, understanding or skills (Cox, 2021). Peer and self-assessment can also be useful strategies that support learners to develop autonomy and deepen understanding of the learning objective(s) and success criteria, and their strengths and areas for development in relation to these thus determining the next steps a learner and teacher should take. The above strategies give useful feedback to the teacher about how the learning is progressing. Hattie (2012) identifies the gathering of such feedback as crucial to becoming an effective teacher.

Once teachers have identified that one or more pupils are not fully on track to achieve the learning objectives(s) for the lesson, they can decide how to intervene. Having gathered this feedback *from* the learners, the teacher may then choose to give feedback *to* the learners. Recent thinking on feedback has expanded the notion of feedback from talking to learners about their work, framing feedback as:

> an instructional scaffold that goes beyond written or verbal comments. Formative feedback can involve *any* verbal exchange (conversation, dialogue, discussion, such as when a teacher responds to a student's incorrect answer with a question) and any instruction or move (e.g. modelling, demonstration). (Ruiz-Primo & Brookhart, 2017, p. 16; emphasis added)

Giving Verbal Feedback to Pupils

Giving high-quality feedback that propels learning forwards is a key part of formative assessment, identified by Hattie (2008) as one of the most powerful influences on learning and widely recognised as a fundamental part of any high-quality teaching. Wiggins (2010) notes that you can't learn without feedback, as it is not teaching that causes learning, but the attempts by the learner to perform that enable learning to happen. This is dependent upon the quality of the feedback and opportunities to respond to it.

In recent years, schools have developed the role of verbal, rather than written, feedback in particular. The advantages of verbal feedback are that it can be given at the point of teaching and thus instantly impact progress.

A review of evidence conducted by the Education Endowment Foundation (EEF) in 2021 concluded that high-quality feedback supports pupil progress by building learning and addressing misunderstandings, thereby closing the gap between where a pupil is and where the teacher wants them to be. However, giving feedback can be a time-consuming process and if it is not high-quality, it can actually harm progress, so any investment made into feedback must be considered carefully. Feedback which focuses negatively on the learners themselves, for example, 'you haven't tried hard enough' has the potential to lead to demotivation and distracts the conversation from the necessary learning focus. Vague comments or general praise are also unhelpful, for example, 'You always write excellent stories' or 'Well done, good work' may temporarily boost a child's self-esteem but don't actually offer them any useful information about how to improve and may in the longer term reduce their motivation (Kluger & DeNisi,

1996). The EEF (2021) suggest that careful thought should be given to how pupils receive feedback as it impacts pupil motivation, self-confidence and teacher–pupil relationships.

Summaries of research into effective feedback demonstrate that feedback must clearly relate to the goal(s) of the lesson, be specific and clear, and be given in a timely way that is useful to the learner. Time must be given for the learner to act on the feedback as soon as possible rather than waiting to do it in their next piece of work. This allows both pupil and teacher to see that the pupil has fully understood the feedback and is more likely to be applied in subsequent work. Black and Wiliam (1998) suggest that feedback can be directive or facilitative. Directive feedback directs the learner clearly to what needs to be changed, for example, 'use an expanded noun phrase to add more detail to your description of the pond so the reader can picture it'. The learner might benefit most from even more directive feedback, for example, 'add an adjective before the word "pond" so that the reader can really picture it'. This may be most helpful when pupils need explicit guidance to show them where they have gone wrong and how to put it right, or in the case of the examples given in this paragraph, how to develop their writing so that it achieves its purpose of being descriptive. Facilitative feedback provides comments and suggestions that help to guide the learner to make their own revisions; this can be helpful in promoting children's independence and metacognitive skills, for example, 'how could you use some expanded noun phrases so that the reader can really imagine what the park looks like?'. This encourages the pupil to revisit their work from a reader's perspective and make changes as and where they think would be best. Therefore, such facilitative feedback may be more appropriate for learners who are confident with key terms and concepts but have simply forgotten to include particular things or need to be encouraged to push themselves further.

Theory Focus: Hattie and Timperley on Feedback

Hattie and Timperley (2007) suggest that for feedback to be effective, it should answer one of three questions for the learner:

1   Where am I going?
2   How am I going?
3   Where to next?

Where Am I Going?

It may seem strange that this question is part of effective feedback, but it is crucial to set the context for learning and thus prepare the ground for meaningful feedback. The teacher sets up the lesson by identifying and sharing a key learning objective and then providing some teaching that shows the children how this can be achieved. High-quality initial instruction will reduce the work that feedback needs to do; formative assessment strategies are required to set learning intentions (which feedback will aim towards) and to assess learning gaps (which feedback will address) (Cox, 2021).

How Am I Going?

This question is most relevant when pupils are engaged in practice tasks and assignments. Feedback given by the teacher, as they are circulating the classroom and reviewing the pupils' efforts, should be aimed at helping the children to see to what extent they are on track in relation to the objectives and success criteria established earlier in the lesson or sequence of learning. The teacher may also set up purposeful peer- or self-assessment opportunities where pupils themselves review and reflect on their work, identifying where they are doing well and any parts where they are not yet successful.

Where to Next?

To answer the final question, the feedback given should inform the learner clearly of where the learner needs to put their attention and energies next so as to maintain progress and motivation.

Hattie and Timperley also assert that feedback is most powerful when it engages the learner in understanding not just the task at hand but the process of learning more widely. For example, if pupils are writing a story, the teacher might notice that their writing would be improved if they added more description to some key parts of their story and so give them feedback such as 'add some more description to the opening of your story'. This can help pupils to make improvements to their work on this occasion, but they may find it hard to transfer learning to other tasks and contexts. However, giving feedback that supports children's understanding of the process of story writing and what makes a good story in general can support the learner in transferring such key principles more easily, for example, by saying 'great stories usually have lots of detail to help the reader imagine they are really there; re-read your setting description and see if there are any more details you could add in'. Here, the feedback quite clearly makes links to story writing in general and so enables the learner to understand the process at a deeper level.

Activity   Making Sure Your Feedback is High-Quality

Look at the examples of feedback and consider whether they fit the criteria for effective feedback. If not, see if you can rewrite them so that they are clearer, more specific and answer one or more of Hattie and Timperley's three questions.

- You've got some direct speech here showing the characters' thoughts. Excellent.
- Try using a simile to describe your character. Maybe 'He ate his food like a pig' or 'He gulped down food like a greedy pelican'.
- That's a great opening. You need to look back at where you've used speech and make sure your punctuation is correct.

(Continued)

- You've used adjectives really well to create a great character. How could you use them to make your story setting better?
- Your writing has definitely improved.
- Use a simile to compare him with something.
- You maintained eye contact throughout your entire speech; now you might work on your expression.

Now consider whether each piece of feedback is directive or facilitative. What impact might this have on the learner? How could you change facilitative feedback so that it is more directive and vice versa?

Feedback as Instructions or Moves

Giving one-to-one high-quality verbal feedback at the point of teaching is a crucial part of effective teaching which should be embedded into every teacher's practice. However, there are times when the teacher might identify that several children are struggling with the same thing and at that point, continuing to give one-to-one feedback is inefficient as the teacher moves between children and gives them largely identical guidance. Instead, the teacher may decide to make a different move that involves either the whole class or a number of pupils who have been identified as struggling. Fletcher Wood's *Responsive Teaching* (2018) identifies four key moves that a teacher might choose to utilize as a response to pupil learning instead of giving one-to-one feedback. These are: to reteach using fresh examples; to revisit the goals of the lesson, for example, by directing the children to go back to any models or checklists which have already been provided; to re-model the process; and to give some additional practice/checking. You can find out more about these in his book, or in this blog post: https://improvingteaching.co.uk/2017/06/18/guiding-student-improvement-without-individual-feedback/. It is well worth finding out more about these ideas and thinking about how to adopt them into your own practice in order to ensure that learning time is used as efficiently as possible.

Summary

This chapter has identified high-quality planning as the foundation of a good lesson and has introduced the key elements of an effective lesson plan. This included the need for teachers to begin planning by considering their choice of learning objective(s) and success criteria and by establishing the children's prior learning and starting points. The need to decide on relevant teaching and learning strategies and activities which engage pupils, to plan for responsive or adaptive teaching, to plan resources and identify key vocabulary, and to plan for formative assessment including effective feedback has also been explored.

Further Reading

1   To see examples of planning a longer sequence of learning for the English curriculum, see
    - James Clements and Mat Tobin's *Understanding and Teaching Primary English: Theory into Practice*, published by SAGE.
    - Eve Bearne and David Reedy's *Teaching Primary English: Subject Knowledge and Classroom Practice*, published by Routledge.
2   To read more about formative assessment, including writing clear learning objectives, read Shirley Clarke's *A Little Guide for Teachers: Formative Assessment*, published by Corwin.
3   To read more about giving effective feedback, read: Hattie, J., & Timperley, H. (2007). The power of feedback. *Review of Educational Research, 77*(1), 81–112. https://www.jstor.org/stable/pdf/4624888.pdf?refreqid=excelsior%3Ac0165edfaeb8a66a3141385124211ea2&ab_segments=&origin=&initiator=&acceptTC=1

References

Alexander, R. (2020). *A dialogic teaching companion*. Routledge.

Beadle, P. (2013). *The book of plenary – Here endeth the lesson*. Independent Thinking Press.

Bearne, E., & Reedy, D. (2017). *Teaching primary English: Subject knowledge and classroom practice*. Routledge.

Black, P., & Wiliam, D. (1998). Assessment and classroom learning. *Assessment in Education: Principles, Policy & Practice, 5*(1), 7–74.

Burden, P., & Byrd, D. (2003). *Methods for effective teaching* (3rd ed.). Pearson Education Ltd.

Carroll, J., & Alexander, G. (2016). *The Teachers' Standards in primary schools: Understanding and evidencing effective practice*. SAGE.

Clarke, S. (2014). *Outstanding formative assessment: Culture and practice*. Hodder Education Ltd.

Clements, J., & Tobin, M. (2021). *Understanding and teaching primary English: Theory into practice*. SAGE.

Coe, R., Rauch, C., Kime, S., & Singleton, D. (2020) *Great teaching toolkit: Evidence review. Evidence based education, in partnership with Cambridge Assessment International Education*. https://greatteaching.com. Accessed on December 9, 2023.

Cox, S. (2021). *Five ways to use diagnostic assessment in the mathematics classroom*. https://educationendowmentfoundation.org.uk/news/eef-blog-five-ways-to-use-diagnostic-assessment-in-the-mathematics-classroom. Accessed on March 14, 2023.

Deunk, M., Jacobse, A., de Boer, H., Doolaard, S., & Bosker, R. (2018). Effective differentiation practices: A systematic review and meta-analysis of studies on the cognitive effects of differentiation practices in primary education. *Educational Research Review, 24*, 31–54.

Department For Education. (2013). *The National Curriculum for England: Key stages 1 and 2 framework document*. Crown Publishing.

DfE. (2016). *Reducing teacher workload: Planning and Resources Group report*. Crown Copyright.

Education Endowment Foundation. (2018). *Preparing for literacy: Improving communication, language and literacy in the early years'*. Education Endowment Foundation.

Education Endowment Foundation. (2021). *Teacher feedback to improve pupil learning guidance report*. Education Endowment Foundation.

Fletcher Wood, H. (2018). *Responsive teaching: Cognitive science and formative assessment in practice*. Routledge.

Florez, M. T., & Sammons, P. (2013). *Assessment for learning: Impact and evidence*. CfBT Education Trust, Oxford University Department for Education.

Grigg, R. (2014). *Becoming an outstanding primary school teacher*. Routledge.

Hattie, J. (2008). *Visible learning: A synthesis of over 800 meta-analyses relating to achievement*. Routledge.

Hattie, J. (2012). Know thy impact. *Educational Leadership, 70*(1), 18–23.

Hattie, J., & Timperley, H. (2007). The power of feedback. *Review of Educational Research, 77*(1), 81–112.

Hawkins, S. (2016). *Outstanding primary teaching and learning: A journey through your early teaching career*. Open University Press.

Heathcote, J. (2023). *Enriching English: Curriculum with soul*. Collins.

Keller, J. (2009). *Motivational design for learning and performance: The ARCS Model approach*. Springer.

Kluger, A. N., & DeNisi, A. (1996). The effects of feedback interventions on performance: A historical review, a meta-analysis, and a preliminary feedback intervention theory. *Psychological Bulletin, 119*(2), 254–284.

Kyriacou, C. (2018). *Essential teaching skills*. Open University Press.

National Advisory Committee on Creative and Cultural Education. (1999). *All our futures: Creativity, culture and education report*. https://sirkenrobinson.com/pdf/allourfutures.pdf. Accessed on September 17, 2022.

Ofsted. (2014). *The Annual Report of Her Majesty's Chief Inspector of Education, Children's Services and Skills 2014/15*. Crown Copyright.

Ofsted. (2022). *Research and analysis research review series: English*. https://www.gov.uk/government/publications/curriculum-research-review-series-english/curriculum-research-review-series-english

Pollard, A., Black-Hawkins, K., Linklater, H., Higgins, S., James, M., Dudley, P., Swann, M., Swaffield, S., Winterbottom, M., & Cliff Hodges, G. (2018). *Reflective teaching in schools* (2nd ed.). Bloomsbury Publishing Plc.

Ruiz-Primo, M., & Brookhart, S. (2017). *Using feedback to improve learning*. Routledge.

Slavin, R. E., Hurley, E. A., & Chamberlain, A. (2003). Cooperative learning and achievement: Theory and research. In W. M. Reynolds & G. E. Miller (Eds.), *Handbook of psychology. Volume 7: Educational psychology* (pp. 177–198). John Wiley & Sons.

Stronge, J. (2018). *Qualities of effective teachers* (3rd ed.). ASCD.

Tomlinson, C., & McTighe, J. (2019). *Integrating differentiated instruction and understanding by design*. Pearson Education Ltd.

Wiggins, G. (2010). *Feedback: How learning occurs*. https://authenticeducation.org/feedback-how-learning-occurs/. Accessed on September 4, 2023.

Wilcox, A. (2017). *Descriptosaurus: Supporting creative writing for ages 8–14*. Routledge.

Wilkinson, D., & Earle, L. (2022). What matters in planning? In C. Carden (Ed.), *Primary teaching: Learning and teaching in primary schools today*. SAGE.

2

Planning for Effective Learning in the Primary English Classroom

Chapter Objectives

This chapter will:

- Consider what the subject of English is for.
- Identify key foundational principles which underpin effective teaching in primary English.
- Explore best practices in the teaching of primary English.
- Explore how to plan for progress in learning in the primary English classroom.

This chapter will also support your development as a reflective practitioner, highlighting some useful tools which will support you in evaluating lesson plans and reflecting on the success of taught lessons.

What Is English for?

Before jumping into the planning of lessons across the primary English curriculum, it is important to consider what the learning and teaching of English in the primary classroom is really all about. This will be helpful in establishing key foundational principles which ensure that planned lessons are meaningful and purposeful for pupils so that they value the learning and are thus motivated to engage fully.

English is both a technical and creative curriculum subject. There are technical aspects to learning how to construct and combine words in order to speak and write, and how to retrieve meaning from words which have been constructed and combined in order to hear and read. It is also highly creative; its authentic purpose is to allow us to create and convey intent and meaning. Words enable us to share our thoughts, ideas, imaginings, interests, concerns and feelings. Having a good command of English allows us to communicate fluently and authentically with others. For some people, articulating their thinking through spoken language or writing allows them to better understand it themselves. Reading the words of others can help us understand ourselves and our world more fully.

As teachers, it can be hard to balance the technical and creative effectively. Sometimes, the priority seems to be on teaching our children to apply the rules of spelling and grammar, use the perfect pen grip to produce perfectly formed and spaced letters, compose a piece of writing that meets a long list of specified criteria and interpret a read text correctly by giving the same answers as can be found in a mark scheme. Whilst accuracy and automaticity in spelling, grammar and handwriting help us write efficiently and communicate our meaning easily to others, meeting checklists of criteria and reproducing correct answers to comprehension questions can hugely threaten the true potential that authentic communication skills contribute to our children's lives, thus robbing them of the pleasure it offers to connect to each other and to the big ideas in the world around us or to the world of imagination that lies beyond our realities.

Planning to Teach English

The National Curriculum in England: English Programmes of Study for Key Stage 1 and Key Stage 2 outlines the end-of-year expectations for pupils in each year group from Year 1 to Year 6. There are three key strands to the English programmes of study: spoken language, reading and writing. The statutory requirements for spoken language consist of 12 statements. Unlike the rest of the curriculum, these are not broken into year group requirements but apply across the Year 1–Year 6 age range, while reading and writing are broken down into programmes of study for Year 1, Year 2, Year 3/4 and Year 5/6. The statutory requirements for reading are broken down into two sub-strands: word reading (decoding) and comprehension and these are presented for each year group. The statutory requirements for writing are also broken down into two sub-strands. These are transcription, which includes spelling and handwriting, and composition, which includes vocabulary, grammar and punctuation. The end-of-year expectations show that there is a place for teaching both the technical knowledge and skills that underpin letter formation, spelling, and sentence and text construction, and the creative knowledge and skills that underpin authentic and meaningful communication with others through speaking, listening, reading and writing.

To prepare to write your own lesson plans, you will probably find it useful to observe learning and teaching in your placement school, to talk to the class teacher and to review others' lesson plans if you can. Because English encompasses three key strands, it is useful to spend some time looking closely at and thinking carefully about learning in the specific strand of English you will be planning. A lesson focused on one or more aspects of writing might look quite different from one focused on one or more aspects of reading or spoken language. Talk to the teacher before and after the lesson too if you can; this will offer invaluable insight into the decisions the teacher has made and into their reflections once the learning has taken place.

Activity   Some Prompts for Observing and Reflecting on the Teaching of Primary English

- How does the lesson start?
- How is the learning focus (and what terminology, e.g., learning objective or intention is used) introduced and/or shared with the children?
- Are any success criteria shared (possibly called steps to success)?
- How does the lesson build on the children's prior learning?
- What models are shared? Does the teacher engage in live modelling or use models that were prepared prior to the lesson?
- Is any key terminology or vocabulary used or introduced? How integral is it to the success of the lesson? How does the teacher ensure that all pupils understand?
- Does the teacher engage in any direct instruction? What? How effective is this?
- What routines are in place (e.g., do the children sit in particular places, get particular resources or do or say things in a particular sequence)?
- What kinds of practice activities does the teacher ask the children to complete?
- How is the lesson paced?
- How does the teacher draw the lesson to a close?
- If there was a plan for the lesson, you could also look at what was planned and to what extent anything differed when the lesson took place.

Schools will plan to achieve a good balance in English in different ways. Initially, there are likely to be two distinct strands to English, teaching the technical skills of transcription, spelling and handwriting through regular and frequent discrete and focused sessions, while encouraging more creative composition skills through the retelling and construction of oral texts. High-quality oral and written texts will likely be shared through whole class, small group and one-to-one reading opportunities. Adults may scribe for children, helping them to see what their words look like written down until their transcription skills are sufficiently developed to allow them to take over.

As children's transcription skills become more proficient, the two strands may become more closely intertwined. However, this is not to say that children should only communicate when they have all the knowledge and skills necessary to do so with complete accuracy. Children's early attempts to put words together, use of mark making as an emergent form of writing, and invented spelling – where they have had a go at representing a word using letter symbols – all support them in developing their knowledge of conventions. It is also worth noting the interconnected nature of the four language modes: speaking, listening, reading and writing. Each one draws on a known bank of words and ideas, with engagement in one language mode strengthening and reinforcing the others. For example, absorbing new vocabulary into spoken language allows us to understand it when reading and use it when writing. New words encountered through reading may be absorbed into our vocabularies for use in speaking, listening and writing. Likewise, developing an understanding of how different written texts are structured through reading provides a resource which can be used to inform our own writing. This implies perhaps that transfer between language modes is natural and automatic. However, skilled and careful curriculum planning is needed to ensure that children see meaningful connections and engage deeply with learning in order to achieve this.

Context is a key concept in the teaching of English. When we think or communicate our thoughts, feelings and ideas, it is always in a specific time and place for a specific purpose and audience. The productive forms of language, speaking and writing, not only have some similarities but also some differences. Unless it is a recorded speech, speaking typically happens in the context of here and now, while writing is typically composed with the expectation that it may be read at another time and in another place. There are non-verbal aspects of communication, which contribute to making meaning understood, such as tone and gesture which are known as paralinguistics. In writing, these must be described as if by a narrator, or perhaps indicated through the use of punctuation and text presentation such as italicised and emboldened fonts.

There are similarities and differences between the receptive language forms of listening and reading. Listening is accompanied by paralinguistics to support meaning-making, and the listener often has the chance to request, either verbally or through their own use of expression and gesture, clarification or repetition. In reading, words can be reread – sometimes this supports understanding but at other times, the reader has to decide for themselves what the writer meant. We may want to use language for a number of purposes, such as to pose questions, narrate, explain, speculate, imagine, hypothesise, explore, include, discuss, argue, reason and justify (Ofsted, 2022). We may want or need to communicate with different audiences, such as our friends and family, other children in the school or more formal audiences such as an authority figure we are writing a letter of complaint to. All of these contexts influence exactly how we use our language resources, and so we need to teach children how to communicate their meaning in each one.

All aspects of the English curriculum are considered in the chapters which follow. However, all are underpinned by some key principles. High-quality English lessons are centred around purposeful opportunities to make and discuss meaning, show children clearly how language works through the use of high-quality models and authentic live modelling, develop children's knowledge of words, sentences, texts and their conventions, and provide good opportunities for children to study, discuss, explore and play with language in a wide variety of contexts, for different purposes and audiences. Learning is typically easier and more enjoyable when children are highly engaged and motivated by the content of lessons, so planning authentic classroom experiences which enable them to explore language in meaningful ways is worth investing in.

Current guidance from Ofsted places great importance on the role of knowledge in the primary curriculum, believing an extensive knowledge-rich curriculum to be a key component of a first-class education (Gibb, 2021). In their recently published research review series, each of which focuses on a different curriculum subject, Ofsted uses different terms to describe different types of knowledge which include:

- Substantive knowledge – 'the content that teachers teach as established fact' (Counsell, 2018).
- Disciplinary knowledge – 'what pupils learn about how the subject's substantive knowledge was established, its degree of certainty and how it continues to be revised by scholars, artists or professional practice' (Counsell, 2018).
- Procedural knowledge – 'knowledge of methods or processes that can be performed'. It can be described as 'knowing how' (Severs, 2022).

In their research review series: English, Ofsted (2022) uses the term 'epistemic knowledge', citing an OECD source for the definition of this term as

> the understanding of how expert practitioners of disciplines work and think...Epistemic knowledge helps pupils to find the purpose of learning, understand the application of learning and extend their disciplinary knowledge. (Ofsted, 2022)

Thus, the terms 'epistemic' and 'disciplinary knowledge' are often used to mean the same thing (Coe et al., 2014). Considering these types of knowledge can initially seem quite daunting. Talking to your class teacher and to your colleagues will help you to develop your understanding of different types of knowledge, and you could have a go at the activity that follows to get you started.

Activity   Considering Substantive and Epistemic/Disciplinary Knowledge in the Primary English Curriculum

- The substantive knowledge (the content that teachers teach as established fact) which must be taught in the primary age phase is presented in *The National Curriculum in England: English Programmes of Study for Key Stage 1 and Key Stage 2.* This includes established facts such as key terminology. Look through the expectations for one year group. What substantive knowledge can you find?
- Within the discipline of history, children learn that historians have continued to learn about the past through the use of historical investigation skills such as the examination of primary and secondary sources of evidence. In English, the epistemic/disciplinary knowledge that must be taught relates to knowledge of how skilled speakers, readers and writers have continued to learn about ways to use language to create, shape and share meaning for different audiences and purposes, thinking both critically and creatively. This typically means sharing, responding to and discussing high-quality models of language, and learning how people create their own verbal and written texts and make meaning from those produced by others. Look at the expectations for one year group to see how disciplinary knowledge could be developed.
- Now look for what procedural knowledge ('knowledge of methods or processes that can be performed') is expected to be learned by pupils in that year group.
- What teaching and learning strategies do you think might be useful for teaching these three types of knowledge to the pupils in that year group?

In addition to epistemic knowledge, the Ofsted document makes many references to specific banks of knowledge that support children's development as they learn to speak, listen, read and write, for example, knowledge of language and knowledge of text structure; each bank of knowledge is discussed in the relevant chapter of this book.

What Is Best Practice in the Teaching of Primary English?

Of course, best practice in the teaching of primary English is strongly related to best practice in effective teaching more widely.

The concept of quality first teaching (QFT) is often mentioned in schools and initial teacher education. A definition of this term was provided by the DCSF (Department for Children, Schools and Families) in 2008 (this government department is currently known as the DfE, Department for Education). A number of more recently published DfE documents refer to the principles of QFT, so a clear understanding of this term is useful to know.

The key characteristics of QFT are:

- Highly focused lesson design with sharp objectives.
- High demands of pupil involvement and engagement with their learning.
- High levels of interaction for all pupils.
- Appropriate use of teacher questioning, modelling and explaining.
- An emphasis on learning through dialogue, with regular opportunities for pupils to talk both individually and in groups.
- An expectation that pupils will accept responsibility for their own learning and work independently.
- Regular use of encouragement and authentic praise to engage and motivate pupils. (DCSF, 2008).

Principles of Effective Teaching

In recent years, much has been done to try to bring together the evidence on the most effective approach to teaching and to create a clear list of key principles.

Coe et al.'s Great Teaching Toolkit Evidence Review (2020)

This review synthesises a range of evidence, identifying four priorities for teachers to invest in order to develop effective teaching. These priorities are:

- Understanding the content they are teaching and how it is learned.
- Creating a supportive environment for learning.
- Managing the classroom to maximise opportunities to learn.
- Presenting content, activities and interactions that activate their students' thinking students develop knowledge and expertise.

Each priority is discussed in some depth, breaking them down into a number of key elements which comprise a useful framework for developing effective practice.

Hattie's Visible Learning (2012)

Hattie also provides a synthesis of evidence on effective teaching, proposing that teaching and learning should be visible to ensure that pupils know what to do and how to do it, and teachers know if learning is occurring or not. Learning goals should be both challenging and explicit, and teachers and pupils should work together to reach goals, provide feedback and evaluate success. Two key principles for Hattie are (i) the need to develop pupils' metacognition and self-assessment and (ii) teachers' engagement with the feedback they gather from the pupils that show them what is working and what is not working in the classroom. Teachers should then take action to make the best use of resources to adapt and maximise learning.

(Continued)

Hattie also concluded that expert teachers:

- Identify the most important ways to organise and represent the subjects they teach, presenting new knowledge in ways that effectively integrate with the pupils' prior learning and supporting pupils to build effective connections between what they know. They also have a repertoire of good strategies to anticipate and respond to possible errors and misconceptions, monitor the impact of their teaching on the pupils' learning, and make effective adaptations to their practice as a result.
- Create an effective classroom climate for learning. This is based on high levels of trust between teacher and pupils in which it is safe for pupils to make mistakes, using these as great opportunities to learn.
- Hold high expectations for all pupils, believing them all quite capable of making good progress. This draws on a growth mindset view (Dweck, 2006) which sees intelligence as something which can be grown through perseverance and engagement.

Rosenshine's Principles (2010)

Rosenshine's synthesis of research into effective teachers, cognitive science, and cognitive supports and scaffolds, identifies a number of research-based principles of instruction. These can be summarised here as:

- Starting lessons with a brief review of previous learning.
- Introducing new learning in small steps, building in time for pupil practice at each step, and guiding this in the initial stages.
- Giving clear and detailed instructions and descriptions.
- Asking questions to check pupils' understanding.
- Modelling the steps that pupils need and using a think-aloud strategy to demonstrate thinking.
- Providing models of worked-out problems and many examples of an idea as a resource.
- Asking pupils to explain what they have learned.
- Checking the responses of all pupils.
- Providing pupils with systematic feedback.
- Devoting a good proportion of classroom time to providing explanations.
- Reteaching key material when necessary.
- Preparing pupils for independent practice time, and monitoring this carefully.

Metacognition

Metacognition is often referred to as learning how to learn. Supporting pupils to develop their metacognitive skills as learners enables them to plan, monitor and evaluate their learning so that they can begin to judge for themselves whether they are on track with their learning. For example, metacognitive skills can be used by learners to check in on their comprehension of a text, asking themselves whether they fully understand what they are reading and if not, what they might do about it (e.g., they may reread a section, look up an unknown word and so on). Metacognition has been identified by the Education Endowment Foundation (EEF) as 'fundamental to learning' and the 'bread and butter of effective teaching' (EEF, 2021).

The EEF suggest that pupils can develop their metacognitive skills through:

- Explicit teaching.
- Teacher modelling.
- Prompts and opportunities for pupils to think about their learning and reflect on how well it is going.

Activity   Reflecting on the Principles of Effective Teaching

Review the principles of effective teaching presented above (you could substitute one if you have an alternative list or policy which is used by your initial teacher education provider or school). What overlaps can you find between the different sources, and what differences?

When you think specifically about the teaching of English, do any sources or individual principles seem more or less relevant?

Can you create your own list of effective principles that relate to teaching English?

How Do These Ideas Relate to the Teaching of English?

Effective teaching in English draws on many of the principles of effective teaching in general, interpreting these within our understanding of what the subject and learning of English is really all about. Medwell et al.'s (2017) synthesis of research into the effective teaching of English suggests the following as principles of high-quality English teaching:

- Make learning goals clear.
- Have high expectations of all children and set targets for groups/individuals.
- Use language purposefully.
- Use demonstration and modelling.
- Provide high-quality models.
- Encourage children to talk about language using a shared vocabulary (meta-language).
- Offer opportunities for children to play with language.
- Provide meaningful contexts for children to practise language and literacy use.
- Encourage independence.
- Give high-quality feedback.
- Celebrate success.

Pressley (2002) suggests that effective teachers of English have classrooms centred around high-quality reading and writing experiences which lead to the active engagement of pupils. The need for teachers to provide authentic and purposeful contexts in which to develop children's knowledge and understanding of all aspects of English is key to the high-quality teaching of English (Cremin, 2015; Medwell et al., 2017). We speak, listen, read and write for a reason, for example, to share our experiences and thoughts through real and imagined stories and recounts, to communicate essential information through shopping lists, recipes, instruction manuals and non-fiction texts, to persuade someone to see a new film, to read a great book, to buy something or to send letters imploring them change their views or behaviour. Authentic and purposeful contexts help children to understand the application of the English curriculum in the real world and can 'make the world meaningful and imaginatively satisfying' (Cremin, 2015, p. 6). This is reflected in the aims of *The National Curriculum in England: English Programmes of Study for Key Stage 1 and Key Stage 2*, which state that:

> English has a pre-eminent place in education and in society. A high-quality education in English will teach pupils to speak and write fluently so that they can communicate their ideas and emotions to others and through their reading and listening, others can communicate with them. Through reading in particular, pupils have a chance to develop culturally, emotionally, intellectually, socially and spiritually. Literature, especially, plays a key role in such development. Reading also enables pupils both to acquire knowledge and to build on what they already know. (DfE, 2013, p. 13)

Learning can also be made meaningful for pupils when it connects to their interests and experiences, supporting their sense of curiosity and wonder about the world around them, and encouraging them to play with ideas and language. These principles should help you design the contexts in which children will learn during each of your lessons.

A further key principle to bear in mind is the idea of the nature of interconnection which underpins the English curriculum. Reading, writing and spoken language are interwoven elements of language development that strengthen and support each other in myriad ways. For example, in a discussion about the most effective adjectives to choose to improve their writing, children may draw on some reading they did earlier in the week. Through discussion, they may debate the extent to which one is more effective in a particular context than others. While doing so, pupils develop an increased understanding of the role and potential of adjectives to support their future writing, deeper comprehension of a range of vocabulary to draw upon in future reading, and greater fluency in their use of spoken language, to draw on in future discussions.

Planning for Progress in English

The word progress is of 'Latin origin, and combines two elements, pro and gradi, meaning to walk forward' (Bossard, 1931, p. 5). In an education context, it suggests the idea of continued advancement towards definite and desirable outcomes in terms of children's knowledge, skills understanding, values and attitudes as they develop and grow. In 2018, the national director of education for Ofsted, Sean Harford, stated that:

> By progress, we mean pupils knowing more and remembering more. Has a child really gained the knowledge to understand the key concepts and ideas? Is this enabling them to develop the skills they need to master?

This remains the definition of progress used by Ofsted. In education, the questions of whether what matters can be measured and whether what can be measured matters continue, as does the fierce debate over the challenges of the influence that national assessments, a quantitative means to measure children's progress in relation to the goals specified by the DfE, have on the curriculum. However, as teachers we undoubtedly want our pupils to keep moving forwards in terms of what they understand and are able to do. We need to gather qualitative information which tells us what strengths and gains have been acquired by each pupil, and we need to know what would be most useful to teach them next to keep that onward trajectory, not least because the sense of growth and development is usually highly motivating for learners.

In brief then, for pupils to make good progress as speakers, listeners, readers and writers, they need to know more about language and its uses in various contexts and be able to use this knowledge to understand and communicate with increasing power. They need to learn some procedural knowledge, for example, about letter formation (see Chapter 16) and sound–symbol relationships (see Chapter 7).

Hattie's concept of visible learning is useful to reflect on here: how can we make the processes that underpin speaking, listening, reading and writing visible to our learners and then to themselves.

A really helpful framework is the gradual release of responsibility model. This was originally proposed by Pearson and Gallagher (1983) in relation to the development of children's reading comprehension skills. The key concept is that of the teacher as the expert who demonstrates the relevant knowledge, understanding and skills required for a particular task, systematically transferring these to the pupils so that their expertise develops in turn.

- The teacher starts by assuming full responsibility for tackling the task, modelling or demonstrating how to approach the task, and using a think-aloud strategy to explain what they are thinking step by step.
- This is followed by some shared work, with the children and teacher working together, taking joint responsibility for tackling the task.
- The next step is guided work. At this stage, the pupils assume more responsibility for tackling the task while the teacher observes closely and steps in as needed to support, aiming to avoid significant disruptions to the learning process which would likely result in feelings of failure or complete demotivation.

- When pupils are well-placed to work with little guidance, they are ready to assume full responsibility for the task and are thus able to tackle it independently.

The first step, teacher modelling or demonstration, enables pupils to see clearly the goal they are aiming to achieve, answering Hattie's question 'Where am I going?' (Chapter 1). In the subsequent stages, the teacher and pupil both monitor the learning as responsibility is gradually transferred. This careful observation and reflection allow both teacher and pupil to see how the learning is progressing (How am I going?) and give feedback to ensure that the learner knows what to do (Where to next?). For these subsequent steps to result in good progress, the teacher must plan rich opportunities for the pupils to practise and apply their learning.

This model is often summarised as 'I do, we do, you do' and has been adopted by others and developed for use beyond the teaching of reading comprehension. For example, Fisher and Frey (2013) have explored how it could be used across subject disciplines, and it forms the basis of the approach used in some schemes of learning.

One of the points noted by Fisher and Frey (2013) is the crucial importance of interaction between the pupil and the teacher, the pupil and the content, and the pupil and their peers, as this new learning is developed. It is also important to note that while these steps form the basis of the teaching approach, they are adhered to with sufficient flexibility to meet the needs of the learners. For example, following some shared or guided work, the teacher may judge that it would be most helpful to return to the initial 'I do' stage by modelling the process again for some or all of the pupils.

It is also important to remember that the shortened version of the gradual release of responsibility model, 'I do, we do, you do' should not discount the critical role of observation. In the first step, the teacher models while the children watch. In the subsequent steps, the teacher increasingly takes on the role of the observer in order to monitor the learning and provide support or challenge as needed.

It is worth reflecting on this sequence of learning when reviewing children's progress as it might be that the case that the responsibility was transferred too suddenly from the teacher to the pupil with insufficient time given for them to take new learning on gradually through shared or guided work. Of course, some children may grasp concepts more quickly, allowing them to move more quickly to independence.

Activity   Reflecting on the Gradual Release of Responsibility Model

Reflect on your experiences of the use of the gradual release of responsibility model in what you have observed and taught in the classroom so far. Which subject disciplines has it been used in and why? How effective was it? Have you seen some parts of the model used more frequently than others?

Revisit the principles of effective teaching and QFT presented earlier. How does this model fit in with those?

How have you or might you use the gradual release of responsibility model in your English teaching? What resources might you need to make effective use of it in all aspects of the primary English curriculum? Does it have any particular implications for the management and organisation of your classroom?

Make a note of your thoughts so you can revisit these when you engage with the chapters that follow.

Teachers as Learners: Reflecting on Your Practice

No matter the level of your teaching experience, there are things that can be learned from every lesson. Your initial teacher education provider or school may require you to complete formal lesson evaluations on a separate proforma or may have a space on the lesson place for your reflections to be recorded after the lesson. With a busy workload to manage, it can be tempting to skip or skimp on the reflection part of the teaching cycle. However, investing time in critical reflection enables teachers to understand the impact of their teaching on the children's learning. Therefore, it is a vital part of their professional growth.

From his synthesis of evidence on the impact of a wide range of influences on pupil learning (2009), Hattie's key message is to 'know thy impact' (2012, p. vii). A crucial part of knowing your impact means reflecting on the learning that has taken place in any one lesson and considering how effective it was for the learners. This enables you to understand both learners and learning more fully, allowing you to develop 'more proactive and informed approaches and responses' (Hawkins, 2016, p. 155), which will continue to increase the effectiveness of your teaching over time. The process of reflection requires teachers to maintain genuine curiosity about learning and teaching, and a willingness to examine classroom practice in-depth, demonstrating an ongoing commitment to the pursuit of excellence and professional learning.

The process of reflecting on teaching after it has happened is termed reflection on action by Schon (1991). This process essentially involves:

- Thinking back to the learning that occurred with particular reference to the pupil outcomes (their achievement, engagement, behaviour and so on).
- Considering what influenced these outcomes (what might have prompted them to come about).
- Considering what to try next time.

Hawkins (2016) outlines a number of useful models for supporting teacher reflection, for example, Kolb's reflective model of experiential learning and Gibbs's reflective cycle. Unless there is an expectation that you use a particular model, it is worth experimenting with a range to see which is most useful to you – and of course it may be that different models are useful for reflecting on different lessons, so again, building a repertoire is desirable.

While of course it is effective for one person to reflect on a lesson by themselves, discussing learning in collaboration with another person, such as a class teacher, mentor or peer, can be very helpful.

That other person, the collaborator, does not necessarily have to observe the lesson themselves to support reflection (this may be especially helpful if the support person is engaged in other activities and cannot be released for any reason). For example, O'Leary's (2022) unseen observation cycle involves discussion between those involved before and after the lesson. Prior to the lesson, the teacher decides on the focus for the lesson and creates a lesson plan which is then shared and discussed with the collaborator. This can be amended in the light of the discussion. The teacher then teaches the lesson and makes reflective notes. These are shared with the collaborator; together they engage in professional dialogue, with the collaborator encouraging 'the teacher to critically reflect on their practice, to delve more deeply into their thinking and decision making by asking probing questions that encourage them to engage reflexively in their professional learning'. O'Leary provides a useful set of prompts which can deepen thinking, supporting reflection. As a result of the discussion, the teacher then decides on what to try next.

A very simple model of reflection is Driscoll's (2007) 'What' model. This involves three simple and clear questions:

- What?
- So what?
- Now what?

Driscoll's questions may appear to be deceptively simple. However, reflecting in-depth on your thoughts is a worthwhile investment of your time. The following example shows how you might reflect on one point from a lesson – in practice, you may well identify a number of points rather than just one.

First, the teacher describes the 'what' uncritically, noting what happened during the lesson. For example, one point might be 'the majority of children took part well in the discussion at the start of the lesson, there were three children that didn't really engage'.

Next the teacher considers those points, reflecting on their impact and introducing the process of analysis – what occurred as a result of those happenings and why this might have occurred. For example, 'the majority of children took part well in the discussion because they were really clear on what I wanted them to talk about. My use of a prompt question and supporting image on the interactive whiteboard seemed to really help them to understand what I wanted and to stay focused. The three children that didn't really engage might have needed longer to process or perhaps it would have been helpful for me to get them started'.

Finally, the teacher asks, 'Now what?'. This looks ahead to how the insights produced can be transferred to future situations. For example, 'Continue to experiment with the use of questions and image to support paired discussions. Plan scaffolding questions to support those who don't engage quickly with their partner and scan to spot them'.

One way of deepening our reflections can be achieved through Brookfield's four lenses framework. This is designed to enable the teacher to increase their understanding of effective practice from four different perspectives: the self-lens, the pupil lens, the colleague lens and the scholarship lens.

The self-lens prompts the teacher to reflect on their own autobiographical experiences as both learner and teacher to consider why they planned and responded to the learning as they did. This draws on research which shows that a teacher's choice of approach frequently mirrors their own experiences as learners, reproducing those strategies they found most helpful while discarding others. This helps us to understand why as teachers we may 'gravitate to certain ways of working and instinctively turn away from others' (Brookfield, 2002, p. 33), and this could be particularly useful in helping us to ensure that we are using an appropriate repertoire of strategies and approaches in order to meet the needs of the diverse range of learners in our classrooms.

The pupil lens prompts the teacher to really consider how the pupils have perceived and experienced the learning. Brookfield states:

> Seeing their practice through learners' eyes helps teachers teach more responsively. Having a sense of what is happening to students as they grapple with the difficult, threatening, and exhilarating process of learning constitutes instructors' primary pedagogic information. Without this information it is hard to teach well. It is obviously important to have a good grasp of methods, but it is just as important to gain some regular insight into what is happening to learners as those methods are put into practice. Without an appreciation of how people are experiencing learning, any methodological choices we make risk being ill informed, inappropriate, or harmful. (Brookfield, 2002, p. 34)

To support reflection on practice through this lens, the teacher may draw on formative assessment evidence as well as their own observations.

The colleague lens makes use of professional conversations between teachers (including student teachers) as a way of reflecting on classroom practice. This involves, as suggested previously, sharing your reflections on a lesson with a colleague and listening to their perspectives; trust and a willingness to talk openly about practice is a prerequisite for such conversations. Brookfield highlights the practical impact of this in helping teachers to challenge their assumptions and interpretations and to develop a repertoire of ways to overcome these. He also notes the emotional impact of this professional discussion; in sharing, teachers often realise that other teachers face (or have faced) similar challenges thus strengthening their sense of competence as teachers.

The scholarship lens involves the use of theory to aid reflection on classroom practice. This helps teachers to connect with the ever-developing body of knowledge about the practice of teaching, perhaps illuminating certain practices or events and expanding their knowledge of the classroom to include multiple perspectives. This is critical for teacher effectiveness and professional growth. It could be that a particular piece of theory, article, list of principles and so on is used as an aide to reflection, allowing the teacher to think more deeply about the learning that has occurred and why. In his 2002 article, Brookfield primarily focuses more on what is known about learners and their emotional responses to learning, suggesting that 'educational literature can provide teachers with an analysis of dilemmas and problematic situations that can be enormously helpful' (p. 35).

All of these tools can provide a useful framework to support you in reflecting on learning after it has taken place in order to gain deeper insight and understanding of learning and teaching, and yourself as a teacher. While it may be tempting to stick to the same one or two, try to find times when you can expand your repertoire to explore the use of a different framework. English is a core element of the primary curriculum, and each lesson you teach will involve some form of speaking, listening, reading and/or writing thus offering you an opportunity to learn more about how to plan good English lessons.

Summary

This chapter has considered what research tells us about the key principles of effective teaching in primary English. The need to plan authentic, meaningful opportunities for children to explore language in a range of contexts and for different purposes and audiences is established. The interconnected nature of the four language modes, speaking, listening, reading and writing, has also been discussed. These principles enable teachers to plan English lessons that are engaging and meaningful for learners and will support them to make good progress from their starting points.

Further Reading

1   Current thinking on effective teaching indicates that developing children's metacognition is really important. Explore the EEF's guidance on metacognition available at https://educationendowmentfoundation.org.uk/education-evidence/guidance-reports/metacognition.
2   Find out more about the gradual release of responsibility model which is a foundation for the effective teaching of English, and has also been adopted by organisations such as White Rose Education to underpin their approach to the teaching of Maths. You could start with this article: https://keystoliteracy.com/wp-content/uploads/2017/08/frey_douglas_and_nancy_frey-_gradual_release_of_responsibility_intructional_framework.pdf.

3   Develop your understanding of how to use lesson observations as effective professional development by reading Matt O'Leary's *Classroom Observation: A Guide to the Effective Observation of Teaching and Learning*, published by Routledge (2020).

References

Bossard, J. (1931). The concept of progress. *Social Forces, 10*(1), 5–14.

Brookfield, S. (2002). Using the lenses of critically reflective teaching in the community college classroom. *Special Issue: Community College Faculty: Characteristics, Practices, and Challenges, 118,* 31–38.

Coe, R., Aloisi, C., & Higgins, S. (2014). What makes great teaching? In *Review of the underpinning research*. Sutton Trust.

Coe, R., Rauch, C., Kime, S., & Singleton, D. (2019). *Great teaching toolkit: Evidence review*. Evidence Based Education. https://assets.website-files.com/5ee28729f7b4a5fa99bef2b3/5ee9f507021 911ae35ac6c4d_EBE_GTT_EVIDENCE%20REVIEW_DIGITAL.pdf. Accessed on May 01, 2023.

Counsell, C. (2018). Taking curriculum seriously. *Impact*. https://my.chartered.college/impact_article/taking-curriculum-seriously/. Accessed on April 2, 2023.

Cremin, T. (2015). *Teaching English creatively* (2nd ed.). Routledge.

DCSF. (2008). *Personalized learning – A practical guide*. DCSF Publications.

Department for Education. (2013). *The national curriculum in England: Key stages 1 and 2 framework document*. https://www.gov.uk/government/publications/national-curriculum-in-england-primary-curriculum. Accessed on May 16, 2022.

Driscoll, J. (2007). *Practising clinical supervision: A reflective approach for healthcare professionals* (2nd ed.). Bailliere Tindall Elsevier.

Dweck, C. S. (2006). *Mindset: The new psychology of success*. Random House.

EEF. (2021). *Metacognition and self-regulated learning guidance report*. Education Endowment Foundation.

Fisher, D., & Frey, N. (2013). *Better learning through structured teaching: A framework for the gradual release of responsibility* (2nd ed.). International Reading Association.

Gibb, N. (2021). *The importance of a knowledge-rich curriculum*. https://www.gov.uk/government/speeches/the-importance-of-a-knowledge-rich-curriculum. Accessed on April 4, 2023.

Hattie, J. (2009). *Visible learning A synthesis of over 800 meta-analyses related to achievement*. Routledge.

Hattie, J. (2012). *Visible learning for teachers: Maximizing impact on learning*. Routledge.

Hawkins, S. (2016). *Outstanding primary teaching and learning: A journey through your early teaching career*. McGraw-Hill.

Medwell, J., Wray, D., Minns, H., Griffiths, V., & Coates, L. (2017). *Primary English: Teaching theory and practice* (8th ed.). Learning Matters.

Ofsted. (2022). *Research and analysis research review series: English*. https://www.gov.uk/government/publications/curriculum-research-review-series-english/curriculum-research-review-series-english

O'Leary, M. (2022). Rethinking teachers' professional learning through unseen observation. *Professional Development in Education*, 1–14.

Pressley, M. (2002). Effective beginning reading instruction. *Journal of Literacy Research, 34*(2), 165–188.

Rosenshine, B. (2010). Principles of instruction; Educational practices series. *The International Academy of Education, 21*(23).

Schon, D. (1991). *The reflective practitioner: How professionals think in action.* Ashgate Publishing Ltd.

Severs, A. (2022). *What are all the different types of knowledge?* https://www.aidansevers.com/post/what-are-all-the-different-types-of-knowledge-part-1. Accessed on March 4, 2023.

3

Planning for Diverse, Inclusive and Adaptive Teaching

Chapter Objectives

This chapter will:

- Develop your knowledge and understanding of what is meant by a diverse, inclusive and adaptive teaching approach.
- Consider some of the needs of key groups of pupils.
- Explore how a teacher can plan and provide effectively for diverse, inclusive and adaptive teaching.

This chapter offers an introduction to the principles of planning effectively for diverse, inclusive and adaptive teaching, exploring them within the context of English. Key ideas will be reflected in later chapters and considered within the focus of each strand of the primary English curriculum.

Introduction

We live in a diverse society where children come from a range of ethnic, linguistic and familial backgrounds (Frederickson & Cline, 2009). We share both similarities and differences with others, for example, in our ethnicity, gender, socio-economic circumstances, age and religious beliefs. Along with our life experiences, our backgrounds have a role in shaping our beliefs and attitudes towards the world. In our practice, we need to both teach *for* diversity and inclusion, by using well-planned strategies to ensure that learning is effectively adapted to meet the needs of the pupils in the class, and teach *about* diversity and inclusion, by using carefully considered resources and contexts to develop children's knowledge and understanding of themselves and the world and its people around them.

Teaching for Diversity and Inclusion

Schuelka (2018) notes that inclusive education is based on the principle that people with disabilities have a fundamental right to education, and their well-being, dignity, autonomy, and contribution to society are valued. This exists within an ongoing process in which barriers to education are eliminated, and reform in the culture, policy and practice in schools to include all students is promoted. Statutory guidance for organisations that supports children with special educational needs (SENs) and disabilities (SEND) is detailed in the SEND code of practice: 0–25 years (DfE, 2015). This document sets out the legal requirements that must be followed without exception, and the statutory guidance that must be followed by law unless there is a good reason not to.

Where a child has been identified as having a SEN and/or disability, you should identify and work with key adults such as the class teacher, Special Educational Needs and Disabilities Co-Ordinator (SENDCo), support staff, parents and external agencies to ensure that you have a good understanding of the child's interests, strengths and learning needs. It will also be helpful for you to develop your knowledge and understanding of any pupils who could potentially have a SEN or disability which has not been confirmed. This should be handled professionally and sensitively by talking to your class teacher in the first instance and following their guidance on whether it is appropriate to discuss this with any other staff members. It is also important that slow progress and/or low attainment are not assumed to be identified as SENs or disabilities.

The National Curriculum Inclusion Statement says that:

> teachers should set high expectations for every pupil, whatever their prior attainment. Teachers should use appropriate assessment to set targets which are deliberately ambitious. Potential areas of difficulty should be identified and addressed at the outset. Lessons should be planned to address potential areas of difficulty and to remove barriers to pupil achievement. (DfE, 2013, p. 94)

The SEND Code of Practice clearly identifies the importance of 'high-quality teaching, differentiated for individual pupils' as 'the first step in responding to pupils who have or may have

SEN'. Additional intervention and support cannot compensate for a lack of good quality teaching (DfE, 2015, p. 99).

Pupils may also require additional support for their learning more generally. The graduated approach is a four-part cycle of assess, plan, do and review in which school staff, typically working with parents and possibly SEND specialists and experts, assess the child's learning needs carefully, agree and plan relevant actions such as interventions, carry these out and then review the impact. While this might also be considered to be the teacher's role as far as all pupils are concerned, this cycle is increasingly personalised for pupils with SEND (Nasen, 2014, p. 2) and will take place separately from daily lesson planning. However, you will wish to draw on this process to ensure that pupils with SEND are carefully planned for so that the benefits of high-quality whole-class learning and teaching are maximised.

Inclusion means valuing and respecting all people, regardless of personal circumstances or characteristics. This is the essential foundation for a fair and just democratic society. In an educational setting, true inclusion should enable all children to participate freely and equally, in order to thrive and develop. For the children in our classes, we can demonstrate our commitment to truly inclusive practice in everything we do in the classroom – from the actions we take to fully include each of them in ways that maximise and build on their strengths to the contexts for learning that we design for them. From a lesson planning perspective, full commitment to inclusive practice means ensuring that adaptations are made to learning and teaching so that pupils make good progress from their starting points. This isn't just relevant for pupils with SEND but applies to all pupils:

> If there is a given in schooling, it is that in any classroom, in any area of study, students are at different points in their development and bring a wide range of experiences to their learning. (Johnston et al., 2016, p. 18)

Adaptive (Responsive) Teaching

> The most important single factor influencing learning is what the learner already knows. Ascertain this and teach him accordingly. (Ausubel, 1968, p. vi)

Adaptive teaching, described as 'both a mindset and a practice' (Glazzard & Green, 2022, p. 277), aims to support pupils to achieve a specific learning objective, thus maintaining high expectations for all. As a mindset, it is underpinned by the understanding that 'no matter how well you describe something, how well you illustrate and explain it, students invent some new way to misunderstand what you have said' (Nuthall, 2007, p. 24). As a practice, adapting learning and teaching to best meet the needs of all pupils requires flexibility and creativity (Parsons et al., 2018). Hattie (2009) refers to this process of altering the teaching in response to what is actually occurring for the learners within the classroom context as improvisation, noting it as a key skill of effective teachers. The teacher must be ready, willing and able to make changes as the lesson unfolds and children grapple with the messy business of learning. For this reason, Fletcher-Wood (2018) uses the term 'responsive teaching' rather than 'adaptive teaching', suggesting that this term better defines the mindset and practice as a blend of planning and teaching which emphasises the interactive nature of teaching by focusing on what pupils have learned and how they can learn more.

A well-planned teacher will have thought through possible adaptations in advance of the lesson and will also monitor and respond to the children's learning carefully so that anticipated strategies can be brought into play along with in-the-moment decisions. This continual monitoring of the classroom and its learning is defined by Duffy et al. (2009) as teacher metacognition. Schön (1983) describes this as reflection-in-action, which enables the teacher to identify and build on pupils' responses (Duffy et al., 2009). Teachers engage in metacognitive thought as they construct and articulate instructional adaptations (Parsons et al., 2018). Experienced teachers may find it easier to make such spontaneous adaptations. As you observe and discuss the practice of experienced teachers, you will be able to make note of effective adaptive learning and teaching strategies that you see, reflecting on what strategies/resources, etc., the teacher made use of, what prompted the adaptations, and what impact they had in order expand your repertoire. You could also discuss this with the teacher after the lesson, using what you learn to help you think through possibilities in advance when planning your own lessons, thus expanding your repertoire of strategies to draw on.

The process of adaptive teaching is underpinned by an accurate understanding of how the children are responding to the learning and therefore uses effective formative assessment strategies, also known as assessment for learning (AfL). Formative assessment involves eliciting evidence of learning from pupils on an ongoing basis so that teaching can be adapted to meet pupils' needs. Fletcher-Wood (2018) suggests that there are three purposes that underpin this kind of in-the-moment assessment for learning: to enable us to check how our pupils are doing, to make sure that we are teaching them the right things and to identify gaps in their learning, noting that 'if we know what students know, we can plan what to remind them of, what to build upon, what to seek to correct' (p. 6).

To achieve this, teachers need to plan some lesson activities that will reveal what pupils are thinking, bringing to light learning gaps or misconceptions. As Fletcher-Wood (2018) states, it is crucial that we 'check content, not confidence' (p. 76), finding out what they actually know and are able to do rather than their perceptions of how well the learning is going. Strategies that can be used include:

- effective questioning;
- quick ways to gather responses from all students where they show you what they know (e.g., through the use of mini wipeboards);
- setting up discussions in pairs or small groups while you listen in;
- carefully designed tasks that aim to assess specific learning gaps such as hinge questions and exit tickets.

Once a teacher has identified a pupil's needs, teaching can be adapted. Aubin (2021) suggests that teaching can be adapted primarily in one of two ways: a change of focus, where a particular aspect related to the learning, such as some key knowledge, would benefit from being targeted; or changing the approach, for example, by using the principles of scaffolding to provide effective support, which should be withdrawn gradually as the pupil gains knowledge and skill. Scaffolding, defined as providing assistance to pupils 'to achieve tasks they cannot yet master on their own' (Muijs & Reynolds, 2011, p. 64), is a key principle within adaptive teaching. This may involve the use of specific resources, and teacher-to-peer and/or peer-to-peer discussions which build pupils' thinking and understanding (Rowe et al., 2012). Other common adaptations include questioning, encouraging, managing, giving feedback, making connections, modelling, explaining and challenging thinking (Parsons et al., 2018).

Adapting Teaching for Some Specific Groups of Learners

All children are individuals and will have their own needs in learning at any one time; teachers may be prompted to adapt learning and teaching in response to their observations of pupil learning, motivation or behaviour (Parsons et al., 2018). The suggestions that follow are not intended to perpetuate stereotypes nor to reduce learning experiences to a routine checklist of strategies which teachers should use as a blanket approach when lesson planning. Teachers should always use their professional judgement and knowledge of the learners they work with in order to design and adapt the best possible learning and teaching actions. However, it is useful to build some background understanding of the possible needs of some specific groups of learners which you may be asked to plan for in advance of a lesson: disadvantaged pupils, pupils with English as an additional language (EAL) and pupils with specific educational needs, and strategies which are effective for one group may also be effective for other learners. There is some reference to quality first teaching in what follows; revisit the discussion on this in Chapter 1 if you need to remind yourself of the principles.

Disadvantaged Pupils

'Disadvantaged pupils' is the term used by Macleod et al. (2015) to describe pupils experiencing familial socio-economic disadvantage. Following concerns over the gap between attainment outcomes for these pupils when compared to their more affluent peers, the UK government set up the Pupil Premium which allocates additional funds to schools for each pupil experiencing socio-economic disadvantage to support their attainment.

According to a report commissioned by the DfE (2015) and carried out by Macleod et al.,

> More successful schools see pupils as individuals, each with their own challenges, talents and interests. Staff work to identify what might help each pupil make the next steps in their learning, whether they are performing below, at, or above expectations. (Macleod et al., 2015, p. 9)

In addition to quality first teaching, strategies that are seen as particularly valuable for disadvantaged pupils include those that encourage high aspirations and independence (such as metacognition), assessment for learning strategies and co-operative learning. This aligns clearly with the Gradual Release of Responsibility model discussed in Chapter 2, where the teacher starts with the use of modelling with think-aloud and develops children's independence through a steady and carefully planned sequence of responsibility as pupils tackle activities together and then with increasing independence while the teacher carefully monitors the learning. It may be worth considering the guided stage of this process to slow it down as needed to support individual pupils in moving from collaboration to independence.

Co-operative Learning

The EEF (2021) identifies co-operative learning as an effective approach to increasing the pace of progress. To be effective, when a small (between three and five) group of pupils work together, activities must be well-designed, carefully structured and typically involve high levels of interaction between learners. The outcomes of the task can be shared or individual; working towards a shared outcome has been shown to bring particularly positive gains to pupils.

The EEF (2021) identify possible benefits such as increased explanation, demonstration, problem-solving and metacognitive skills, and suggest that pupils may benefit from sharing the load of challenging tasks. They also note that the following aspects must be thought through with great care:

- All pupils, particularly pupils with low prior attainment, are supported to fully participate.
- The make-up of pairings and groups is considered.
- Teachers promote good practice in collaboration – for example, modelling high-quality discussions so that collaborative activities are productive.
- Teachers carefully monitor collaborative activities and support pupils that are struggling or not contributing.

There is a broad range of approaches to collaborative or cooperative learning involving different kinds of organisation and tasks across the curriculum. Not all of the specific approaches to collaborative learning adopted by schools have been evaluated, so it is important to evaluate any new initiative in this area. Professional development is likely to be required to maximise the effectiveness of approaches and monitor the impact of different approaches in the classroom.

Ways in which collaborative discussions can be supported are explored in Chapters 4 and 5.

The current UK government view reading as a key vehicle for improving the educational outcomes for disadvantaged pupils. This view is underpinned by findings from The Organisation for Economic Co-operation and Development's (OECD) Programme for International Student Assessment (PISA) (2021) which identified a correlation between children's engagement in reading and their performance which mediates the influence of their socio-economic status. As knowledge and understanding of vocabulary are key aspects of good reading, ensuring that any disadvantaged pupil who is not yet confident and fluent in reading is a key priority. Alongside good teaching of reading, the reading demands and opportunities for development within the design of a specific lesson are important to consider in adaptive teaching. As established in Chapter 6, the accessibility of a text is influenced by the reader's background knowledge of the topic or theme of the reading, the way in which the text is presented, and the reader's vocabulary knowledge. Therefore, the teacher could consider:

- Ways to activate and possibly increase background knowledge in advance or at the start of the lesson. This might include paired discussions in response to a stimulus such as a picture, quote or statement. It may require more sensory experiential learning such as participation in a related drama activity or watching some audio-visual resources.
- How the text is presented. It should be in a well-sized and easy-to-read font. It could be helpful to allow enough space for note-making depending on the age of the child, and supporting illustrations might be considered.
- Key vocabulary. This could be explored through individual or small group work as a pre-reading activity or provision of a glossary.

In general, it is helpful for learners to be able to discuss their general understanding of a text in pairs or small groups before they progress to using it as part of their learning.

Pupils With English as an Additional Language (EAL)

The Department for Education defines a pupil as having EAL if 'she/he is exposed to a language at home that is known or believed to be other than English' (DfE, 2020, p. 4). These pupils may be bilingual or multilingual. Franson (2011) identifies the following:

- The learner's first or home language is a valuable resource for the learner which plays a key cognitive, linguistic and socio-cultural role in supporting the learning of an additional language.
- The learning of a second language does not necessarily proceed along an orderly and linear path; each learner's prior linguistic, learned and world knowledge will influence and interact with their new learning.
- Typically, learners who have EAL acquire a practical level of English in the first two years of learning the new language but will need longer to develop the full proficiency needed to engage successfully with the full curriculum.

- Learning a language is not solely about the words; a pupil with EAL is also learning to understand a particular culture and society. This is linked to the development of their identity. (Franson, 2011)

A key thinker in the field of EAL is Jim Cummins. His research led him to propose the idea that language learners first acquire basic interpersonal communicative skills (BICS), which enable them to use oral language to communicate effectively with native speakers. This may typically develop over one or two years and may lead people to consider the language learner as fully fluent and proficient. However, Cummins noted that the process of acquiring proficiency in the use of cognitive and academic language (CALP) was needed to achieve complete proficiency.

Pupils will of course vary in their stage of acquisition of the English language. They may be:

- Quite new to the language, primarily listening in and building their receptive understanding.
- Beginning to join in, participating with increasing independence as they build their confidence and competence, typically expressing more as they do so.
- Building or already having acquired fluency, perhaps using English proficiently.

The learner may also be experiencing some form of trauma, for example, if they have arrived as a refugee from another country or been separated from their home or important family members. It is helpful not to pressure the learner to talk until they are ready. Some schools have useful resources for new EAL arrivals, such as lanyards with keywords and symbols that allow them to communicate some simple needs. In some cases, an English-speaking buddy can help support understanding and the use of key vocabulary, and can include them in games and activities in the early days. Many learners with EAL begin to talk as they build confidence in their new surroundings, but if this does not happen, it is worth seeking advice from colleagues such as the inclusion coordinator or local authority/academy sponsor.

Any learner or user of language may engage in what is known as code-switching, using words or phrases from the different languages they know in their oral communication. This may be because a word in one language is more readily available, or perhaps it has slightly different connotations which seem more pertinent in a particular context. Code-switching enables a person to draw on all of their linguistic resources to express their ideas. Recognising and valuing this practice can support children's confidence and belief in themselves as learners.

Another key idea proposed by Cummins is the notion of common underlying proficiency. This sees the surface levels of language that an individual holds as an iceberg projecting from the sea, with one iceberg tip for each language the individual can speak. However, under the surface of the water, it is clear that these tips come from the same iceberg, which represents the body of knowledge and understanding that the learner has acquired, underpinning what they communicate in each language. This concept is key to understanding the importance of using all of a child's languages as a resource for developing both vocabulary and understanding of the world.

Gathering detailed information about any pupils with EAL, such as what is known about their home background and the language(s) they speak, as well as their interests, will be really useful. The Bell Foundation website is an excellent resource which includes assessment tools and suggested activities for language and learning for pupils. These exemplify principles of effective practice and can easily be adapted to suit different contexts for learning. Resources can be accessed at https://www.bell-foundation.org.uk/resources.

Designing Learning for Pupils With EAL

To aid thinking when designing learning, Cummins (1984) suggests that the teacher should consider:

- The context for the learning, identifying the extent to which this is concrete or abstract.
- The level of cognitive demand within a learning task.

Concrete and Abstract Learning Contexts

Concrete learning contexts (also referred to as context embedded) typically have high levels of support to help learners make sense of key ideas. For example, a first-hand experience is concrete in that it allows the learner to experience something themselves using their senses. Abstract learning contexts (also referred to as context reduced) typically have much lower levels of support. For example, a learning discussion between peers which uses only words (rather than stimuli such as pictures, etc.) is abstract. Depending on the stage of language acquisition the pupil is at, Conteh and Brock (2006) highlight the importance of considering learning design which moves from concrete to abstract understanding, gradually fading out the scaffolding strategies. For example, following the first-hand experience of visiting a Victorian house and taking on the role of a Victorian servant, the children could role-play again back in school, recount what they did by telling someone else, discuss some audio-visual materials about Victorian servants, discuss some materials in non-fiction books with pictures and then have a discussion in pairs or small groups with no supporting materials. In this way, children have moved from concrete to abstract understanding and are then much better placed to begin to write.

The Level of Cognitive Demand Within a Learning Task

According to Tsarpalis (2014), 'the cognitive demand of a mental task, such as a problem, is related to the complexity of the task/problem... A problem increases in complexity in terms of what information has to be held and what process has to be performed'.

Low cognitive demand tasks typically involve memorisation tasks such as recalling facts and following simple procedures (Van De Walle et al., 2013), for example, matching words and pictures. They don't typically demand any explanation or understanding.

High cognitive demand tasks typically involve much more thinking, for example, requiring pupils to make connections to relevant knowledge, analyse information and draw conclusions (Smith & Stein, 1998), for example, analysing a poem. It is important to ensure that tasks are at an achievable level of cognitive demand for pupils with EAL, and that the learning context offers the right support.

Building Vocabulary for Pupils With EAL

Because vocabulary is quite possibly going to present a barrier to learning, the British Council (online) suggests pre-teaching the language learners need before an activity. For example, if the children are going to watch an audio-visual clip of an aspect of the geography curriculum, they could be taught a few keywords in advance, perhaps matching the words to simple definitions and/or making use of pictorial support.

Conteh and Brock (2006) also highlight the role of talk in promoting the development of understanding and language, suggesting that pupils are prompted to talk about what they are doing at every stage of the activity. They also suggest that pupils are given models of how to use new language in context. Explicit discussion about word meaning, grammar and other features of different languages will also support language learning; this can be achieved through effective practice in the teaching of spoken language, reading and writing as it is laid out in *The National Curriculum in England: English Programmes of Study for Key Stage 1 and Key Stage 2*.

In addition to the principles of quality first teaching and more general adaptive teaching strategies highlighted in this chapter, Crolla and Treffers-Dalla (2017) suggest that listening activities can also be scaffolded, for example, by giving pupils keywords or ideas in image form to listen out for. They also suggest the use of strategies that support learner independence such as writing frames, word banks, and sentence banks and stems which model the language structures and key vocabulary to be learned.

Designing Learning for Pupils With SEND

Effective provision for pupils with SEND is of course much broader than individual lesson planning and, as outlined at the start of the chapter, should take a holistic view of the child which involves the voice of the child themselves, parents or carers, key school staff and possibly representatives from external agencies. Many local authorities now provide very clear guidance on how to scaffold and support learning for pupils with a wide range of SENs and disabilities. I will not try to replicate these here but instead will introduce some key principles to lesson planning which you can build upon in the light of sources relevant to your school and pupils. Broadly, lesson adaptations for learners with SEND take account of one or more of the following:

- A child's physical or sensory needs, ensuring that the child has the right conditions and resources for learning.
- A child's communication and interaction needs, ensuring that language is modelled well, instructions are clear and simple, time is given for processing, and alternative ways of recording and communicating are provided as appropriate.
- A child's social and emotional needs, supporting these through the use of social stories, visual timetables, now and next boards, and carefully planned paired and group work when appropriate.
- A child's cognition and learning needs, supporting these tasks are well-structured, broken down into small steps and carefully ordered and paced, and key vocabulary and resources are supported with the use of visual and/or audio materials and pre-taught if necessary.

The strategies for adapting learning considered so far have also centred around providing additional support for pupils. Of course, some pupils (who may or may not fall within the groups already identified) may find the planned learning runs very smoothly and so requires stretch and challenge.

Designing Learning for Stretch and Challenge

There are two ways in which the term 'stretch and challenge' is currently used in teaching. The first relates to all pupils, as laid out in the Teachers' Standards (DfE, 2011) with the expectation that teachers will 'set goals that stretch and challenge pupils of all backgrounds, abilities and dispositions'. This is set within an ethos of ambition and aspiration for all learners to continue to make good progress from their starting points and involves:

- Using intentional language to promote challenge – for example, by encouraging contributions from all pupils, prompting deep thinking, exploring excellence, promoting resilience and resourcefulness, and giving high-quality feedback.
- Designing tasks which support achievable but challenging outcomes – for example, by using live modelling to demonstrate processes and metacognition, planning for children's differing needs, barriers, rates of learning, and levels of prior knowledge, offering choice where possible, and holding a high focus on promoting independence.
- Supporting pupils to master challenging content – for example, ensuring adults can scaffold learning effectively when needed, providing resources which can be used independently, carefully sequencing learning so it builds on prior learning, encouraging pupils to make connections to existing knowledge and skills, providing models and worked examples as resources, and using sentence stems to structure thinking and discussion.

The second use of the term stretch and challenge is the main focus of this section. It relates to how teachers extend classroom learning for some pupils who are ready to go beyond the main learning of the lesson. Medwell et al. (2017) suggest that there are three primary ways in which additional stretch and challenge can be provided for pupils who are ready for it:

- by adding breadth, for example, enriching the children's learning through a broader range of contexts, tasks and resources;
- by increasing depth, for example, by providing a more complex task;
- by accelerating the pace of their learning, for example, noting that they are ready to move on more quickly than others in the class who require more time to consolidate their learning.

It can sometimes be hard for learners who are ready for stretch and challenge to do an additional task which does not really inspire or motivate them. This can lead to some underachievement should they decide to work more slowly to avoid this kind of extra work in the future. Again, it is important to know your learners and understand what they are interested in or motivated by. Watson suggests that consideration is given to the following at the planning stage:

- The design of the task – getting the level of pitch and stretch right is likely to be engaging; the task should make them think, not just be busy.
- Flexible learning – do the pupils who are ready for a stretch and challenge need to stay with the whole class for each part of the lesson, or could they get started on independent work more quickly and then work with you to extend them from there?
- Might they work towards a different outcome (e.g., verbal not written, or using some form of graphic representation), use different resources, or in different groupings?
- When and how you might prompt their reflective and metacognitive skills.
- How could they apply the main learning focus of the lesson in a different context and what opportunities are there for them to take their thinking further? (Watson, n.d.)

At the point of teaching, the teacher could use reframing to provide greater stretch, for example, rewording questions so that the child could use higher level vocabulary to articulate their thinking or to elaborate on their answers. You could also extend the children's thinking by prompting them to read more widely or explore different perspectives, or to investigate whether there is more than one answer or possibility or whether all possibilities are equally effective. You could also give children a statement or question to investigate. There are some good examples of these on the 'once upon a picture' website at https://www.onceuponapicture.co.uk/the-challenge-book/.

Getting Started With Adaptive/Responsive Teaching

It takes time to develop the knowledge and skills needed to adapt teaching effectively for all learners, and not all strategies will be effective for all lessons. It is also important that the adaptations you make are meaningful and manageable, and not so complicated to implement that they tie you up with one group of learners to the detriment of the others (although sometimes you may well want to spend time with one group when you know the others can work well independently on a meaningful task).

Think of a lesson that you are planning to teach. Think of one simple adaptation for each group of learners that is easy to implement. Either talk this through with a colleague at school or a peer and see if you think your adaptations will be effective in practice, or try them out in the classroom and evaluate their impact.

Teaching About Diversity and Inclusion

As well as teaching for diversity and inclusion through adaptive teaching strategies, English is an excellent vehicle for teaching about diversity and inclusion. The DfE's Character Education Framework (2019) asks: 'Do we enable young people from all backgrounds to feel as if they belong and are valued?' Through the choices we make regarding the high-quality spoken and written texts we choose to share with our classes and the themes and issues we present them to watch, read, discuss and write about, the English curriculum can help shape their attitudes, values and understanding of the world and its rich diversity:

> In excellent schools, there is no tension between a rigorous and stretching academic education on the one hand and outstanding wider personal development on the other.

> This is most effective when schools also actively promote good behaviour and positive character traits, including for example courtesy, respect, truthfulness, courage and generosity. Schools with…well-planned provision for character and personal development can help promote good mental wellbeing. (DfE, 2019, p. 4)

High-quality spoken and written texts also support teachers in fulfilling their duty to 'actively promote the fundamental British values of democracy, the rule of law, individual liberty, and mutual respect and tolerance of those with different faiths and beliefs' (DfE, 2014).

Wilson (2020) suggests this can be achieved by fostering an ethos of respectful curiosity, compassion, kindness and empathy which goes beyond merely tolerance to promoting acceptance and understanding of diverse views and experiences, thus supporting children's holistic development. In addition to promoting acceptance, she proposes four further principles to support teaching for about diversity and inclusion:

- Increasing visibility.
- Encouraging celebration.
- Creating belonging.
- Enabling learning.

Promoting Acceptance

Of course, building a positive relationship with each pupil is the best way to promote acceptance and is an essential part of effective teaching in any curriculum subject and within any age phase. However, within the context of the primary English classroom, as highlighted in *Development Matters: Non-Statutory Curriculum Guidance for the Early Years Foundation Stage* (DfE, 2021), high-quality children's books (and other texts) are an effective resource to help children understand the rich diversity of the world around them:

> Books create belonging. They help us see each other and understand one another. They shine a light on the world. It's vital that the books we read in our formative years reflect the rich diversity of the society we live in. (Elliott et al., 2021)

The Centre for Literacy in Primary Education's (CLPE) annual Reflecting Realities Survey of Ethnic Representation within UK Children's Literature explores the extent and quality of ethnic representation in children's literature, showing that both extent and quality are increasing. This is hugely helpful in allowing teachers to avoid stereotypical, superficial and/or tokenistic representations, and this succinct and accessible report supports teachers in developing their understanding of meaningful representation within high-quality literature. Rochman (1993) highlights the crucial importance of choosing high-quality representations in the texts we choose to share with our children:

> Books can make a difference in dispelling prejudice and building community; not with role models and little recipes, not with noble messages about the human family, but with enthralling stories that make us imagine the lives of others. A good story lets you know people as individuals in all their particularity and conflict; and once you see someone as a person – flawed, complex, striving - then you've reached beyond stereotype. Stories, writing them, telling them, sharing them, transforming them, enrich us and connect us and help us know each other (p. 19).

There are several useful booklists online which can offer a good starting point to support teachers' book choices, for example by the National Literacy Trust and the Penguin Publishing Houses. Your school and/or local children's librarians are usually an excellent resource, along with a school's local authority. As always, it is useful to draw on a range of text formats including age-appropriate picture books, short and longer fiction novels, non-fiction texts, poetry, graphic novels and comics, songs and rhymes.

Increasing Visibility

Increasing visibility is about ensuring children see and hear a diverse range of faces and voices in what we share with them. Including a range of high-quality texts written by a diverse range of authors demonstrates an authentic commitment to the principles of diversity and inclusion, promoting the creative achievements of these authors and establishing their place in a powerful curriculum. We learn about the world by seeing ourselves in books and other forms of printed text as well as in oral texts such as speeches, songs, presentations, podcasts, adverts and so on; so, it is vital that all pupils in our classes are represented in the texts we share with them. This is also crucial in supporting high expectations for all pupils, presenting role models to support our high aspirations for them and theirs for themselves.

Encouraging Celebration

There are many opportunities in the school year to encourage celebration. Wilson suggests that this includes celebrating religious festivals as well as national and international days such as World Mental Health Day and so on. Again, high-quality texts can support children's understanding of these, offering a powerful context in which to come together and celebrate diversity. There are also several key dates related to the English curriculum, such as National Poetry Day, Libraries Week, World Book Day, National Writing Day and National Storytelling Week. A list of these along with other key dates, including special events happening in a particular year, is available at https://literacytrust.org.uk/resources/literacy-teaching-calendar/. Again, considering diversity and inclusion when celebrating each event will offer good opportunities to enrich children's knowledge and understanding of the world's infinite variety. These practices should be consistently embedded to avoid being tokenistic.

Creating Belonging

Wilson's fourth suggestion of creating belonging focuses on the idea of adjustments that we might make to our classroom layout or styles of communication in order to fully include all children in the class. These have already been discussed in this chapter. However, she also suggests that teachers can create belonging through carefully considered language choices, ensuring that the words we choose to use are fully inclusive, enabling us to fulfil our responsibility as educators to promote sensitive and inclusive language from which our children can learn.

Enabling Learning

Wilson's final principle, enabling learning, builds on the principles of creating belonging. She notes that 'It is our responsibility to keep reading, to keep learning, and to grow in confidence when it comes to diversity, equity and inclusion. We need to check our power and our privilege and actively listen to understand. We need to consciously diversify our thinking, be aware of our biases, and diversify the circles we move in. By pushing ourselves out of our comfort zones, we will meet people who challenge us and whom we will learn from'. As teachers of English, it is our role to model and thus equip our children with the language, values, attitudes, knowledge and understanding that they need to become committed and responsible members of a truly inclusive society.

Summary

This chapter has considered what research tells us about how to ensure our teaching takes account of the principles of diverse, inclusive and adaptive teaching. The importance of reflecting on the identities and experiences of the pupils in our classes and expanding their knowledge and understanding of the world to consider those of others is established. Ways in which teachers can show their commitment to these principles through the choice of high-quality texts, considered use of language and understanding of the broad needs of different learners have been explored. These principles will be built upon in the coming chapters to show ways in which they can be applied within the specific strands of the primary English curriculum.

Further Reading

1   Find out more about effective provision for pupils with SENs and disabilities here: https://www.gov.uk/government/publications/send-code-of-practice-0-to-25.
2   Find out more about supporting pupils who have EAL in *Promoting Learning for Bilingual Pupils 3-11: Opening Doors to Success* by Jean Conteh and Avril Brock, published by SAGE.
3   Read CLPE's Reflecting Realities Survey of Ethnic Representation within UK Children's Literature and/or the findings of their other research. The most recent publications can be found at https://clpe.org.uk/research.

References

Aubin, G. (2021) *Scaffolding: More than just a worksheet.* https://educationendowmentfoundation.org.uk/news/scaffolding-more-than-just-a-worksheet. Accessed on May 3, 2023.

Ausubel, D. (1968). *Educational psychology: A cognitive view.* Holt, Rinehart and Winston.

CLPE. (2022). *Reflecting realities: Survey of ethnic representation within UK Children's Literature 2017–2021.* https://clpe.org.uk/system/files/2022-11/CLPE%20Reflecting%20Reality%202022%20WEB_0.pdf. Accessed on March 22, 2023.

Conteh, J., & Brock, A. (2006). *Promoting learning for bilingual pupils: Opening doors to success.* SAGE.

Crolla, C., & Treffers-Dalla, J. (2017). *A guide to supporting EAL learners.* Oxford University Press.

Cummins, J. (1984). *Bilingualism and special education: Issues in assessment and pedagogy.* Multilingual Matters.

Department for Education. (2011). *Teachers' standards.* https://www.gov.uk/government/publications/teachers-standards. Accessed on May 2, 2023.

Department For Education. (2013). *The National Curriculum for England: key stages 1 and 2 framework document.* Crown Publishing.

Department for Education. (2014). *Promoting fundamental British values as part of SMSC in schools: Departmental advice for maintained schools.* Crown Copyright.

Department for Education. (2015). *Special educational needs and disability code of practice: 0 to 25 years Statutory guidance for organisations which work with and support children and young people who have special educational needs or disabilities.* Crown Copyright.

Department for Education. (2019). *Character education framework guidance.* Crown Copyright.

Department for Education. (2020). *English proficiency of pupils with English as an additional language: Ad hoc notice.* Crown Copyright.

Department for Education. (2021) *Statutory framework for the early years foundation stage.* https://www.gov.uk/government/publications/early-years-foundation-stage-framework--2. Accessed on November 22, 2022.

Duffy, G., Miller, S., Parsons, S., & Meloth, M. (2009). Teachers as metacognitive professionals. In D. J. Hacker, J. Dunlosky, & A. C. Graesser (Eds.), *Handbook of metacognition in education* (pp. 240–256). Lawrence Erlbaum.

EEF. (2021). *Collaborative learning approaches.* https://educationendowmentfoundation.org.uk/education-evidence/teaching-learning-toolkit/collaborative-learning-approaches. Accessed on December 15, 2022.

Elliott, V., Nelson-Addy, L., Chantiluke, R., & Courtney, M. (2021). *Lit in colour: Diversity in literature in English schools research report.* The Runnymede Trust and Penguin Books.

Fletcher-Wood, H. (2018). *Responsive teaching: Cognitive Science and formative assessment in practice* (1st ed.). Routledge.

Franson, C. (2011). *Bilingualism and second language acquisition.* https://www.naldic.org.uk/eal-teaching-and-learning/outline-guidance/bilingualism/. Accessed on June 1, 2023.

Frederickson, N., & Cline, A. (2009). *Special educational needs inclusion and diversity.* McGraw-Hill Education.

Glazzard, J., & Green, M. (2022). *Learning to be a primary teacher: Core knowledge and understanding* (2nd ed.). Critical publishing.

Hattie, J. (2009). *Visible learning: A synthesis of over 800 meta-analyses related to achievement.* Routledge.

Johnston, P., Dozier, C., & Smit, J. (2016). How language supports adaptive teaching through a responsive learning culture. *Theory into Practice, 55,* 189–196.

Macleod, S., Sharp, C., Bernardinelli, D., Skipp, A., & Higgins, S. (2015). *Supporting the attainment of disadvantaged pupils: Articulating success and good practice research report.* Crown Copyright.

Medwell, J., Wray, D., Minns, H., Griffiths, V., & Coates, L. (2017). *Primary English: Teaching theory and practice* (8th ed.). Learning Matters.

Muijs, D., & Reynolds, D. (2011). *Effective teaching: Evidence and practice* (3rd ed.). SAGE.

Nasen (2014). *SEN support and the graduated approach.* Nasen.

Nuthall, G. (2007). *The hidden lives of learners.* NZCER Press.

Parsons, S., Vaughn, M., Scales, R., Gallagher, M., Parsons, A., Davis, S., Pierczynski, M., & Allen, M. (2018). Teachers' instructional adaptations: A research synthesis. *Review of Educational Research, 88*(2), 205–242.

Rochman, H. (1993). *Against borders: Promoting books for a multicultural world.* American Library Association.

Rowe, N., Wilkin, A., & Wilson, R. (2012) *Mapping of Seminal Reports on Good Teaching (NFER Research Programme: Developing the Education Workforce).* NFER. http://www.nfer.ac.uk/publications/RSGT01. Accessed on September 2, 2022.

Schön, D. (1983). *The reflective practitioner: How professionals think in action.* Temple Smith.

Schuelka, M. (2018). *Implementing inclusive education.* K4D Helpdesk Report. Institute of Development Studies.

Smith, M., & Stein, M. (1998). Selecting and creating mathematical tasks: From research to practice. *Mathematics Teaching in the Middle School, 3,* 344–350.

Tsaparlis, G. (2014). Cognitive demand. In R. Gunstone (Ed.), *Encyclopedia of science education.* Springer.

Van de Walle, J., Karp, K., & Bay-Williams, J. (2013). *Elementary and middle school mathematics: Teaching developmentally* (8th ed.). Pearson.

Watson, K. (n.d.). *Getting started with challenging 'more able' learners.* https://my.chartered.college/early-career-hub/getting-started-with-challenging-more-able-learners/. Accessed on May 14, 2023.

Wilson, H. (2020). *5 tips for teaching diversity, equity and inclusion* https://www.innovatemyschool.com/ideas/tips-for-making-your-school-truly-modern. Accessed on March 18, 2023.

4

Planning Lessons That Develop Children's Spoken Language Skills

Chapter Objectives

This chapter will:

- Consider what spoken language is and what knowledge and skills children need to develop.
- Explore the key components of language development, highlighting the relationships between developing children's language and developing them as readers and writers.
- Consider the environment for developing children's knowledge and understanding of what spoken language involves, fostering the skills they need to become effective oral communicators.
- Explore the key components of spoken language which underpin the structure of the national curriculum.
- Explore what the effective teaching of spoken language looks like, highlighting what effective teachers of spoken language do.
- Consider how to support children whose progress may not keep pace with age-related expectations.

Introduction

You may have heard the idea that reading and writing float on a sea of talk that has been widely attributed to Britton. No matter how adept they are at decoding words on the page, children will not be able to make sense of them unless they can match them to meaning from the knowledge of language that they have gained through speaking and listening, and in order to write a sentence, they must first have used their knowledge of language to think through what they want to write down. Children's understanding of language, then, is a crucial foundation for their reading and writing, as is recognised in *The National Curriculum for English:*

> Spoken language underpins the development of reading and writing. The quality and variety of language that pupils hear and speak are vital for developing their vocabulary and grammar and their understanding for reading and writing. (DFE, 2013, p. 3)

As well as being a vital resource for children's development as readers and writers, developing children's knowledge of and skills in the use of spoken language is also highly valuable in their own right. Spoken language is a powerful force. It is described by Bearne and Reedy (2017, p. 13) as

> the bedrock of children's personal, social, cultural, cognitive, creative and imaginative development...a means of thinking through ideas as well as a medium of communication and the most important resource for teaching and learning in and beyond the classroom.

In recent years, there has been a renewed focus on developing children's spoken language. This has highlighted its role in:

- deepening learning by supporting thinking and reasoning skills crucial to learning across the curriculum;
- raising both achievement and attainment;
- preparing pupils more effectively for the workplace;
- empowering pupils as agents of change;
- building relationships and emotional development.

Of course, we may well work with children who primarily or exclusively use other forms of communication, but for many, spoken language is used to share their thoughts, ideas, feelings, wishes and dreams, build relationships, and explain and develop their knowledge within the various communities to which they belong. It is a powerful medium which holds social and cultural value as well as being a primary channel through which they learn.

Activity   Reflecting on Your Own Spoken Language Skills

Make a list of all the occasions when you have used spoken language over the last two days, noting who you were speaking with (the audience, for example, friend, barista. . .) and the reason for speaking with them (the purpose, for example, social catch up, to order a coffee. . .).

How did each context for spoken language differ in terms of how you used language or the kinds of words you chose? For example, when catching up socially with friends, you might use more expressive language, including more exclamations (No! He didn't!) or words to convey your thoughts and feelings. Meanwhile, when interacting with a barista, you may use more transactional language (I'd like a..., Could I have that to take away?) to efficiently accomplish the task of ordering your favourite drink.

To what extent does the range of contexts you engaged in for your talk over the past 48 hours reflect your use of spoken language more generally? In what other contexts do you use spoken language? How do the purposes of and audiences for these contexts differ?

Are you comfortable talking in a wide range of contexts and with a wide range of people? What is it that makes you feel more or less comfortable in some contexts than in others? How might this affect you as a teacher of spoken language?

Now think about children you have worked with. With a new class, it is worth talking to their teacher, or previous teacher if you are an Early Career Teacher (ECT), to see how confident and skilled the children are, and to find out what kinds of opportunities they have had in the past to develop their spoken language skills.

Reflect on this activity as you read through this chapter.

Learning to Talk and Talking to Learn

While many children will arrive at school already able to talk, they will continue to develop their uses of language, learning to talk by becoming more proficient oral communicators in a wide range of contexts and for a variety of audiences. Through high-quality adult interactions and carefully planned learning and teaching, they will extend their knowledge and under-standing of words, phrases and language conventions which will support them not only in their verbal communication but also in the ability to read and write increasingly sophisticated texts. Learning to talk will be explored in more depth in the next chapter which looks at planning lessons that aim to develop children's spoken language. However, it is imperative to consider the role of spoken language in talking to learn more widely as it is likely to be a crucial element of lessons right across the curriculum in its role as a pedagogical tool for facilitating and extending learning. Spoken language is then 'not only the basis of reading and writing but also has a repertoire of its own which deserves equal attention in teaching' (Bearne & Reedy, 2017, p. 13).

Alexander (2020, p. 15) describes the power of talk for learning:

> ...of all the tools for educational intervention in students' development, talk is perhaps the most pervasive in its use and powerful in its possibilities. Talk vitally mediates the cognitive and cultural spaces between adult and child, among children themselves, between teacher and learner of any age, between society and the individual, between what the learner knows and understands and what he or she has yet to know and understand. Language not only manifests thinking but also structures it, and speech shapes the higher mental processes necessary for so much of the learning which takes place, or ought to take place, in school. So, one of the principal tasks of the teacher is to create interactive opportunities and encounters which directly and appropriately engineer such mediation.

Alexander's view here demonstrates why talk is such a powerful tool for scaffolding learning – it is through talk that we can negotiate back to what the learner already knows to take them forwards. Sometimes this is about using questions thoughtfully to ascertain what is known, and sometimes it is about rephrasing ideas in words that the learner can grasp. Therefore, every lesson is likely to both involve talk for learning and offer opportunities to develop children's proficiency in using spoken language.

Although the term 'spoken language' is used in the current version of the National Curriculum, it has previously been referred to as speaking and listening, and some teachers may be more comfortable with this as it highlights both elements essential for effective verbal communication. Recently, the use of the term 'oracy' has gained traction. This is attributed to Andrew Wilkinson in the 1960s. According to The Oracy All-Party Parliamentary Group,

> Oracy is our ability to communicate effectively using spoken language. It is the ability to speak eloquently, articulate ideas and thoughts, influence through talking, listen to others and have the confidence to express your views. These are all fundamental skills that support success in both learning and life beyond school. Oracy isn't just any talk that is happening - it is purposeful classroom talk which develops children's speaking and listening skills, and enhances their learning through the effective use of spoken language. (All-Party Parliamentary Group, 2021)

It's important to note that oracy is not just about formal uses of spoken language, for example, through debates or public speaking, but also includes all the ways in which people interact verbally, for example, through sharing information in learning or social situations, solving problems collaboratively and so on.

What Are the Components of Spoken Language?

Spoken language skills fall into two broad categories: receptive and expressive language. Receptive language skills involve the ability to understand what others say – either through speech or writing. At the vocabulary level, receptive vocabulary refers to all the words that can be understood by a person whether in spoken, written or signed form. This involves understanding words and sentences, and making sense of them so that their meaning is fully recognised. At the vocabulary level, expressive vocabulary refers to the words that a person can express or produce, for example, by speaking or writing them. Expressive language skills allow the speaker to share thoughts by constructing and articulating words and sentences, and communicating these so that meaning can be understood by others.

However, there is more to effective communication than words and sentences. A really useful resource which identifies all the components of effective communication is The Oracy Skills Framework developed by Oracy Cambridge and Voice 21, a national education charity which aims to transform the learning and life chances of young people through talk so that all children can use their voices for success in school and life. The Oracy Skills Framework defines the skills that underpin the effective use of spoken language in a wide variety of contexts. The skills are organised into four strands: physical, linguistic, cognitive, and social and emotional.

The Physical Components of Talk

The physical strand comprises ways in which people can use their voices and body language to support communication. In terms of voice, this includes our pace, tone, clarity of pronunciation and voice projection. Body language supports verbal communication using posture and gesture, eye contact and facial expression; these may have cultural significance, for example, in some cultures, nodding is a recognised, and even expected, polite way of communicating that you are listening and understanding. These aspects of spoken language communication that don't involve words are known as paralinguistics. We might be particularly aware of these aspects of talk in more formal contexts, such as presentations and interviews, but we also use them when talking with others to gain and keep their attention, emphasise particular ideas, and so on.

The Linguistic Components of Talk

The linguistic strand comprises our choice of vocabulary and register which should be appropriate to the context, purpose and audience, for example, using more formal language when presenting information as an expert and using more informal language when chatting to friends. A proficient speaker is likely to try to gauge how much the person they are speaking to knows (or cares) about a particular subject and may well alter the vocabulary used to take account of this (Macrory, 2021). It also draws on our knowledge of grammar so that we order and present our words in a way that can be easily understood. When talk involves conversation between two or more people, it is constructed at a given point in time between participants to achieve a collective purpose. There are a number of ways in which spoken and written language differ, for example, in dialogue with one or more people, spoken language uses a smaller pool of words, it typically has words with fewer syllables and uses more interjections such as 'Wow!' 'Really?', and colloquial or non-standard words (McCroskey et al., 2003). Ellipsis is often used

– that is the process of omission. In writing, this is often signified by the use of ... whereas in speech, it may be indicated by a pause, or not explicitly indicated at all but used for example in an answer to a question such as:

What you doing tonight?

Going to the cinema

The words 'Tonight' and 'I am' are omitted from the reply as full understanding is likely to have been established through the context. Spoken language also offers speakers and listeners opportunities to repair breaks in comprehension (Macrory, 2021) such as from the listener 'Wait, say that again', or 'So where were you when that happened?' and from the speaker in response to a blank look, 'You know that house with the big windows? The one by the duck pond. Just by the pub'.

You will see from the conversation extracts provided that people often talk in what are called utterances rather than full sentences. The rules, or accepted, grammar for spoken language may well differ from that used in written language. The final component of the linguistic strand of speech is the use of rhetorical techniques such as metaphor, humour, irony and mimicry. Rhetoric is simply the art of speaking persuasively or to convey a particular meaning. This helps to build rapport between speaker and listener, and good use of rhetorical techniques can support this, for example, using metaphor to explain someone as having a heart of gold aims to persuade you that this person is very kind, or using humour or anecdote to make someone laugh and share examples of how something works in practice.

The Cognitive Components of Talk

The cognitive strand refers to the conscious mental actions that are involved in any type of interaction, including contexts where the audience is more of a silent partner such as in a presentation. This includes the content the speaker chooses to talk about to fulfil their goals regarding what meaning they are trying to convey or what intention they are trying to fulfil. This content then has to be structured and organised in the best possible way. This will help to ensure that what is said is clear and easy to follow. Again, this will be highly influenced by the context and purpose of the talk, and the speaker will find it helpful to draw on their knowledge of typical conventions used in that situation. For example, when starting a conversation with someone, it is conventional to start by saying hello and asking them how they are before delving into the substance of what you want to say to them, whereas if you are presenting a two-minute speech on one of your hobbies, you might say hello but it is not expected that you ask each member of the audience how they are. Other cognitive skills include knowing when to clarify or summarise as a speaker (e.g., if the listener looks confused or bored), and recognising when to seek clarification or ask for a summary as a listener. Reasoning is another component of the cognitive strand of spoken language. This involves any participant in the dialogue in examining ideas critically and possibly prompting someone to give reasons to support their views. The final component of the cognitive strand is self-regulation. Both speaker and listener must take steps to monitor their focus and bring it back on track if needed, and/or use strategies to seek clarification.

The Social and Emotional Components of Talk

The final strand is the social and emotional one. As interaction involves more than one person, skilled use of spoken language requires developing awareness of the audience's needs. This includes being able to listen and respond appropriately to maintain connection, developing confidence to engage in both speaking and listening roles, and being engaging when in the speaker role. It also involves managing dialogue through turn-taking, enabling and extending conversations by making contributions, encouraging others to contribute, and checking back with the focus and purpose of the talk to see if it is on track, among other skills.

The authors of *The Oracy Framework* state clearly that they do not believe that it should be used as an assessment tool, but it is helpful in considering what successful communication is really made of, and indicating how children's skills can be developed through effective teacher modelling and discussions which will raise children's awareness and understanding of these components. These could be explored in a range of contexts, for example, using online resources such as Newsround or BBC Class Clips as a basis for class discussions on how effectively presenters employ specific components, evaluating live and online performances and visiting speakers, and using drama to set up different contexts in which the children explore different ways of trying out the various components.

The components of the four strands of *The Oracy Framework* all relate to pragmatics – the use of language and word choices within a particular context. Every context for spoken language requires the skills listed above to be adapted to suit. The National Curriculum for English highlights the importance of developing children's spoken language or oracy skills across the whole curriculum. Well-planned opportunities for children to use and develop their spoken language skills in all subjects will provide a wide range of authentic and meaningful contexts for purposeful oracy. The vast majority of learning, especially in the primary years, both relies on and offers rich opportunities to develop spoken language use, for example when making predictions in scientific investigations, discussing points of view in history, or giving instructions on technology.

Of course at first glance, classrooms often appear to centre around talk, particularly in some parts such as the opening of the lesson. Lessons typically involve some teacher talk and quite possibly some pupil talk. Teachers may ask questions, give feedback and guide learning, while children may answer the teacher's questions, perhaps ask some of their own, and discuss ideas with a partner or in a small group. However, this does not guarantee that the talk is of high quality or that it is really moving children's spoken language skills forwards as they may just be using already-known words and language structures. With younger pupils, we emphasise the value of high-quality interactions, considering how the teacher can support the children's thinking and language development when they are engaged in self (also known as child) -initiated learning. As pupils get older, we typically use the terms 'teacher' and 'pupil' 'talk'. However, teachers of Year R and Year 1 pupils need also to be skilled in planning and using high-quality teacher and pupil talk for the times when pupils are engaged in teacher-led, directed and supported learning, and teachers of older pupils need to be skilled in how to develop high-quality interactions with pupils for the times when they are working independently or in small groups.

Effective Pedagogy for Teaching Spoken Language

In ensuring that provision for spoken language is of high quality, Bearne and Reedy identify the following aspects:

- Teacher modelling of high-quality talk and how to listen and respond to pupils' (and others') utterances.
- Effective scaffolding and supporting of talk that enables children to become proficient in their spoken language skills, creating rich and authentic opportunities for talk to be stimulated and developed.
- Fostering an environment in which spoken language flourishes.

The teacher's role in being curious and enthusiastic about talk and language, understanding the different audiences we address, recognising the different purposes for which we talk, and acknowledging the roles of both the speaker and the listener is key. Bearne and Reedy (2017) also highlight that spoken language plays a crucial role in showing how we value the individual identities of our pupils by responding to the things that pupils talk about.

Key principles of effective pedagogy which will underpin high-quality learning and teaching of spoken language within a language-rich environment are:

1   Showing Real Interest in Children's Talk

This can be achieved by listening carefully to their ideas and feelings, and responding genuinely and supportively to foster an atmosphere of trust and enjoyment in interactions. A sensitive intervention will extend pupils' understanding, for example, by encouraging them to elaborate so that they add detail and description to things they are talking about, or by asking questions and providing statements to positively challenge and extend their thinking, engaging them in reviewing or justifying their thinking as well as expanding it to consider 'what if?'. This supports the development of pupils' metacognitive and critical thinking skills, as they begin to internalise ways in which thinking can be challenged. Teachers need to be highly skilled listeners themselves so that they can judge when and how to promote, prompt, probe, enrich, build, extend and challenge the children's thinking and verbal expressions. Showing genuine interest in and enthusiasm for words spoken by pupils and adults, and those found in a wide range of fiction and non-fiction publications, will also support the development of a language-rich environment.

2 Provide Authentic, Engaging and Meaningful Opportunities for Pupils to Talk Across the Full Curriculum

Planning where rich discussions can take place, for example, when children are devising practice activities and games in physical education (PE), debating the character strengths or impact of people and events in history, and making predictions about what might happen when planning a scientific experiment, will all provide strong opportunities for pupils to develop their language skills. Within the context of English, carefully posed questions which enable children to explore and discuss their understanding of or responses to a book, poem, song, performance, video or experience offer language-rich opportunities, as do the use of drama and other indirect planning opportunities in preparation for writing.

3 Teach Vocabulary Explicitly

All areas of the curriculum offer opportunities to build a wealth of high-quality vocabulary which will extend the precision with which children talk about ideas, events and experiences. Curriculum subjects offer opportunities for children to explore disciplinary thinking, for example, historians develop knowledge and understanding of people and places over time by using language related to chronology as well as historical concepts such as cause and consequence, and similarity and difference. They also use language to enable them to make connections, ask questions, search for clues, synthesise and make deductions from sources of evidence, and construct plausible narratives. High-quality reading materials include a wealth of rich vocabulary to extend children's knowledge and understanding, enabling them to develop a deeper understanding of characters, settings and plots in fiction, and many different aspects of the world in non-fiction. Skilful teaching which engages children meaningfully with new words in and from these contexts so that they become part of the children's own spoken vocabulary enables them to become a resource for their own speaking and writing.

4 Model High Standards of Spoken Language

Finally, it is critical that the teacher and other adults are excellent models of high-quality spoken language, using a rich variety of words and sentence stems to express themselves clearly and with intent, and highlighting how talk changes in different contexts. This will support children's implicit knowledge and understanding of language, which can then be drawn out explicitly for learning. This modelling will include the demonstration and use of waiting time (sources differ on this but typically suggest 3–5 seconds for closed questions and longer for open questions) to allow the listener space to think about what they have just heard and to compose a response thoughtfully.

These aspects of effective pedagogy for teaching spoken language should be embedded in classroom practice to provide strong foundations on which purposeful learning of spoken language can be built.

Developing High-Quality Interactions With Children

Engaging children in effective adult–pupil interactions which genuinely support their thinking and language skills is a really important teaching skill. There are many opportunities within the school day when skilled adult–pupil interactions could foster children's development, and a number of approaches which could be taken, such as sustained shared thinking (SST) and back-and-forth talk.

Sustained Shared Thinking

Research carried out by Siraj-Blatchford et al. (2002) highlighted the role of SST as a particularly valuable way of developing children's learning and a consistent feature of excellent provision. SST has typically been considered within the context of younger pupils' learning; however, the principles apply to effective interactions throughout primary school. The authors define SST as,

> An episode in which two or more individuals "work together" in an intellectual way to solve a problem, clarify a concept, evaluate activities, extend a narrative etc. Both parties must contribute to the thinking and it must develop and extend. (2002, p. 8)

SST is characterised by the use of open questioning and prompts as a way of stimulating children's imaginations and extending their thinking and uses of language while they are involved in exploration or play-based learning. The authors note that activities initiated by the children themselves may be particularly powerful vehicles for SST. The Education Endowment Foundation (EEF, 2018) summarised the following techniques that adults might use to encourage SST:

- Tuning in – listening carefully to what is being said and observing what the child is doing.
- Showing genuine interest – giving whole attention, eye contact, and smiling and nodding.
- Asking children to elaborate – 'I really want to know more about this'.
- Recapping – 'So you think that…'.
- Giving their own experience – 'I like to listen to music when cooking at home'.
- Clarifying ideas – 'So you think we should wear coats in case it rains?'
- Using encouragement to extend thinking – 'You have thought really hard about your tower, but what can you do next?'
- Suggesting – 'You might want to try doing it like this'.
- Reminding – 'Don't forget that you said we should wear coats in case it rains'.
- Asking open questions – 'How did you?', 'Why does this…?', 'What happens next?'. (EEF, 2018, p. 9)

Genuine interest from the teacher is key as this typically communicates significant encouragement, signalling an atmosphere of trust and encouragement to enable the child to feel confident to explore in response to the questions and prompts. More recent guidance from the EEF suggests an approach called ShREC, which draws on many of the principles of SST. The ShREC approach involves:

1 **Sh**aring attention by showing interest and tuning into what a child is focused on.
2 **R**esponding sensitively to them once they are engaged with you.
3 **E**xpanding their understanding of words and spoken language by modelling slightly more complex responses (e.g., the child says 'dog' and the adult says 'Yes, it's a small dog'.
4 **C**onversing in a sustained way involving back-and-forth contributions. They highlight the role of commenting (e.g., narrating something that the child is doing) here rather than asking too many questions. (James, 2022)

Secure knowledge and understanding of the curriculum in relation to the child's individual development is an essential element of highly effective practice; without this, the teacher may not be able to prompt the children in an authentic and meaningful way thus lessening the value of this approach.

Recent guidance from the Department for Education (DfE) has also focused on the importance of children's spoken language. In The Reading Framework (DfE, 2023), key principles for effective adult–pupil interactions are defined through the use of back-and-forth talk.

Document Summary: Back-and-forth Talk in the Reading Framework (DfE, 2023)

The Reading Framework identifies the need for a language-rich environment, defined as,

> one in which adults talk with children throughout the day. The more children take part in conversations, the more they will understand once they can read and the more vocabulary and ideas they will have to draw on when they can write. ... [These] form the foundations for language and cognitive development. The number and quality of the conversations they have with adults and peers throughout the day in a language-rich environment is crucial. (DfE, 2023, p. 21–22)

These back-and-forth interactions involve the adult in:

- thinking out loud, modelling new language for children;
- paying close attention to what the children say;
- rephrasing and extending what the children say;

(Continued)

- validating the children's attempts at using new vocabulary and grammar by rephrasing what children say if necessary;
- asking closed and open questions;
- answering the children's questions;
- explaining why things happen;
- deliberately connecting current and past events ('Do you remember when. . .?');
- providing models of accurate grammar;
- extending children's vocabulary and explaining new words;
- connecting one idea or action to another;
- helping children to articulate ideas in well-formed sentences.

The document highlights that developing and extending children's language takes careful, deliberate planning in each area of learning, focusing on:

- What do we want children to know and think about?
- What vocabulary is associated with this knowledge and thinking?
- How can we engage the children in back-and-forth talk that supports their knowledge and thinking?
- What photos could we take that would reinforce the vocabulary and language after an activity or visit?
- Which books could be read aloud and shared before and afterwards?
- Which songs might introduce or reinforce the vocabulary?

You will see that back-and-forth talk is presented here as a more directive approach than SST. It is important to think about the purpose of interacting with a child at any time and drawing on the most relevant aspects of either or both frameworks to support children's thinking and language development in any given context.

High-Quality Teacher Talk

Sometimes, the teacher will want to talk for an extended period of time, for example, when modelling something, or engaging in other types of talk such as giving instructions which require the children to listen. However, there are times when teachers use questions to elicit children's understanding and aim to take their learning forward through dialogue. Research shows that most of this kind of talk in classrooms is dominated by teachers and often takes the form of interactions known as initiation–response–feedback (IRF) or initiation–response–evaluation (IRE). IRF/IRE exchanges are described by Sinclair and Coulthard: 'A typical exchange in the classroom consists of an initiation by the teacher, followed by a response from the pupil, followed by feedback to the pupil's response from the teacher...' (Coulthard, 1992, p. 3) and can be seen in the following example:

> T: ...And er, I've got this here. What's that? Trevor. (initiation)
>
> P: An axe. (response) T: It's an axe yes. What do we cut with the axe? (follow-up)/ (initiation) P: Wood, wood (response)
>
> T: Yes I cut wood with the axe... (follow – up) (Sinclair & Coulthard, 1975, p. 94)

Alexander (2020) notes that research such as this demonstrates a number of limitations with much classroom talk between pupils and teachers. For example, exchanges are often short rather than sustained, and teacher questions are often closed, requiring one correct answer and prompting low-level recall rather than deeper thinking. Concerns over pace and participation may influence teacher talk, with teachers feeling a need to move on quickly with the lesson or to get others involved, which may result in a lack of waiting time being given for pupils to formulate their responses. Feedback is often evaluative so that everyone knows whether the response was right or wrong but may contain little useful information beyond that to consolidate and develop pupils' learning.

An alternative to these limited IRF/IRE exchanges is offered through Alexander's suggested approach, dialogic teaching. Alexander (2020) details why adopting a dialogic approach to teaching is so valuable:

> It harnesses the power of talk to engage their interest, stimulate thinking,
> advance understanding, expand ideas and build and evaluate arguments, empowering
> them for lifelong learning and democratic engagement. Being collaborative and
> supportive, it confers social and emotional benefits too. Dialogic teaching helps
> teachers. By encouraging students to share their thinking, it enables teachers to
> diagnose needs, devise learning tasks, enhance understanding, assess progress
> and assist students through the challenges they encounter. (Alexander,
> 2020, p. 1).

Alexander suggests that to enable dialogic teaching, teachers should develop a repertoire for talk which enables them to expand beyond the limited patterns described above and instead develops a broader range of strategies and skills which can be utilised according to the teacher's professional judgement.

Alexander's Repertoire for Teacher Talk

Alexander's repertoire for teaching talk comprises these eight purposes:

- **Rote** (teacher-class): memorising facts, formulae and routines through constant repetition.
- **Recitation** (teacher-class or teacher-group): using short teacher question/student answer sequences to recall what has previously been encountered, or to test what is presumed or required to be already known or to cue pupils to work out the answer from clues provided in the question.
- **Instruction** (teacher-class, teacher-group or teacher-individual): telling pupils what to do, and/or how to do it.
- **Exposition** (teacher-class, teacher-group or teacher-individual) imparting information, and/or explaining ideas or procedures, narrating.
- **Discussion** (teacher-class, teacher-group or pupil-pupil): exchanging ideas and information and juxtaposing viewpoints.
- **Deliberation** (teacher-class, teacher-group or pupil-pupil): weighing the merits of ideas, opinions or evidence.
- **Argumentation** (teacher-class, teacher-group or pupil-pupil): making or testing a case by reference to reasons or evidence.
- **Scaffolded dialogue** (teacher-class, teacher-group, teacher-individual or pupil-pupil): working towards common understanding through structured questioning, probed and elaborated responses and an interactive dynamic that strives to be collective, reciprocal and supportive as well as cumulative, deliberative and purposeful. (Alexander, 2020, p. 145)

In *Talk for Teaching and Learning: the Dialogic Classroom,* Reedy and Bearne provide a helpful example to show how some of the purposes for teacher talk identified by Alexander can be applied within a Year 3 lesson focusing on reading comprehension. In this example, the teacher and pupils are working together to develop their understanding of the text *The Worst Witch* by Jill Murphy, focusing on the character of Miss Hardbroom:

- **Recitation** – Teacher asks children to recall what has happened in previous chapters and what they know about the main characters, particularly Miss Hardbroom.
- **Exposition** – The teacher reads aloud the new chapter, clarifying unfamiliar vocabulary and checking the children have understood what has happened.
- **Discussion** – The class or group discuss what they've discovered about Miss Hardbroom in the chapter.
- **Deliberation** – Consider whether it has changed their view of her as a character.

- **Whole class plenary** – Children are asked to share their ideas and the teacher probes their responses, prompting them to justify their answers using argumentation to challenge their thinking by citing evidence from the text. (Reedy & Bearne, 2021, p. 13)

The teacher starts by using recitation to check the children's prior knowledge and prompting recall to tune them into the lesson's focus. The teacher then shares the stimulus for thinking, using exposition. This also provides a good model of fluent reading for the pupils. The teacher then leads a discussion – this could involve the whole class or may involve the children talking in small groups. It can be helpful to set a clear end goal for the discussion, perhaps in the form of a succinct question or provoking statement. For example, in this context, it could be that the pupil discussion aims to answer a question such as 'What are the positive and negative aspects of Miss Hardbroom's character?', or it could aim to argue for or against a statement such as 'Miss Hardbroom is mean'. The teacher then uses deliberation to support the children's ability to reflect on their learning and see whether it has changed anything in their views.

Activity   Reflecting on Teacher Talk

Take a lesson plan, either that you have taught (or intend to teach) or one that has been constructed by someone else.

Highlight any places where there is a planned teacher talk. You could include any key questions indicated.

Using the list of eight purposes for teacher talk, see if you can match the teacher talk and questions to the purposes. Consider the aim of each instance of teacher talk and the demands made on the children's language skills. Does each type of teacher talk match the aim? Are there opportunities where other kinds of teacher talk could be useful? In the lesson, are the children's spoken language extended or will they only be drawing on the language they already know?

The aim of this is not to get all types of teacher talk into each lesson, nor necessarily to ensure that children learn new words and phrases in every lesson. Instead, it is to reflect on teacher habits and determine whether the purpose of the teacher talk achieves its aims. Of course, over time lessons will need to foster children's spoken language development explicitly if they are to make good progress, so you could expand your review to look at lessons taught over a week.

If by looking at your chosen lesson plan you have identified that the teacher relied on a more limited range of talk, or that it probably drew only on language that the children already knew, reflect on how you might aim to extend the teacher talk repertoire, and/or how explicit teaching may help children's spoken language development.

Pupil Talk

As well as identifying eight types of teacher talk, Alexander (2020) identifies eight purposes for children's talk:

- **Transactional**: to manage encounters and situations.
- **Expository**: to narrate, expound and explain.
- **Interrogatory**: to ask questions of different kinds and in diverse contexts.
- **Exploratory**: to venture, explore and probe ideas.
- **Deliberative**: to reason and argue.
- **Imaginative**: to contemplate and argue what might be.
- **Expressive**: to put thoughts into words, nuance ideas, articulate feelings and responses
- **Evaluative**: to deliver opinions, form and articulate judgements. (Alexander, 2020, p. 143)

As you can see, there is some overlap with the teacher talk here. Again, the aim is not to teach our children to be able to list these types of talk. Instead, we should think about the kinds of talk we are asking of our children to identify how best to scaffold their learning so that they can use each type of talk with increasing fluency and confidence. Reedy and Bearne's excellent *Talk for Teaching and Learning: The Dialogic Classroom* explores these ideas in some depth, giving lots of practical ideas for how these types of talk can be developed in the classroom.

Giving children sentence stems, the opening few words of a sentence, can really help to support their thinking (it needs to be modelled in context first). Children can also be supported through explicit vocabulary teaching. In the example we looked at above, the teacher could choose to extend the children's language, perhaps by including some vocabulary work on adjectives to describe characters, or the use of sentence stems to help the children to structure their ideas, for example, 'I believe that...' before putting forward an idea about Miss Hardbroom, and 'I agree with...' or 'I disagree with', 'On the other hand...', to help them to build on each other's thinking. Use of sentence stems should be carefully planned to build on the children's prior knowledge and skills and introduced judiciously so as not to overload them.

Activity   Reflecting on Pupil Talk

Take a lesson plan, either that you have taught (or intend to teach) or one that has been constructed by someone else (this could be the one you used to reflect on teacher talk). This could be within the context of an English lesson, or you could instead consider a different curriculum subject as a way to reflect on how effectively high-quality talk for learning is planned and supported.

Highlight any places where there is a planned pupil talk.

Using the list of eight purposes for pupil talk, see if you can match this to any of the eight purposes. Consider the aim of each instance of pupil talk and reflect on what they need to know to be able to communicate effectively. Will it extend the children's knowledge of spoken language and skills in its use or will they only be drawing on what they already know?

The aim of this is not necessarily to dictate that children learn new words and phrases in every lesson, but to reflect on whether the purpose of the pupil talk achieves its aims and explicitly fosters children's spoken language development over time.

Reflect on how the children's repertoire of talk could be extended, considering what components of spoken language could be developed and how this could be scaffolded to secure good progress.

Developing the skills needed to teach spoken language effectively is challenging and will take time to embed. You may find it helpful to choose one or two ideas at a time and/or to focus on one curriculum subject at a time. It is worth focusing your attention and practice to get one or two particular aspects right at a time and make sure they are fully embedded in your practice rather than to employ a more general scattergun approach which lacks quality and staying power. Choosing small goals to master will soon add up to you making a real difference in the quality of teacher and pupil talk in both your teaching of English and across the curriculum.

Supporting Children Whose Progress May Not Keep Pace With Age-Related Expectations

Of course some children will involve themselves more readily in talk activities than others, and some may be keen to join in but find it challenging to engage fully. If you have concerns about any particular pupil, you need to talk to your class teacher and possibly the SENDCo to get some advice which is tailored to the individual. It is always good to start from a position of understanding so spending time talking with and observing the child to determine their specific strengths and next steps will be of most value in helping you to plan how to support them during talk activities and determine whether a specific intervention programme is needed. However, the following scaffolds might enable pupils who are less confident or proficient in their use of spoken language to participate well in learning activities:

- Make sure that visual supports are in place – would the child benefit from their own set of prompt cards to support an activity, or could you display key images or questions for discussion on the interactive whiteboard so that they don't also need to remember what they are talking about?

- Consider whether concrete learning experiences would help the child to develop key vocabulary and give them more time to engage with an idea so that they have plenty of time to prepare for pair, group and class discussions.
- Consider the needs of shyer children – would they benefit from practising in advance, working in smaller groups and/or feeding back quietly to an adult rather than to the whole class?
- Support their understanding by using non-verbal gestures clearly.
- Think really carefully about where to seat pupils so that they can see and hear really clearly.
- Make sure that you give a pupil enough time to think before they respond. If children are working in pairs or small groups, you might need to talk to them about this so that they can support each other effectively.
- Make sure all children have had enough time to think and talk about their ideas before they start writing – they may also benefit from other forms of indirect planning such as drawing and drama. Some children may find using a planning proforma helpful.
- Make sure that all children have had plenty of time to talk about anything they have read in general terms so that they understand the text clearly before they move on to answering more challenging questions about it.
- Always say the child's name and make sure you have their attention before giving an instruction so they know you are talking to them and can tune in.
- Make sure that ground rules for talk are in place and the children are familiar with them. Think about whether using an object to pass around might help children who find it hard to remember to take turns.
- Consider whether the use of sentence stems (these could be on the interactive whiteboard (IWB) for most pupils but some may also benefit from having their own cards) to help pupils express their ideas.
- Make sure that adults model good spoken language and listening skills, and that any child whose progress causes concern has plenty of opportunity to see these models, and to interact with these adults.
- Make sure all talk activities have a clear goal (e.g., to explain why the Three Bears were so upset with Goldilocks). Break down discussions as needed – for example, you could give them two minutes to talk about the story, then a further two minutes to talk about the bears found when they arrived home, and then two minutes to talk about what the bears said and did that showed how they felt about what they found. Sometimes, this might be followed by asking the children to decide on one sentence that answers your question which they could practise orally before feeding back or sharing with the class.

Planning for Diversity, Inclusion and Adaptive Teaching

- As far as possible, ensure that the models you share and discuss with pupils represent a diverse range of voices from different backgrounds, and include positive role models which reflect society in full.

- Ensure that analysis of talk is always respectful and celebrates strengths as well as exploring aspects that could perhaps be even better.
- Make sure that you have provided for the individual learning needs of any pupils with SEND so that they can access and participate in activities.

Summary

This chapter has considered an evidence-informed approach to the teaching of spoken language, focusing on ways in which teachers can build both their own and their children's understanding of and repertoires for the use of talk to support learning. Key principles that underpin the teacher's role in supporting the development of high-quality spoken language are presented, and key approaches for ensuring quality interactions with pupils are suggested.

Further Reading

1   To find out more about teacher and pupil talk, read *A Dialogic Teaching Companion* by Robin Alexander, published by Routledge.
2   To find out more about different types of pupil talk and how these can be planned for successfully within primary English, read *Talk for Teaching and Learning: The Dialogic Classroom* by David Reedy and Eve Bearne, published by the United Kingdom Literacy Association.
3   Look at the EEF's guidance on supporting children's language skills. The need to develop pupils' oral language is a key principle in their improving literacy guidance which can be found at: https://d2tic4wvo1iusb.cloudfront.net/production/eef-guidance-reports/literacy-early-years/Preparing_Literacy_Guidance_2018.pdf?v=1693806440 for pupils in EYFS; https://educationendowmentfoundation.org.uk/education-evidence/guidance-reports/literacy-ks-1 for pupils in Key Stage 1; and https://educationendowmentfoundation.org.uk/education-evidence/guidance-reports/literacy-ks2 for pupils in Key Stage 2.

References

Alexander, R. (2020). *A dialogic teaching companion*. Routledge.

All-Party Parliamentary Group. (2021). *Speak for change: Final report and recommendations from the Oracy All-Party Parliamentary Group Inquiry*. https://oracy.inparliament.uk/files/oracy/2021-04/Oracy_APPG_FinalReport_28_04_21_4.pdf. Accessed on January 15, 2023.

Bearne, E., & Reedy, D. (2017). *Teaching primary English: Subject knowledge and classroom practice*. Routledge.

Coulthard, M. (1992). *Advances in spoken discourse analysis* (pp. 1–34). Routledge.

Department for Education. (2013) *The national curriculum in England: Key stages 1 and 2 framework document.* https://www.gov.uk/government/publications/national-curriculum-in-england-primary-curriculum. Accessed on May 16, 2022.

Department for Education. (2023). *The reading framework.* Crown Copyright.

Education Endowment Foundation. (2018). *Preparing for literacy: Improving communication, language and literacy in the early years.* Education Endowment Foundation.

James, F. (2022). *The ShREC approach – 4 evidence-informed strategies to promote high quality interactions with young children.* https://educationendowmentfoundation.org.uk/news/eef-blog-the-shrec-approach-4-evidence-informed-strategies-to-promote-high-quality-interactions-with-young-children. Accessed on March 27, 2023.

Macrory, G. (2021). *Learning to talk: The many contexts of children's language development.* SAGE.

McCroskey, J., Wrench, J., & Richmond, V. (2003). *Principles of public speaking.* The College Network.

Reedy, D., & Bearne, E. (2021). *Talk for teaching and learning: The dialogic classroom.* UKLA.

Sinclair, J. M., & Coulthard, M. (1975). *Towards an analysis of discourse: The English used by teachers and pupils.* Oxford University Press.

Siraj-Blatchford, I., Sylva, K., Muttock, S., Gilden, R., & Bell, D. (2002). *Researching effective pedagogy in the Early years.* https://dera.ioe.ac.uk/id/eprint/4650/1/RR356.pdf. Accessed on April 24, 2023.

5

Planning to Teach Spoken Language

Chapter Objectives

This chapter will:

- Identify the key elements of a high-quality spoken language curriculum.
- Consider what effective pedagogy for teaching spoken language might look like.
- Demonstrate ways to approach planning for the development of children's spoken language skills.

This chapter looks at the requirements for teaching spoken language. The key knowledge and skills children need are introduced and explored, along with principles of effective pedagogy that underpin high-quality teaching.

Introduction

The school day is a very busy one, with teachers and children continually challenged to cover the full curriculum and attain increasingly high proportions of pupils meeting and exceeding age-rated expectations. It is perhaps for these reasons that spoken language is not yet consistently planned explicitly and systematically in all schools. However, as we saw in the previous chapter, high-quality learning and teaching in spoken language has a strong impact on many aspects of children's academic, personal and social development. For all these reasons, it is good to see that professional discussions about spoken language are becoming much more frequent in schools. It is, therefore, important that teachers know how to plan effectively for this element of the English curriculum.

Document Focus: The Oxford Language Report

The Oxford Language Report presented the results of a survey of around 1,300 primary and secondary school teachers, carried out in 2017/2018. Its aim was to explore the idea of what is known as 'the word gap' – the view that pupils who experience socio-economic disadvantage have a smaller vocabulary than their more affluent peers. Specifically, the survey aimed to find out teachers' perceptions of:

- How many children are affected by the word gap in the UK in primary and secondary schools?
- The root causes of the word gap and how this impacts pupils' academic achievement and life chances.
- What successful strategies schools have put in place to close the word gap?

A number of the 473 primary teachers surveyed reported concerns around different levels of vocabulary which they felt affected their children's learning, resulting in

> weaker comprehension skills and slower than expected progress in reading and writing...86% of primary teachers...responded that they thought it was very or extremely challenging for pupils with a limited vocabulary to read national test papers. (OUP, 2018, p. 6)

A number of teachers also reported that they felt the word gap was increasing. Over half of the primary teachers surveyed felt that the word gap impacts negatively on children's self-esteem, likelihood of staying in education, and behaviour, while around a quarter thought it made it more difficult for them to make friends and impacted negatively on their school attendance.

The report suggests that ways to develop children's language include:

- using a rich variety of words in interactions with children, including when giving them instructions;
- sharing lots of high-quality texts through read-alouds;

- talking about books;
- giving children opportunities to play around with language.

Ways to help children to develop an ear for language include:

- oral storytelling;
- performing poetry;
- using audiobooks.

The report also suggests a need for the early identification of children who may need intervention takes place and emphasises that high-quality teaching will support effective development.

Whilst surveys like the Oxford Language Report can be useful in sharing teachers' perceptions of critical issues in learning and teaching, it is important to note that some people are highly critical about the terminology that can be used in relation to vocabulary and pupils experiencing socio-economic disadvantage (e.g., see Cushing, 2020). Their view is that the idea of a gap suggests a deficit model in which pupils are seen to be lacking. It is worth being mindful of this, and thinking about how you will support children's language development in a positive way which doesn't discredit home background and practices. Look at what they already know as a starting point and show interest in the ways that they express themselves, aiming to expand their repertoire, rather than communicating that one way is right or wrong.

Curriculum Continuity and Progression

The Department for Education's (DfE) *Development Matters* (2023) guidance highlights the importance of developing children's spoken language as a foundation for all other learning, impacting children's language and cognitive development across the curriculum. This development takes place within the context of a language-rich environment which is characterised by rich interactions between adults and children, reading to and with children, exposing them to high-quality stories, songs, rhymes, poems and non-fiction texts, and storytelling and role play.

As we saw in the previous chapter, language skills can be divided broadly into two main categories. Receptive language skills are those needed for someone to be able to understand what others say or read to them, or what they have read for themselves. Expressive language skills involve the ability to communicate thoughts and ideas to others, typically through speech and/or writing. As effective communication is a two-way process between speaker and listener, both receptive and expressive language skills are needed.

In Year R, children should be taught the skills of:

- careful listening;
- questioning to check their understanding;

- using and responding to social phrases;
- listening to and talking about stories;
- retelling stories.

They will also learn a range of new vocabulary and use it throughout the day. Additionally, they will learn to describe events in some detail, and connect ideas using words such as 'because'.

Spoken language is also identified or implied in a number of other areas of learning:

- In the area of personal, social and emotional development, children will be taught to build constructive and respectful relationships, express and manage a range of feelings, think about the perspectives of others, and talk about different factors that support their overall health and well-being.
- In physical development, children will extend their knowledge of words that describe fundamental movement skills such as rolling, crawling and walking.
- In literacy, children will learn to read letters and words by saying and blending individual sounds (phonemes). In developing or extending their love of reading, they are likely to discuss books, and in learning to write short sentences, they are likely to use the skill of oral rehearsal so that they compose a sentence aloud using spoken language before writing it.
- In mathematics, children will learn a range of mathematical vocabulary to help them learn to count, talk through their mathematical thinking, and use the language of comparison when talking about measures such as length and weight.
- In understanding the world, children will extend their vocabularies when learning to understand the world around them, talking about their families and communities, describing people who are familiar to them and beginning to understand the past. They will also explore similarities and differences between life in this country and in other countries.
- Finally, in expressive arts and design, children will develop vocabulary relating to artistic effects such as colour, shape and texture, learn to express their feelings about music, art, dance and performance, and create storylines in their pretend play.

Children who have met the Early Learning Goals (ELGs) by the end of Year R will have demonstrated their ability to do the following:

1 **Listening, Attention and Understanding ELG**
    - Listen attentively and respond to what they hear with relevant questions, comments and actions when being read to and during whole class discussions and small group interactions.
    - Make comments about what they have heard and ask questions to clarify their understanding.
    - Hold conversation when engaged in back-and-forth exchanges with their teacher and peers.

2   **Speaking ELG**

- Participate in small group, class and one-to-one discussions, offering their own ideas, using recently introduced vocabulary.
- Offer explanations for why things might happen, making use of recently introduced vocabulary from stories, non-fiction, rhymes and poems when appropriate.
- Express their ideas and feelings about their experiences using full sentences, including the use of past, present and future tenses and making use of conjunctions, with modelling and support from their teacher. (DfE, 2023, p. 19)

Moving into Year 1, children in most schools will follow *The National Curriculum in England: English Programmes of Study for Key Stage 1 and Key Stage 2* (DfE, 2013). The expectations for spoken language are particularly interesting here as, unlike in the other subjects or strands identified, there is no clear progression, just the same set of 12 statements which apply to all pupils from Year 1 to Year 6. This means that a school and its teachers will decide how to ensure that these statements are pitched at a level which is appropriate to the age of the pupils and build effectively on what has come before. A useful resource to support possible lines of progression from Year 1 to Year 6 has been produced by The Communication Trust (see https://speechandlanguage.org.uk/talking-point/for-professionals/the-communication-trust/more-resources/communicating-the-curriculum/communicating-the-curriculum-resource-page/). Whether a school has based their spoken language curriculum on this guidance or not, the progression might help with pitching a lesson as you can reflect on the various statements to identify a reasonable starting point based on your assessments of what you know your pupils can already do, or through discussions with the class teacher.

The 12 statements which outline what pupils should be taught are:

1 Listen and respond appropriately to adults and their peers.
2 Ask relevant questions to extend their understanding and knowledge.
3 Use relevant strategies to build their vocabulary.
4 Articulate and justify answers, arguments and opinions.
5 Give well-structured descriptions, explanations and narratives for different purposes, including for expressing feelings.
6 Maintain attention and participate actively in collaborative conversations, staying on topic and initiating and responding to comments.
7 Use spoken language to develop understanding through speculating, hypothesising, imagining and exploring ideas.
8 Speak audibly and fluently with an increasing command of Standard English.
9 Participate in discussions, presentations, performances, role play, improvisations and debates.
10 Gain, maintain and monitor the interest of the listener(s).
11 Consider and evaluate different viewpoints, attending to and building on the contributions of others.
12 Select and use appropriate registers for effective communication. (DfE, 2013, p. 7)

By grouping these statements into similar themes, we can see that the spoken language curriculum aims to develop children's proficiency in oral communication by teaching them to:

- Develop effective listening skills (statements 1 and 10).
- Monitor their understanding of what they hear (statements 2 and 6).
- Build their knowledge of words (statement 3).
- Develop their knowledge and understanding of the different purposes for using spoken language (statements 4, 5, 7, 9 and 11).
- Develop their understanding of standard and non-standard forms and different registers for language use (statements 8 and 12).

In *The National Curriculum in England: English Programmes of Study for Key Stage 1 and Key Stage 2* (DfE, 2013), the guidance states that it is the intention that the 12 statements are 'reflected and contextualised within the reading and writing domains which follow'. As in all aspects of the English curriculum, it is important that spoken language is developed within purposeful and authentic classroom contexts. Examples of such contexts include discussing children's understanding of and responses to reading materials (see Chapters 8 and 9), listening to and talking with adults and peers in a range of curriculum subjects, and as a crucial part of the writing process (Chapters 10–12).

In this chapter, we will explore these statements, and consider some contexts and activities that teachers can use to support learning and teaching in the classroom. These will be explored in the order of how they have been grouped above, rather than as they appear in the National Curriculum. Before that, it is worth quickly recapping the principles of effective pedagogy which will underpin high-quality learning and teaching of spoken language within a language-rich environment, as established in the previous chapter:

- Show real interest in children's talk.
- Provide authentic, engaging and meaningful opportunities for pupils to talk across the full curriculum.
- Teach vocabulary explicitly.
- Model high standards of spoken language.

Developing Effective Listening Skills (Statements 1 and 10)

Listening and Responding Appropriately to Adults and Their Peers (Statement 1)

Listening is a key skill which supports children's social, cultural and cognitive development and engagement. As children progress through primary school, they typically become increasingly able to listen for longer periods of time and are steadily more successful at managing competing distractions. They also become more skilled at dual-channelled attention – the ability to carry out an activity while listening actively to information being presented verbally. This supports them in carrying out classroom instructions and listening to more complex and detailed texts. Active listening is the practice of engaging closely with what a speaker is saying in order to develop a full understanding.

Ellis (2019) suggests that there are two key components for the effective teaching of listening: making listening necessary and encouraging active listening. To make listening necessary, they suggest that planning activities where careful listening is necessary to success is key. Other useful points are to avoid repeating yourself where possible, making sure that children answer the exact question asked, encouraging children to speak clearly and loudly enough for everyone to hear, and sometimes speaking quietly yourself can all help children to learn to tune in and listen effectively. However, it is of course important to note that in all spoken language learning, showing professional judgement and sensitivity to children's needs is key. Therefore, it might be right to repeat yourself at times if this is best for the learner at any given moment. Rather, these are principles which can guide your general behaviour to encourage the children's development as good listeners, but you judge the time and place when it is right to reinforce them.

To encourage active listening, Cambridge Assessment International Education (CAIE) suggests drawing children's attention to and making use of the physical aspects of communication such as non-verbal gestures and variations in your pace, tone and volume. They also recommend using questions to structure listening and asking children to paraphrase what they have just heard, as well as building opportunities for children to reflect on their listening.

The progression outlined in *Communicating the Curriculum* suggests that children learn to identify and keep track of key points when listening. By the end of Year 6, they should be able to follow increasingly complex instructions, listen in turn to more than one speaker, and compare different points of view. Of course, a natural context for developing this skill is listening to a range of texts being read-aloud, and watching or listening to talks and presentations such as those found in the BBC's teaching resource https://www.bbc.co.uk/teach.

Whilst listening skills are best developed through carefully planned authentic and meaningful learning tasks in the main, there are some games which can help to develop children's learning skills. Barrier games involve children working in pairs with a barrier of some sort between them so that the listener cannot see the speaker. The speaker gives a set of instructions, for example, getting the listener to draw something, following a route on a map, building something and so on. Instructions must be clear and precise and listening must be active. There are also some great turn-taking games where again children work in pairs to create or retell a story (or historical narrative/explain a scientific process that they know well etc.), either taking turns word by word, sentence by sentence or until the teacher says 'switch'. To succeed, they have to listen carefully to what their partner has said in order to provide continuity. For older learners, you could play radio games such as 'Just a Minute' where the speaker talks on a given topic for up to a minute and their fellow panellists listen carefully to decide if the speaker has hesitated or repeated themselves. Any player who makes a successful challenge, can take over for the remaining time. Another idea is to ask the children to work in small groups (a maximum of four is suggested) using a starting line as the opener to some improvisation work. For example, ask the children to create a series of short scenes which start with the line 'I didn't borrow my brother's favourite jacket yesterday'. For each new scene, the children should emphasise a different word in the opening line. Each scene may involve the children creating new characters, or not.

Gaining, Maintaining and Monitoring the Interest of the Listener(s) (Statement 10)

This statement also refers explicitly to listening. This is a challenging skill where speakers aim to become increasingly aware of how to watch the listener while speaking and, if they look confused or inattentive, make some changes. Some changes might be physical ones, for example, if there is suddenly background noise and the listener can't hear you clearly, you may raise your voice. This draws on social and emotional aspects of learning, for example, noting whether the listener doesn't have the level of understanding you thought they would, realising that they already know this or recognising that you have talked for too long and it would help to give them a turn to talk. This relies on both linguistic and cognitive skills – you might have to rephrase something, add more information, go back over one or two key points, work out how to jump ahead, or think about how to cue them in naturally so they can take over the conversation for a bit. Using a think-aloud strategy is helpful here – you can model how to monitor the audience's reaction and make a conscious decision to adapt your spoken language to them. You can also draw the children's attention to this by using audio-visual clips of people talking. Flexibility in the use of spoken language will come from lots of opportunities for children to use discussions in their learning, and will develop as they extend their vocabularies and understanding of grammar.

Monitoring Their Understanding of What They Hear (Statements 2 and 6)

Asking Relevant Questions to Extend Their Understanding and Knowledge (Statement 2)

This statement supports the children's development of metacognition in which they monitor their own learning and identify where reparation is needed, for example, identifying where they have not understood and asking questions to clarify or to seek additional information. Progression identified in *Communicating the Curriculum* suggests that children begin by identifying when they have not understood something, gradually refining this skill until they can identify clearly which points do not yet make sense to them. Children can also begin to ask questions, building on this so that they are able to use a range of questions to clarify and extend their understanding. In Voice 21's *The Oracy Framework,* the skill of clarification falls within the cognitive component.

Reading provides excellent opportunities for developing children's strategies for seeking clarification, presenting an authentic context in which children can monitor and question their understanding of a text, as well as responding to questions posed by others. It is important that questions are rich and meaningful, not simple recall questions or ones in which the teacher (or a mark scheme) has defined one specific answer which is to be given (there is more on this in Chapter 8). Rich opportunities are also offered across the curriculum, again making use of audio-visual resources, or when children are engaging in first-hand experiences, or with guest speakers and teacher presentations.

Drama strategies can also support this skill, for example, the use of hot seating, where someone adopts a role such as from a story, or a moment in history and so on, and the others ask questions to find out more about them or what has just happened. Teachers could also use interesting words, objects, pictures or photographs as a starting point for generating curious questions, and of course, generating questions about a new topic or the front cover of a book is a great way in. It is useful to link this skill with the listening statement above – when children are asked a question, they need to listen to the answer and then identify whether they feel the question was answered in full. It will be helpful if the teacher models how to ask relevant questions, either making use of a think-aloud strategy (e.g., 'As I am looking at this book cover, I am wondering who the two people are...') or a genuine question ('Thank you for that interesting talk. Could you just explain the part about...again? I wasn't sure I fully understood it'.).

Maintaining Attention and Participating Actively in Collaborative Conversations, Staying on Topic and Initiating and Responding to Comments (Statement 6)

Again with the right teaching and opportunities, this skill will develop considerably over the primary age phase. Younger pupils will start by listening and answering each other's questions or expressing their views in response to someone else's, and over time children will be able to listen for longer periods of time and retain information, giving more extended responses. Some resources aim to build this explicitly. For example, the ABC method (there are various sources which explain more about this on the internet) involves children in agreeing, building or challenging each other's comments. Each is introduced in turn, and it is often helpful to think of some sentence starters such as 'I agree with ...'s point because...', 'I would like to build on what...has just said by adding...', or 'I would like to challenge that idea because...'. The children are then given something to discuss. This might involve the whole class – particularly when getting started as it is often the case that not everyone contributes to whole class discussions (and it might take too long if they did), but it will offer useful modelling which can then be attempted in groups. Pupils can use sentence starter cards to remind them of the possibilities. As they become more skilled, you could perhaps randomise the three positions so that the children have to turn over a card (e.g., agree, build or challenge, whether that's would they really think or not!). This can be really effective with older pupils, getting them to think quickly. There are other ways of scaffolding children's ability to work productively in groups. For example, a resource from the British Council uses the roles of builder, instigator, challenger, clarifier, prober and summariser (https://www.britishcouncil.org/

sites/default/files/its_good_to_talk.pdf). It is important to remember that these skills should be built up gradually. Children will benefit from seeing them modelled clearly, both live and perhaps analysing their use through watching shared audio-visual clips. They should also practice these skills in supported situations before working more independently in groups. The focus of the discussion should always be carefully planned; the children must be able to engage properly with the content if they are to sustain discussions.

Building a Knowledge of Words

Using Relevant Strategies to Build Their Vocabulary (Statement 3)

Vocabulary is the knowledge of words and word meanings. There has been much focus on the teaching of vocabulary in recent years. According to Lane and Allen (2010), strong vocabulary knowledge is associated with success in reading and, more generally, in school achievement. Law et al.'s research (2017) showed it to be one of the factors linked to future employment. In terms of reading, Berne and Blachowicz (2008) note that both literal and inferential comprehension rests on the reader's understanding of the majority of words in a text. When children are decoding words, they only experience real success if they can then match the word to a plausible meaning; therefore, the word must exist first within children's language comprehension.

This has clear implications for learning and teaching. According to the DfE (2013, 6.4),

> Pupils' acquisition and command of vocabulary are key to their learning and progress across the whole curriculum. Teachers should therefore develop vocabulary actively, building systematically on pupils' current knowledge.
>
> They should increase pupils' store of words in general while making links between known and new vocabulary and discuss the shades of meaning in similar words. Pupils can then expand the vocabulary choices that are available to them when they write.
>
> In order for pupils to improve their comprehension, it's also vital that they understand the meanings of words they meet in their reading across all subjects.

In a highly influential text, Beck et al. (2013) showed that words could be classified into three tiers. In the first tier (tier one), there are the most basic words that children typically learn through experience. This includes words to describe things such as house, car, dog and toy, actions such as run, walk, and emotions such as happy and sad. In the third tier (tier three), there are words that come from specific content domains such as triangle, simile, photosynthesis and morpheme. These could be considered to be subject-specific technical vocabular words, which teachers tend to teach within context. For example, when teaching children about shapes in mathematics, the teacher introduces key vocabulary and encourages the children to practise using these words in their own talk (and perhaps writing). You will note that some words in this tier represent some quite challenging processes (e.g., osmosis) while others are quite simple (e.g., triangle).

This leaves us then with the second tier (tier two) words which broadly encompass everything in between, for example, all the other ways related to the basic concept of 'walk' such as 'amble', 'shuffle' and so on. These words are key to reading comprehension. Although people do use such words in their everyday speech, they tend to be more prevalent in reading materials. These materials are a source of rich vocabulary but also typically demand that the reader makes meaning from a much wider bank of vocabulary than is needed to navigate their everyday world through talk. Discussion has also centred around academic content words such as 'describe', 'evaluate' and so on as understanding these words is key to academic success, particularly in the later years of education. It is also possible for words to belong to more than one tier. For example, the word incubate is a tier three word in terms of its meaning within the domain of biology but also has tier two connotations when considering the notion of incubating an idea.

It is a daunting task to think about all the words that exist within the English language and consider teaching them! Because it is not possible to teach every word, teachers need to make careful decisions about which words to teach. Sometimes, teachers will identify words which they know children will meet, for example, in a class read-aloud or presentation, and which require a simple explanation (e.g., through pre-teaching or prior to re-reading) to minimise any disruption to the children's receptive vocabulary as they listen. However, teachers will also want to identify words that will be valuable in extending the children's vocabularies, therefore investing time in embedding them in children's receptive and expressive vocabularies. Beck et al. (2013) note that exploring more sophisticated ways to understand and express a concept such as walking develops vocabulary breadth by adding to the number of the words the child knows, and also develops depth as new words are linked to the more familiar concepts, enhancing understanding of both the new and old words.

When teaching a new word, it is essential to think of the children's prior learning – what vocabulary do they already know in relation to this concept? There is no particular hierarchy within tier two words themselves. So, if we want to teach children more ways to express the idea of happy (the tier one concept word), we can choose from delighted, ecstatic, jolly, pleased, etc. – as long as they understand the concept using a tier one word, they will be able to add a word which is related in meaning to extend their vocabulary.

To ensure that learning does not just take place at a superficial level where we bombard children with lots of words but they retain none of them, it is important to plan for meaningful encounters that are deep and revisited sufficiently. This allows children to embed new vocabulary in their long-term memories helping them to make use of this knowledge in their speaking, listening, reading and writing.

There are broadly three recognised ways in which children's vocabularies can be developed: indirect teaching, explicit teaching and cultivating word consciousness (Quigley, 2018).

Much vocabulary is learned through children's everyday experiences of language. Such indirect learning takes place then through conversations, listening to read-alouds and in their own reading. When the same word pops up a number of times, it may well be absorbed naturally into a child's lexicon. However, this is reliant on sufficient exposure and a certain level of attention being paid to the word.

Explicit teaching ensures that children learn word meanings and subtle differences between words. This involves carefully planned learning opportunities where explanations of word meanings are given and discussed. Children engage actively with the words and their meanings, considering whether they are suitable for a given context. They may compose sentences collaboratively on small wipeboards or sentence strips. Additionally, they are exposed to words multiple times over an extended period of time. This may involve analysis of words, for example, breaking them down into morphemes (parts of the word which carry meaning such as in the word 'disappear' where the prefix 'dis' means 'not' and the root word 'appear' means 'to be seen').

Finally, word consciousness refers to the teacher's interest in words and how this is communicated to the children. For example, the teacher shows enthusiasm when he or she, or one of the children, identifies a word they don't know. They are curious to look it up together and talk about it before modelling attempts to use it in context. Some classes have word displays on a working wall or create class word books where new words can be collected and referred back to.

Three Quick Ideas for Increasing Children's Exposure to Recently Learned Vocabulary

- Charades – newly discovered words are put onto cards and children take one and have to act it for the others to guess. You could mix in different old ones from time to time to embed them.
- Picture challenge – display a picture (e.g., book illustration/cover or a free image from the internet) and challenge the children to use one or more specified new words in sentences that fit them (again this could be done collaboratively using wipeboards).
- Get the children to make a graphic organiser for one or more words. You could choose from asking children to compose their own definition of the word, draw a picture that represents it, list some synonyms (words which mean the same or nearly the same), identify an antonym (word that means the opposite) or compose a sentence which uses it.

Many more games and activities can be found at https://global.oup.com/education/content/dictionaries/key-issues/word-gap/primary-resources/.

Developing Knowledge and Understanding of the Different Purposes for Using Spoken Language (Statements 4, 5, 7, 9 and 11)

Articulating and Justifying Answers, Arguments and Opinions (Statement 4)

This may well start with encouraging children to express their likes and dislikes, and being able to say why. It may well link into children's work on grammar through the use of conjunctions such as 'but' and 'because' and increasing use of phrases to build cohesion such as 'My reasoning here is. . .'. Again, this has clear links to reading where children can discuss themes, plots and characters as well as author choices, perhaps in response to a rich question, for example, 'Why do you think Jim did that? Was it the right thing to do?' or provocative statements such as 'Jim is a really selfish character'. Providing rich opportunities across the curriculum will enable the children to build their language in meaningful ways, for example, discussing issues of climate and coastal erosion in geography or opinions on historical events and rulers. However, it is important to teach this skill carefully. It relies on a bank of knowledge about how to express opinions and arguments clearly but also sensitively and appropriately. This must be modelled by the adults in the room, and the responsibility should be gradually released to the pupils to work in groups only when they are really ready to do so effectively. Arguments which aim to persuade may be a good starting point. Corbett and Strong (2020) identify some good activities to help children to tune in to this kind of language. For example, they suggest asking the children to work in pairs, where one of them tries to persuade the other, who has taken on the role of a snowman, to come in from the cold. An excellent resource to support children's ability to articulate and justify their answers, arguments and opinions can be found at https://noisyclassroom.com/developing-students-oracy/. This has a wealth of skill-building games as well as ideas for more formal debates across the curriculum. It is also worth considering whether drawing up some ground rules for talk would be useful.

Establishing Ground Rules for Talk

Establishing ground rules to support effective classroom talk is a really useful strategy to help children to understand how to talk productively in a learning environment. As is often the case, it is better to create such rules with the children who typically have much better buy-in when they have been involved in producing them. However, one possible example of ground rules is:

- Partners engage critically but constructively with each other's ideas.
- Everyone participates.
- Tentative ideas are treated with respect.
- Ideas offered for joint consideration may be challenged.
- Challenges are justified and alternative ideas or understandings are offered.
- Opinions are sought and considered before a decision is taken.
- Knowledge is made publicly accountable (and so reasoning is visible in the talk). (Mercer & Dawes, 2008, p. 66).

Giving Well-Structured Descriptions, Explanations and Narratives for Different Purposes, Including for Expressing Feelings (Statement 5)

This skill enables children to present ideas with increasing depth, organising and sustaining their talk to keep the listener interested. The word narrative means to give an account of connected events. This may be fictional (such as a made-up story) or the recount of a real experience (your own or someone else's, for example recounting an experience such as a school trip or recounting a famous event such as the Great Fire of London from an eye-witness's perspective). Descriptions might relate to objects, places or interests, while explanations may be drawn from reading, for example, giving a clear explanation of a character, or from across the curriculum, for example, to explain a geographical or scientific phenomena such as tornadoes. Again, this is likely to develop in line with children's understanding of grammar – children learn in Year 1 to sequence simple sentences to form short narratives, and in Year 2 to use expanded noun phrases, which will embellish their accounts. This is built on in Year 3 where pupils learn how to use conjunctions, adverbs and prepositions to determine time, place and cause, further developed in Year 4 where they learn to use fronted adverbials such as 'Later that day,...', and enhanced through their work in Year 5 and Year 6 on cohesive devices.

Scaffolds, such as story strings, can support children to remember the structure when talk is planned; children draw a series of pictures, one from each part of their story or talk. Younger children may draw one for each sentence, while older children might draw one for each section, and fix these to a piece of string. They then take out the string whenever they are going to tell their story, using the picture prompts to remind them.

A similar idea can be used to create a journey stick in outdoor learning (see this and many more engaging ideas for outdoor learning at the Learning Through Landscapes web resource found at https://ltl.org.uk/). Practising the skills of narration, description and explanation can be done through a range of games, for example, using sentence starters such as 'Once there was', 'One day', 'Suddenly', 'Luckily' and 'Finally' (these could be displayed on cards) and asking the children to make up their own stories or retell known ones using props, maps, puppets and so on. This can be adapted to support the development of curriculum knowledge. For example, once the children have learned about different animals and their life cycles, you could number the animals from 1 to 6 and get groups to take turns to roll the dice and explaining the life cycle of the corresponding animal. The talk could be scaffolded or extended by giving sentence opener cards, and you could include a sand timer to add an extra element of challenge (or make sure that the pace doesn't drop).

You could also consider planning some talks over the school year that the children can prepare in advance, either as homework or following some research carried out in school time, for example, giving a two-minute talk on their favourite hobby, book, or a topic of their choice.

Using Spoken Language to Develop Understanding Through Speculating, Hypothesising, Imagining and Exploring Ideas (Statement 7)

This statement represents a number of different ideas which are connected to different uses of language. Children might use their receptive skills to develop their understanding of what is being said to them, as well as their expressive skills to try out ideas in their own words, and of course, this is closely linked to the ability to monitor their own understanding and ask questions to clarify. Using language to imagine might be developed authentically through the context of written composition at the indirect planning stage when children are thinking about what they will write and how their pieces will develop. They may also speculate, hypothesise and explore ideas in the context of reading comprehension, for example, considering why a character might choose to do a certain thing or what might happen if he or she does.

When we use spoken language in the ways outlined in the statement, we are usually working with one or more others to explore an idea, leading to the term 'exploratory talk', originally coined by Douglas Barnes. As this idea has been developed more recently, there are now definitions of exploratory talk which differ a little; however, its value is not disputed. Mercer's work (2008) defines exploratory talk as that in which everyone listens actively and is encouraged to contribute, ask questions and share relevant information, build on each other's contributions and may challenge each other's ideas, giving reasons for this.

Crucially within Mercer's view of exploratory talk, the aim of the discussion is for the group to reach a consensus. Mercer suggests that instead of exploratory talk, pupils often engage in what he calls disputational talk, in which there is disagreement but no effort to try to understand each other's points or reach an agreement, or cumulative talk, where pupils accept what each says, perhaps elaborating further but not thinking critically about each other's points. As a result of these two types of talk, learning is limited, whereas with exploratory talk, purposeful learning is achieved. Exploratory talk is, therefore, a useful vehicle for developing children's abilities to explore ideas, speculate and hypothesise.

Using talk to imagine, though, is not always linked to reasoning and so a different type of talk such as Wegerif's notion of playful or creative talk (2018) is useful. Wegerif defines playful talk as making verbal puns and imaginative associations with words. For example, imagine you are having a conversation with someone and trying to find the right words to express an idea. You each make suggestions and eventually hit upon the idea that feels right to both of you. You have not used necessarily explicit reasoning here but through your talk, you have developed your thinking until you find the best way to express what is in your mind. Thus, talk is used creatively. When children are working together in drama or to compose pieces of writing such as stories, poems and non-fiction texts, they are able to practise their ability to use spoken language to explore imaginative ideas and thinking.

Participating in Discussions, Presentations, Performances, Role-Play, Improvisations and Debates (Statement 9)

This statement covers a broad range of contexts in which spoken language skills may be used quite differently and overlaps with a number of the other statements in the Spoken Language curriculum. For example, discussions, role play, improvisations and debates offer opportunities to develop close listening skills whereas presentations and performances may offer more opportunities for pupils to practise and refine their command of some of the physical components of talk. These contexts draw on different purposes for and thus types of pupil talk as explored in the previous chapter. It is important for teachers to consider this range and ensure that they have found relevant and authentic cross-curricular stimuli for all of these contexts to develop children's spoken language skills meaningfully so that they become increasingly confident and adept in using language across the curriculum. Contexts can become increasingly formal. For example, pupils may first give short presentations to each other (in pairs, small groups and then whole class) on a hobby or interest of theirs, or in conjunction with some book talk activities (see Chapter 9). They may then start to give presentations to other audiences, for example, presenting their work in assemblies or inviting their parents in to share an aspect of their learning. Similarly, performances may be to each other within the class, as in a Poetry Show (see Chapter 14), or to a wider audience through the performance of a play. Opportunities for developing role play and improvisation skills can be developed through the use of drama across the curriculum, for example, to explore key scenes within texts they are reading or to re-enact or imagine a great historical event. A great resource to support the teaching of spoken language skills as used in debates is the Noisy Classroom (visit https://noisyclassroom.com) which offers a wealth of ideas, games and more formal activities.

You may also like to join in with national initiatives such as the annual National Storytelling Week. More details can be found at: https://literacytrust.org.uk/resources/national-storytelling-week/.

Consider and Evaluate Different Viewpoints, Attending to and Building on the Contributions of Others (Statement 11)

Again there is overlap with other spoken language statements here. This statement requires children to listen carefully to what another person has to say and respond to it; this may involve keeping track of several points and using summarisation skills to identify and track the most important ones. Responses might involve making a relevant comment, asking questions to find out more, stating that you agree or disagree with some or all of what was said and saying why. Modelling good listening in both social and learning talk will support children in developing the initial parts of this skill, and reinforcing through the use of focused praise is also helpful. To develop it more formally within learning, you could adopt a strategy such as the ABC strategy explained earlier in this chapter. You could practise these skills using a circle game where one child starts by sharing an opinion (e.g., 'I love pizza because...' or 'I think school uniforms should be banned because...') and each person agrees with the statement, giving one idea in support. When the children are familiar with the game, you could introduce the idea of building on and finally challenging it. When the children are really good, you could mix it up by using some sort of signal or card to get them to switch between agreeing, building and challenging. Of course, there will also be many opportunities to practise and develop this skill across the curriculum, for example, when discussing key ideas in History and Geography, and in discussions about books.

Developing an Understanding of Standard and Non-standard Forms and Different Registers for Language Use (Statements 8 and 12)

Speaking Audibly and Fluently With an Increasing Command of Standard English (Statement 8)

Speaking audibly and fluently requires children to become increasingly skilled at managing the physical components of talk such as their pace, tone, clarity and volume (Voice 21). It will typically involve the social and emotional aspects of confidence and of course draw on children's language and cognitive skills as they order their words and ideas so that they are presented fluently. To become skilled and proficient users of language, children need to learn how to talk for different purposes, in different contexts and to different audiences. Although there are some variations in definitions of Standard English, it is broadly true to say that Standard English is the form of English which follows what are viewed as the correct rules of grammar (e.g., 'I did it' rather than 'I done it') and is thus the form that is taught as a major world language. It tends to be associated with more formal forms of communication, although in the glossary which accompanies *The National Curriculum in England: English Programmes of Study for Key Stage 1 and Key Stage 2* (DfE, 2013), it is noted that 'some people use Standard English all the time'. Standard English avoids the more regional forms of language, which may use different words or grammatical forms, instead using words which are widely understood to be the 'correct' words (see https://www.bbc.co.uk/bitesize/topics/z86qsbk/articles/z3wx6g8 for an interesting tour around the UK to see some different ways in which people might ask for a bread roll filled with chips!).

These different ways of using words are dialects, different forms of language that are spoken in a particular part of a country. In the National Curriculum, Standard English is defined as one dialect of English which, as it uses the standard forms of English grammar, is likely to be understood most widely by other users of English:

> The aim of the national curriculum is that everyone should be able to use Standard English as needed in writing and in relatively formal speaking'. (DfE, 2013, p. 16)

Standard English is the form of English that is typically seen in information texts and is required for exam situations. Therefore, as Reedy and Bearne note, it is seen as 'the gateway language to academic attainment' which children need to be able to use when required (2021, p. 5).

Early on, children need to learn that when we write, we often use language differently from when we speak. For example, in speech, it is quite acceptable for people to express ideas in words and phrases rather than complete sentences all the time. Because spoken language often occurs between two or more people, there is a context of time and place, whereas a piece of writing may be read at a different time and in a different place and so needs to be communicated differently. This is linked to the notion of oral rehearsal where children compose and practise a sentence out loud before writing it down. It is also important to be mindful of the fact that how we speak, and the words we may instinctively use are linked to our personal identities and the groups we belong to. For example, families often have their own phrases, and some expressions and vocabulary are key aspects of cultural and social identity. The principle of showing enthusiasm and interest in what we say and how we say it is really useful for this statement. If the classroom is well established as a place in which we have enthusiasm for and explore the different ways we use language, it is much easier to talk about what Standard English is. We can show or ask children to say it in that form without them feeling as if they have said it wrong. It would be quite easy to set up a book or display area where you can display Standard and non-Standard words and phrases which are used in the school's location or known to the pupils as helpful reminders. You might have some good discussions around the ways different characters speak in the stories that you read and draw the children's attention to the way in which the language in a non-fiction book is more formal than the language we might use to explain something to a friend. Poetry is often a rich source of language play, and you might find some great examples of non-Standard English there to discuss and perform. You could also play around in drama improvisations, asking children to work in pairs or small groups where they have to speak in Standard or non-Standard English as directed so that they can practise these different forms.

Key Idea: Code-Switching

Code-switching refers to a speaker's use of different language codes. In the context of teaching spoken language, this means switching between the 'codes' of standard and non-standard English, and between formal and informal registers. This is usually determined by the audience and purpose of the talk. In addition, pupils who speak more than one language may switch between them. For example, I once worked with three Year 5 girls who were fluent in Polish and English. When talking to me (as their teacher), they would use

English but when talking together they would typically speak in Polish. Similarly, I may choose to use a more informal code when talking to my peers but a more formal one when teaching. Code-switching can happen at the sentence and word level too, for example, when you can't find the right word in one code you might draw on your knowledge of another code to get your meaning across. The more familiar you are with the language of different codes (in this context, the levels of formality and standard and non-standard English forms of language), the easier it is to switch between them. This is where drama activities could be particularly useful in allowing children to practise and play around with speaking in different codes.

Selecting and Using Appropriate Registers for Effective Communication (Statement 12)

The register is the level of formality in language use that is best for the audience and context of some talk. For example, giving public presentations and speeches typically requires a more formal register, while chatting to a friend may work best with a more informal one. Sometimes, the idea of a register gets confused with the idea of Standard English. However, in *The National Curriculum in England: English Programmes of Study for Key Stage 1 and Key Stage 2* (DfE, 2013), it is noted that

> Some people use Standard English all the time, in all situations from the most casual to the most formal, so it covers most registers'. (p. 95)

The glossary gives these examples:

> I did it because they were not willing to undertake any more work on those houses [formal Standard English];

> I did it cos they wouldn't do any more work on those houses' [casual Standard English with the use of the words 'cos' and 'wouldn't do' instead of 'because' and 'were not willing to undertake'];

> I done it cos they wouldn't do no more work on them houses' [casual non-Standard English with the use of the words 'done', 'no' and 'them' instead of 'did', 'any' and 'those'].

Some teachers make use of visual supports such as a washing line or other ways of showing a continuum with the least formal on the left and the most formal on the right. They can then explore examples of words and phrases with the children, deciding where to put them.

Activity   Exploring the Idea of a Register

Look at these ways of greeting someone:

Hi   Hiya   Hello   Good morning   Yo bruv

Order them from least to most formal.
Which of these forms use Standard English and which use non-Standard?
Create a similar list of ways of saying goodbye and thank you.
Think of some classroom routines where you typically give the children instructions, for example, lining up. How could you express this in more and less formal registers? Are there ways which include Standard and non-Standard forms of language? You could make a game of these ideas, for example, asking the children to set you the challenge of speaking in different registers and using different forms of language, and sometimes you could turn the tables on them!

As well as drawing children's attention to this, and making use of examples from everyday life, books and audio-visual clips, Reedy and Bearne (2021) suggest the use of drama and role-play to support, giving the children a range of contexts in which to explore different forms and registers of spoken language. For example, more formal uses of Standard English can be explored through role-play contexts such as being a newsreader or weather forecaster, while less formal contexts might include friends chatting on the walk to school. It is worth having class discussions when opportunities to use spoken language in different contexts occur, for example, if they are asked to show visitors around the school, or when a guest speaker arrives.

Summary

This chapter has explored the National Curriculum expectations for the teaching of spoken language, presenting key concepts and terminology as well as principles of effective pedagogy. Practical ways in which learning and teaching might be developed in the classroom in relation to each of the National Curriculum statements have been suggested.

Further Reading

1   Explore the resources produced by The Communication Trust. These are available at: https://speechandlanguage.org.uk/talking-point/for-professionals/the-communication-trust/more-resources/.

2   Read out more about talk roles and other ideas to support talk produced by the British Council. Available at: https://www.britishcouncil.org/sites/default/files/its_good_to_talk.pdf.

3   Listen to Neil Mercer talking about exploratory talk at: https://www.youtube.com/watch?v=u9DdfTmT29E.

References

Beck, I., McKeown, M., & Kucan, L. (2013). *Bringing words to life: Robust vocabulary instruction.* Guildford Press.

Berne, J., & Blachowicz, C. (2008). What reading teachers say about vocabulary instruction: Voices from the classroom. *The Reading Teacher, 62*, 314–323.

Corbett, P. and Strong, J. (2020). *Talk for Writing Across to Curriculum: How to Teach Non-fiction Writing to 5–12 Year-olds.* (Revised Edition). Maidenhead: Open University Press.

Cushing, I. (2020). The policy and policing of language in schools. *Language in Society, 49*(3), 425–450.

Department for Education. (2013). *The national curriculum in England: Key stages 1 and 2 framework document.* https://www.gov.uk/government/publications/national-curriculum-in-england-primary-curriculum. Accessed on May 16, 2022.

Department for Education. (2023). *Development Matters: Non-statutory curriculum guidance for the Early Years Foundation Stage.* https://assets.publishing.service.gov.uk/government/uploads/system/uploads/attachment_data/file/1180056/DfE_Development_Matters_Report_Sep2023.pdf. Accessed on November 19, 2023.

Ellis, P. (2019). *Learning to listen.* Cambridge Assessment International Education. https://blog.cambridgeinternational.org/learning-to-listen/. Accessed on December 13, 2023.

Lane, H., & Allen, S. (2010). The vocabulary-rich classroom: Modeling sophisticated word use to promote word consciousness and vocabulary growth. *The Reading Teacher, 63*(5).

Law, J., Charlton, J., Dockrell, J., Gascoigne, M., McKean, C., & Theakston, A. (2017). *Early language development: Needs, provision, and intervention for preschool children from socio-economically disadvantaged backgrounds.* Education Endowment Foundation. https://educationendowment foundation.org.uk/public/files/Law_et_al_Early_Language_Development_final.pdf

Mercer, N. (2008). *3 kinds of talk.* https://thinkingtogether.educ.cam.ac.uk/resources/5_examples_of_talk_in_groups.pdf. Accessed on April 20, 2023.

Mercer, N., & Dawes, L. (2008). The value of exploratory talk. In N. Mercer & N. Hodgkinson (Eds.), *Exploring talk in school: Inspired by the work of Douglas Barnes* (pp. 55–73). SAGE.

Oxford University Press. (2018). *Why closing the word gap matters: Oxford language report.* https://www.oup.com.cn/test/word-gap.pdf

Quigley, A. (2018). *Closing the vocabulary gap.* Routledge.

Reedy, D., & Bearne, E. (2021). *Talk for teaching and learning: The dialogic classroom.* UKLA.

Voice 21. (n.d.). *The Oracy Framework.* https://voice21.org/oracy/#:~:text=The%20Oracy%20Framework%20Through%20a%20high%20quality%20oracy,to%20learn%20the%20skills%20needed%20to%20talk%20effectively. Accessed on September 10, 2020.

Wegerif, R. (2018). *What are types of talk?* https://www.rupertwegerif.name/blog/what-are-types-of-talk. Accessed on May 13, 2023.

6

Planning Lessons That Develop Children as Readers

Chapter Objectives

This chapter will:

- Consider what reading is and what knowledge and skills children need to develop to become proficient readers.
- Explore the key components of reading which underpin the structure of the National Curriculum.
- Explore what the effective teaching of reading looks like, highlighting what effective teachers of reading do.
- Consider how to support children whose progress may not keep pace with age-related expectations.

Introduction

Learning to read transforms lives. According to the World Literacy Foundation (2018), reading broadens our knowledge, enables us to engage with our culture and is a foundation for success in the workplace. Low levels of literacy contribute significantly to inequality within and across society, increasing 'the likelihood of poor physical and mental health, workplace accidents, misuse of medication, participation in crime, and welfare dependency, all of which also have substantial additional social and economic costs' (World Literacy Foundation, 2018).

The DfE (2013) state that:

> Reading widely across both fiction and fiction develops [children's] knowledge of themselves, and the world in which they live, to establish an appreciation and love of reading, and to gain knowledge across the curriculum. Reading also feeds pupils' imagination and opens up a treasure-house of wonder and joy for curious minds.

Learning to read and then using that reading to learn is therefore a vital and powerful skill; the teaching of reading is central to the primary curriculum.

Activity   Reflecting on the Knowledge and Skills Involved in Reading

Long, long ago there lived, in Japan, a brave warrior known to all as Tawara Toda, or 'My Lord Bag of Rice'. His true name was Fujiwara no Hidesato, and there is a very interesting story of how he came to change his name.

One day, he sallied forth in search of adventures, for he had the nature of a warrior and could not bear to be idle. So, he buckled on his two swords, took his huge bow, much taller than himself, in his hand, and slinging his quiver on his back started out. He had not gone far when he came to the bridge of Seta-no-Karashi spanning one end of the beautiful Lake Biwa. No sooner had he set foot on the bridge than he saw lying right across his path a huge serpent-dragon. Its body was so big that it looked like the trunk of a large pine tree, and it took up the whole width of the bridge. One of its huge claws rested on the parapet of one side of the bridge, while its tail lay right against the other. The monster seemed to be asleep, and as it breathed, fire and smoke came out of its nostrils.

At first, Hidesato could not help feeling alarmed at the sight of this horrible reptile lying in his path, for he must either turn back or walk right over its body. He was a brave man, however, and putting aside all fear went forward dauntlessly. Crunch, crunch! He stepped now on the dragon's body, now between its coils, and without even one glance backwards he went on his way.

(from Japanese Fairy tales Kindle Edition – Yei Theodora Osaki 1908)

Now take some time to reflect on the reading you have just done. What did you need to know to be able to make meaning from this text? What skills did you demonstrate? How did you feel during the experience? Were any aspects of the task easy or hard for you? Do you feel you fully understand the text? Are there any things that you don't know? Would anyone reading this text come away with the same understanding of it?

As you read through this chapter, continue to reflect on the ideas presented and consider how much they match your reading experiences.

The Simple View of Reading

In *The National Curriculum in England: English Programmes of Study for Key Stage 1 and Key Stage 2* (DfE, 2013) and the more recently published *Reading Framework* (DfE, 2023), the approach to reading is based on a theoretical model proposed by Gough and Tunmer (1986) called The Simple View of Reading. This comprises two key elements: word recognition processes, encompassing the knowledge and skills needed to decode each word, and language comprehension processes, involving the knowledge and skills needed to match that word to meaning.

Knowledge for Reading

For readers to make sense of the written symbols and conventions on the page, they must draw on orthographic knowledge which builds the understanding that each symbol corresponds with a sound which can be blended in the correct order with the following symbols to produce a word. Once the word has been decoded, the reader then sifts through the vast store of known words and their meanings in his or her head and attempts to match them. Of course, many words have more than one meaning, so the relevant meaning of a particular word is often determined by the context. For example, in the story extract above, the word 'nature' has more than one meaning and in this context, the words 'of a warrior' are key to understanding the text. It is important to note here the difference between reading comprehension and language comprehension. Reading comprehension is built on language comprehension – you need to know what a word means in your language vocabulary before you can match it securely to meaning when reading.

The reader also needs syntactic knowledge – this is knowledge of how sentences are formed and the grammar rules they follow (Foorman et al., 2016). Sentences often have elements such as pronouns which readers need to learn to navigate. For example, in the story of My Lord Bag of Rice, you had to make sense of the pronouns 'him' and 'it' to follow the story fully. Readers also need to be able to navigate words whose job is to link groups of words such as clauses together, for example (from the same story), conjunctions such as 'and', 'so' and 'for', prepositions such as 'on' and 'against', and adverbs such as 'at first'.

Readers also draw heavily on their background knowledge of the world; this is typically built from a range of experiences including first-hand participation and observation, discussion, as well as engagement with a wide range of texts. For example, you may have drawn on your background knowledge of Japan, warriors, swords, bows, quivers and rice in just the first few sentences of the story.

To help them to navigate and tune in to a text, the reader also draws on their knowledge of texts. In this case, the reader will have drawn on their knowledge of stories and story structure and is likely to have anticipated that the start of the story will aim to set the scene, introducing the setting and one or the main characters. The very first few words, 'Long, long ago there lived' may have suggested to the reader that this is a traditional tale of some sort, drawing on language forms and cueing up some ideas of what might happen in such a tale.

All of these sources of knowledge support the reader to make sense of the text. In addition, the reader also draws on their understanding of what it means to be a reader – knowing how texts work, that words and letters are oriented in a particular direction, that pages may be read left to right and must be turned over when you reach the bottom of the right-hand one, and that pictures may contribute to meaning or just be there for embellishment.

To develop this knowledge, the reader needs to have many exposures to meaningful reading and needs to see all aspects of the reading process being modelled explicitly. As children read, they will draw on these stores of knowledge and expand them further, adding further examples of genres, language use and so on to consolidate and develop their understanding.

People read for many different purposes. Sometimes, they read to gain knowledge or provoke thinking, while at other times, they read for enjoyment. Reading can inspire and feed the imagination, and often engages our emotions. Some reading does these things together. It is important that when we plan to teach reading in the primary classroom, purpose and meaning are at the heart of the learning and teaching.

Skills for Reading

Knowledge of reading must be accompanied by effective reading skills. The reader needs to:

- Be able to decode the marks on the page and match them to meaning.
- Keep track of what they are reading so that they can continue to build meaning over sentences, paragraphs and pages. This means being able to recognise the key ideas and using inference skills to make sense of the text.
- Be able to navigate a text quickly, understanding how its layout is related to its purpose so that they can use it efficiently, for example, understanding that a story is best understood by starting at the beginning and reading through in order, but a non-fiction text may be better navigated by the use of the contents and index pages, headings and subheadings, etc.
- Make connections between texts and their own experiences (text to self), to other texts that they have read (text to text) and to their background knowledge of the world (text to world). Good readers make connections as they read, linking what they read to what they already know, helping them to make meaning (Harvey & Goudvis, 2007; Keene & Zimmermann, 2007).

- Monitor their reading so they can check they understand and repair meaning when they don't, for example, by re-reading or checking with another part of the text.

The knowledge and skills children need to become proficient readers are supported by a high-quality reading curriculum which is based on:

- an increasingly wide range of high-quality texts;
- plentiful opportunities to see good reading modelled well;
- meaningful discussions which support pupils to make sense of texts and learn more about their language and structure;
- purposeful and authentic opportunities to respond to what they read.

Activity   Reflecting on Yourself as a Reader

Think about your own practices as a reader. What do you like to read? Do you like to read different things at different times or in different places? How do you like to read? Do you like silence or can you tune out background noise? How has your engagement with reading changed over different periods of your life? What don't you like to read? Why not? Who has influenced your reading over your lifetime, and what other influences have been present? How do you decide what to read next?

Think about what being a reader means to you. How might this differ for your pupils? What implications does this have for you as a teacher?

Effective Teachers of Reading

Research tells us that reading is taught most effectively through:

- The use of a balanced approach which develops both word reading (decoding) skills and comprehension in a way that values the importance of reading as a form of communication in which the central aim is to gain meaning.
- A focus on each child's skills, interests and experiences gathered through high-quality interaction and close monitoring of individual progress.
- Providing encouragement and rich and plentiful opportunities for pupils to engage with reading. (Dombey, 2010)

According to Elborn (2015), effective teachers of reading:

1   Read to their pupils, dedicating precious classroom time to share high-quality texts that aim to engage and inspire the children, and providing an excellent model of what good reading sounds and feels like.

2   Read with their pupils, sharing reading as a class and guiding their reading in small groups, showing children how to read, and how good readers make meaning from texts.
3   Read alongside their pupils, working one to one to support them and providing rich opportunities for them to practise key skills.

Clay emphasises the value of seeing reading as an active process, defining reading as 'a message-getting, problem-solving activity which increases in power and flexibility the more it is practised' (1991, p. 6). Therefore, children need to develop cognitive strategies to help them solve the problem. These are discussed in more depth in the two chapters that follow.

Reading Aloud to Children

Westbrook et al. (2019) suggest that reading aloud throughout children's schooling is one of the most important things that a teacher can do. When learning to read, teacher read-alouds provide an excellent model of the reading process, and when reading to learn, teacher read-alouds extend the children's understanding of how both fiction and non-fiction texts are structured and the language within them. They can draw on this understanding of a wide range of texts to develop their knowledge across the curriculum and help them see how they can explain and communicate their ideas effectively.

It is important to include the reading aloud of non-fiction across the curriculum if children are to gain sufficient understanding of and familiarity with this genre. There is an increasing wealth of high-quality non-fiction texts which children need to hear. Typically, non-fiction texts may be seen as resources to dip into rather than to read from start to finish. Children may particularly enjoy reading non-fiction texts with a friend, as the way in which the text is presented often makes it easier to share.

Of course, children's fiction texts are also great to read aloud. Clements and Tobin (2021) suggest that stories can:

• Invite readers to grow and develop emotionally and socially by presenting them with the opportunity to self-reflect and self-construct.
• Allow readers to step into the shoes of others and experience the world through different eyes, developing a strong sense of empathy and understanding of different cultures.
• Offer a form of escape, a way of relieving stress, of improving general knowledge and knowledge of ourselves.
• Invite readers to become part of a community.

The Reading Framework (DfE, 2023) emphasises the value of reading aloud to pupils, providing explicit guidance on what they believe an effective read-aloud should look like. This guidance is worth exploring.

Choosing a High-Quality Text for Reading

The texts you choose to read to and with children will have a profound influence on the children's engagement and motivation to learn to read, so they must be chosen carefully. You might sometimes want to choose texts with the children; this offers them an opportunity to share in the process of choosing and allows them to teach you what they are interested in, and what catches their eye. Research findings from the Centre for Literacy in Primary Education (CLPE, 2020) show that teachers should:

- Build a collection of books from a wide and diverse range of authors, illustrators and forms.
- Choose books and multimodal texts with quality artwork which complement, support or extend the story.
- Select texts that present information in a variety of interesting ways.
- Allow children to see themselves reflected in what they read and to have the opportunity to investigate other perspectives.
- Respect children's choices, ensuring that chosen texts support their experience of literature as well as their current interests.
- Choose books that are worth re-reading and provide the opportunity to respond in a variety of cross-curricular ways.
- Select books that include rhythm and pattern, encouraging children to play with language so that they see reading as a meaningful and fun process.

Guidance from the DfE (2023) is also useful, suggesting that teachers consider whether a book:

- Elicits a strong response – curiosity, anger, excitement, laughter and empathy?
- Has a strong narrative that will sustain multiple readings?
- Extends children's vocabulary?
- Has illustrations which engage and reflect children from all backgrounds and cultures?
- Helps children connect with who they are?
- Helps children to understand the lives of people whose experiences and perspectives may be different from their own?

The books you choose for your classroom will have a significant impact on the quality of learning and teaching that takes place. How do you keep up with the latest publications and ways to extend your own knowledge of high-quality children's literature (including non-fiction, poetry, comics, graphic novels and so on)? In such a busy profession, it is hard to allocate time to the myriad of tasks that teachers must or could complete, so it is worth thinking about the role of existing networks and resources here so that you use your time efficiently with maximum benefit – there are some suggested sources in the further reading section of this chapter.

It is also well worth talking to colleagues and peers about any sources they have come across that help them to continue to develop a broad knowledge of children's literature. Try to decide on a regular time that you will set aside for this and enlist your peers and colleagues to make it social and fun.

A Language-Rich Environment

Many texts on teaching reading highlight the critical importance of a language-rich environment to support effective learning and teaching. A language-rich environment is one which celebrates and provokes authentic and meaningful language use. Often such environments are also print-rich – that is they display print for children to read and to inspire their talk and writing. Characteristics of such environments typically include the following:

- Clearly labelled resources (these also promote independence and responsibility for the children).
- An inviting book area where children can choose and share books. They may also interact with displays, for example, reading and writing their own reviews and recommendations.
- Areas for children to share their knowledge of topics and vocabulary, perhaps using post-it notes to share facts they have learned or to write an unfamiliar word when they come across it.
- Thought-provoking questions, perhaps through interactive displays.
- A collection of words, phrases and sentences that have been created by the children themselves or come across in their reading (often the second inspires the first!) and captured as a resource.
- Model texts that have been composed by teachers and pupils together
- Examples of the children's writing to be celebrated.
- Working walls which provide a useful resource for pupils to draw on.

The examples above refer to the written word (be careful not to overload the children – sometimes less is more – and use print that is relevant and meaningful to avoid it becoming mere wallpaper). Ofsted (2022) also use the term 'literature-rich environment'. This is defined as one which includes high-quality interactions between adults and children, and has plentiful opportunities for pupils to listen, discuss and learn by heart stories, poems, rhymes and songs. Of course, if we want children to become skilled in reading and writing non-fiction too, our choice of high-quality texts for reading aloud, sharing and independent reading should reflect this clearly.

It is worth taking time to step back and try to look at your classroom through fresh eyes, whenever possible, to check that it communicates the messages about language and print that you want it to.

Curriculum Continuity and Progression

The National Curriculum in England: English Programmes of Study for Key Stage 1 and Key Stage 2 identifies specific expectations for pupils in each year group in the main body of the document through two strands: word reading and comprehension.

Word Reading

If a child has met the relevant early learning goals for the end of Year R, they will be able to:

- Read and understand simple sentences.
- Use phonic knowledge to decode regular words and read them aloud accurately.
- Read some common irregular words.

From Year 1 onwards, the curriculum aims to build children's knowledge, understanding and skills in relation to phonics, by learning to read the grapheme–phoneme correspondences for 40+ phonemes, including some alternative sounds for graphemes. Children should also be taught the skills of blending, and by the end of the year, should be able to read aloud phonically decodable texts.

In Year 2, pupils should build on their developing phonic knowledge and skills so that they are able to decode words so that reading is fluent. They will extend their knowledge of alternative grapheme–phoneme correspondences, read exception words, read most words quickly and accurately without overt sounding and blending, and read aloud books closely matched to their improving phonic knowledge, sounding out unfamiliar words accurately, automatically and without undue hesitation.

In Key Stage 2, it is expected that the priority for teaching will shift to reading comprehension, as most pupils will be able to decode fluently. Therefore, the emphasis on word reading diminishes, and teaching within this strand aims to support children to:

- Apply their growing knowledge of root words, prefixes and suffixes (etymology and morphology) as listed in the *English Programmes of Study Appendix 1*, both to read aloud and to understand the meaning of new words they meet (Year 3/4 and Year 5/6).
- Read further exception words, noting the unusual correspondences between spelling and sound, and where these occur in the word (Year 3/4 only).

Any pupil who is not yet able to decode fluently should continue to have this as a focus for learning and teaching, although it is likely that this will take place through additional, targeted intervention and support in the classroom.

Word reading is discussed in more depth in Chapter 7.

Comprehension

If a child has met the relevant early learning goals for the end of Year R, they will be able to:

- Listen to stories, accurately anticipating key events and respond to what they hear with relevant comments, questions or actions.

- Answer 'how' and 'why' questions about their experiences and in response to stories or events.
- Demonstrate an understanding when talking with others about what they have read.

From Year 1, a few threads of progression can be seen within the comprehension strand of the National Curriculum, developing:

1 Pleasure, motivation, vocabulary and understanding through a range of reading.
2 Familiarity with texts.
3 Engagement with poetry and performance.
4 Understanding of non-fiction.
5 Ability to engage in book talk.
6 Understanding of authorial intent.
7 Prediction, questioning, clarification and summarisation skills.
8 Ability to draw connections from texts.
9 Vocabulary.
10 Ability to infer.

The first four (1–4) of these threads relate to the range of texts that children are introduced to and engage with, enabling them to build their familiarity with a range of genres. This range increases as the pupils progress through the primary age phase.

The next two (5 and 6) build on the first four. The increasingly wide range of texts stimulates interesting discussions about books, and from Year 3 onwards, supports children's understanding that authors make deliberate word choices to capture the reader's interest and use language to provoke an impact on the reader.

The final four (7–10) relate to the strategies and skills that good readers employ to comprehend a text effectively. These are discussed in more depth in Chapter 8.

Fluency

One key component of effective reading is fluency. This is highlighted in the National Curriculum which states that:

> It is essential that, by the end of their primary education, all pupils are able to read fluently, and with confidence, in any subject in their forthcoming secondary education. (DfE, 2013, p. 4)

Readers who are fluent and automatic in their decoding will be able to read at a fairly rapid pace, with expression. As well as making the reading flow well, fluency is key to comprehension – when pupils' word reading flows, they are much more able to devote time and energy towards thinking about what the words mean. To comprehend a text effectively, readers often need to gain meaning across multiple sentences which can only happen when they are able to read it fluently (Cain, 2010). In the National Curriculum, re-reading books are presented as the key to developing children's fluency and confidence.

Rasinski and Smith (2018) suggest that fluency arises from three distinct components:

- Accuracy in word decoding.
- Automaticity in word recognition.
- Prosody (appropriate phrasing and expression).

Progression in Fluency

Pupils in Year 1 should:

- Read aloud accurately books that are consistent with their developing phonic knowledge and that do not require them to use other strategies to work out words.
- Re-read these books to build up their fluency and confidence in word reading.
- Pupils' reading and re-reading of books that are closely matched to their developing phonic knowledge, and knowledge of common exception words, supports their fluency, as well as increasing their confidence in their reading skills.

In Year 2, pupils should:

- Continue to apply phonic knowledge and skills as the route to decode words until automatic decoding has become embedded and reading is fluent.
- Read aloud books closely matched to their improving phonic knowledge, sounding out unfamiliar words accurately, automatically and without undue hesitation.
- Re-read these books to build up their fluency and confidence in word reading.

In Year 3/4 pupils should:

- Prepare poems and play scripts to read aloud and to perform, showing understanding through intonation, tone, volume and action.
- Be encouraged to use drama approaches to understand how to perform plays and poems to support their understanding of the meaning. These activities also provide them with an incentive to find out what expression is required, so feeding into comprehension.
- Be able to read (books written at an age-appropriate interest level) accurately and at a speed that is sufficient for them to focus on understanding what they read rather than on decoding individual words.

As decoding skills become increasingly secure, teaching should be directed towards developing vocabulary and breadth and depth of reading, making sure that they become independent, fluent and enthusiastic readers who read widely and frequently.

In Year 5/6 pupils should:

- Prepare poems and plays to read aloud and to perform, showing understanding through intonation, tone and volume so that the meaning is clear to an audience.

During years 5 and 6, teachers should continue to emphasise pupils' enjoyment and understanding of language, especially vocabulary, to support their reading and writing. Pupils' knowledge of the language, gained from stories, plays, poetry, non-fiction and textbooks, will support their increasing fluency as readers.

By the end of Year 6, pupils' reading and writing should be sufficiently fluent and effortless for them to manage the demands of all subjects in the Year 7 curriculum.

What Makes a Quality Fluency Activity?

Rasinski (2005) notes that effective teaching of fluency should be designed around the following elements:

- Quality Texts – texts with a good voice and clear phrasing lend themselves to being read orally with expression, for example, poetry, play scripts and narratives work are particularly useful.
- Oral Reading – teachers must model good fluency so that pupils can hear what good reading sounds like. The use of expression should reflect the text's meaning. Reading aloud also supports silent reading. When reading aloud is effortless, reading naturally transfers to becoming an automatic process that can happen silently in the head.
- Feedback – this can come from the teacher or other adult, a peer, or the reader themselves. Rasinski and Smith (2018) suggest that feedback can be focused on the use of expression and intonation, the automaticity of word reading, the use of rhythm and phrasing, and the smoothness of the reading. A useful tool to support the assessment of reading fluency can be found in the Education Endowment Foundation's Improving Literacy at Key Stage 2 (Bilton & Duff, 2021) (this can be used to support pupils across the primary age range).
- Repetition – repeated reading has a strong impact on pupils' fluency in reading.
- Motivation – fluency activities can be engaging as there is often a sense of playfulness about them and repeated reading leads to success which supports motivation. However, the text choice is key; pupils should find the text itself engaging when reading it themselves, achieved through the planning of rich opportunities for them to engage with the characters, setting, plot and themes (in the case of fiction texts) and ideas it contains.

Key Activities to Promote Fluency

Choral Reading

- Choral reading involves reading aloud together with a class or group of pupils.
- It helps build confidence, motivation and fluency by providing a model for fluent reading, giving less confident readers a chance to practice before reading alone and should improve sight vocabulary.
- Choose a text extract which is at the independent reading level of the majority of the pupils.
- Give each a copy to follow.
- Read aloud, modelling fluent reading as pupils follow along, perhaps using a finger to track the words.
- Re-read asking all pupils to join in together.

Paired Reading

- Paired reading involves pupils reading aloud to each other.
- Children can be paired in different ways, for example, more fluent readers could be paired with less fluent readers, or children who read at a similar level could be paired together.
- Pupils read together or take turns to read a sentence, paragraph, etc.
- The process needs to be modelled. Pupils should be clear about how they will ask each other for help or resolve any errors.
- Encourage re-reading to build fluency.

Readers Theatre

- Readers' theatre involves pupils reading scripts – this is like a radio play, involving only voice acting.
- The text should be shared together first before pupils begin working on it in their readers' theatre groups.
- They don't memorise their part but should work from a printed copy which they rehearse (re-read) several times to develop fluency skills.
- Pupils may want to mark their texts with prompts and so on.

Reading Along

- Reading along with books using audiobooks or alongside teachers helps pupils to develop confidence and reading skills to help build fluency including proper phrasing and expression, as well as sight recognition.
- This approach allows them to hear the tone and pace of a skilled reader.
- With audiobooks, pupils can re-listen until they feel comfortable reading the text unaided.

Shared Reading

- This is an interactive strategy that allows pupils to share reading while supported by a teacher.
- The teacher models the skills clearly first, then the teacher and pupils may re-read together.
- Start by giving a book introduction, discussing the title, cover and author.
- Read aloud to pupils, modelling expression and fluency.
- Pupils can join in for a re-read or read independently following the modelled read.

One-to-one Reading

- The pupil reads one-to-one with an adult (e.g., teacher, teaching assistant, trained volunteer and so on).
- The adult reads the text first, providing the pupil with a model of fluent reading.
- Then, the pupil reads the same passage to the adult with the adult providing assistance and encouragement.
- The pupil rereads the passage until the reading is quite fluent. This should take approximately three to four re-readings.

Echo Reading

- The teacher reads a sentence, and pupils then echo it back using the same prosody.
- Repeat until they do this well.
- If necessary, it might be helpful to break down longer sentences into smaller parts and practising these elements discretely before putting the whole sentence back together.

Curriculum Design for Reading

Perhaps when you were reflecting on your own reading, you found that the conditions in which you like to read (e.g., in silence curled up in a soft chair, always reading to the end of a chapter before you put the book down) don't really seem conducive to classroom life. In my experience, this is often a real challenge for teachers – becoming a reader is in many ways a very personal journey underpinned by what we want to read and how we like to experience reading – and this can be at odds with the challenges of curriculum expectations and the school environment. We can't always reconcile the many components that we have to juggle for all the children in our classes, but we can be aware of them, we can talk to our children about them, and sometimes, we might be able to find time to provide for them. Because reading is a crucial skill, we owe it to our children to keep reflecting, keep talking with them and keep trying. Mixing things up a little from time to time, participating in national initiatives, such as World Book Day, the National Literacy Trust's (NLT) 'Picture this!' reading challenge, Libraries Week, National Poetry Day, Non-Fiction November and so on, will help to keep things fresh for the children. Teachers communicate clear messages about reading through what they share about themselves as readers, how much they value reading, how they engage with it and gain purpose and pleasure from it, as well as how they share what reading is and why it matters. These messages will also be communicated through how books are displayed, how they are introduced, how they are discussed, and what happens to them when someone has finished reading them. They will be communicated in the atmosphere created during read-alouds, reading lessons and reading times. They will be communicated through teachers' actions – what happens when someone is taking too long to choose their next read, or giggling in the reading corner, or can't think of what to read next, or wants to re-read a book or read all the others in a set, or when a child that we know isn't yet strong on word reading skills wants to read the book that everyone else is reading even though it is too hard. It is helpful to think through these scenarios in advance and to talk them through with teachers in your school. This way, you will know what to do when they occur.

As well as all those implicit messages, the more explicit reading curriculum comprises:

- The texts we choose to use to develop children's word reading (decoding) knowledge and skills.
- The texts we choose to use to develop children's reading comprehension knowledge and skills.
- The texts we choose to share to develop children as readers for pleasure.
- The learning and teaching opportunities, activities, resources, approaches and strategies that we make use of.

As well as the sources that were shared earlier in this chapter, you might want to make use of resources that give guidance on high-quality books for particular year groups or on particular themes. You might want to start with https://clpe.org.uk/books/booklists, https://justimagine.co.uk/book-lists/ or https://www.booksfortopics.com/booklists/recommended-reads/. You will find many more through an internet search. Don't forget to make good use of your school, County Council or initial teacher education provider's children's librarians – they have extensive knowledge and a real passion for supporting reading which are well worth tapping into.

Supporting Pupils to Keep Up with Age-Related Expectations

Guidance from the DfE (2023) is very clear about learning to read as a key priority for pupils. Throughout Year R and Year 1, teachers should find ways to help pupils keep up with the pace of classroom phonics learning through carefully planned interventions (these may take place outside dedicated phonics/English time). This should continue for pupils into Year 2 and beyond, with the foundational principle of keeping up and the strategy for learning and teaching being the development of phonic knowledge and skills. Talk to your class teacher, English or Reading Subject Leader and/or the SENDCo if you have any concerns about pupil progress.

It is also important to be clear about the focus of your teaching of reading. When the focus is on comprehension, all pupils should participate in class lessons, with appropriate scaffolding in place to support them with any decoding needs. This allows them to continue to work towards age-related expectations unless there is a specific reason why this would not be appropriate for them.

Promoting Diversity and Inclusion

- Choose texts carefully, ensuring that they are relevant to your children's learning needs, interests and identities. Include a diverse range of authors, topics, characters and settings and consider how they are presented – is there any danger that they might perpetuate stereotypes? If so, how might you use this as a discussion point in the classroom?

Adaptive/Responsive Teaching

Considerations could include the following:

- Making sure that words, sentences and texts selected for teaching word reading (decoding) are appropriate to the child's learning needs.
- Providing scaffolding to support pupils' decoding when teaching comprehension, for example, use carefully planned pairings audiobooks or provide your own audio to support pupils in any parts of the lesson when they have to read independently of you. Make sure that all pupils can see a text clearly when they need to, adapting printed materials as necessary.
- Considering carefully how to introduce texts so that children's background knowledge is activated. Identify whether any key information such as vocabulary, context or ideas within a text would benefit from being taught in advance. Provide supporting visual materials for pupils who have English as an Additional Language (EAL) if this would help them.
- Considering whether pre-reading a text (e.g., with a teaching assistant or another child) in advance would help one or more children to engage with discussions or shared or guided reading.
- Considering how to extend children's understanding of a text by adding breadth and/or depth to any planned activities, for example, might some children broaden their knowledge of texts by reading an extract from a book with a similar or contrasting character or setting, or that provides additional factual information, or presents similar information in a different way? Could you use a provocative statement for some children to think about to deepen their knowledge of a text (see The Challenge Book at https://www.onceuponapicture.co.uk/the-challenge-book/for examples)?

Summary

This chapter has considered an evidence-informed approach to the teaching of reading. It has considered the value of learning to read and presented reading as an active process in which the fundamental aim is to gain meaning. It has explored the knowledge and skills children need to develop to become proficient readers, examining decoding and comprehension as the key components of reading which underpin the structure of the National Curriculum. Key principles of effective teaching have been explained, with suggestions given as to how to support children whose progress may not keep pace with age-related expectations

Further Reading

1   Just Imagine shares their knowledge through a blog, podcast series and YouTube events which can be accessed from: https://justimagine.co.uk/blog/, https://justimagine.co.uk/podcasts/ and https://www.youtube.com/@nikkigamble1. These offer a wealth of information on children's books and excellent advice and guidance for teachers.

2   An organisation called Booktrust works with the children's laureate – a children's author is appointed for three years and shares lots of ideas to inspire pupils. Find out more at https://www.booktrust.org.uk/what-we-do/childrens-laureate/

3   Several websites review books and provide other resources to support learning and teaching, for example, https://www.lovereading4kids.co.uk/ and https://www.booksfortopics.com/

4   Some websites have a wealth of audio-visual and other resources from children's authors to inspire young readers, including https://authorfy.com/ and https://www.penguin.co.uk/brands/puffin.html

5   Some schools participate in or shadow popular children's book awards. This involves the children in reading and discussing books that have been longlisted and/or shortlisted. You can find out more at https://schoolreadinglist.co.uk/resources/childrens-literature-awards/ and https://ukla.org/awards/ukla-book

References

Bilton, C., & Duff, A. (2021). *Improving Literacy in Key Stage 2 Guidance Report*. Education Endowment Foundation.

Cain, K. (2010). *Reading development and difficulties*. John Wiley & Sons Ltd.

Clay, M. (1991). *Becoming literate: The construction of inner control*. Heinemann.

Clements, J., & Tobin, M. (2021). *Understanding and teaching primary English: Theory into practice*. SAGE.

CLPE. (2020). *Choosing & using quality children's texts: What we know works*. CLPE.

Department for Education. (2013). *The national curriculum in England: Key stages 1 and 2 framework document*. https://www.gov.uk/government/publications/national-curriculum-in-england-primary-curriculum. Accessed on May 16, 2022.

Department for Education. (2023). *The reading framework*. Crown Copyright.

Dombey, H. (2010). *Teaching reading: What the evidence says*. UKLA.

Elborn, S. (2015). *Handbook of teaching early reading: More than phonics*. UKLA.

Foorman, B., Beyler, N., Borradaile, K., Coyne, M., Denton, C., Dimino, J., Furgeson, J., Hayes, L., Henke, J., Justice, L., Keating, B., Lewis, W., Sattar, S., Streke, A., Wagner, R., & Wissel, S. (2016).

Foundational skills to support reading for understanding in kindergarten through 3rd grade. U.S. Department of Education.

Gough, P., & Tunmer, W. (1986). Decoding, reading and reading disability. *Remedial and Special Education, 7,* 6–10.

Harvey, S., & Goudvis, A. (2007). *Strategies that work: Teaching comprehension to enhance understanding and engagement.* Stenhouse.

Keene, E., & Zimmermann, S. (2007). *Mosaic of thought: The power of comprehension strategy instruction.* Heinemann.

Ofsted. (2022). *Research and analysis research review series: English.* https://www.gov.uk/government/publications/curriculum-research-review-series-english/curriculum-research-review-series-english

Rasinski, T. (2005). The role of the teacher in effective fluency instruction. *New England Reading Association Journal, 41,* 9–12.

Rasinski, T., & Smith, M. (2018). *The mega book of fluency.* Scholastic.

Westbrook, J., Sutherland, J., Oakhill, J., & Sullivan, S. (2019). *'Just reading': The impact of a faster pace of reading narratives on the comprehension of poorer adolescent readers in English classrooms.* University of Sussex.

World Literacy Foundation information. (2018). *The economic & social cost of illiteracy: A white paper by the world literacy foundation.* https://worldliteracyfoundation.org/. Accessed on September 10, 2022.

7

Planning to Teach Phonics

Chapter Objectives

This chapter will:

- Identify the key elements of a high-quality phonics curriculum.
- Consider what effective pedagogy for teaching phonics might look like.
- Demonstrate one way of approaching the planning of a phonics lesson.

Introduction

Phonics is a way of teaching children how to read and write by developing their knowledge and understanding of the relationship between the sounds that make up words (phonemes) and the way those sounds look when they are written (graphemes). In England, it has been statutory for all maintained schools to teach pupils to read and write using a systematic synthetic phonics approach. This followed the Rose Report (2006), which recommended the teaching of phonics as the prime approach for tackling unfamiliar words and that children should be taught to apply their phonic skills and knowledge within the context of a broad and rich language curriculum.

The most recent guidance on the Department for Education's view of what makes effective phonics teaching can be found in The Reading Framework (2023). There are a number of DfE-validated Systematic Synthetic Phonics Schemes (SSPs), which schools may buy into, or they may choose to create their own. It is most likely that any school you are in will have a clear and systematic approach to the teaching of phonics which you should follow carefully to ensure consistency for the children. It is helpful to observe carefully how a school teaches phonics before planning and teaching your own lessons.

Useful Terminology

The Reading Framework (DfE, 2023) suggests that letters are a kind of code – a way of writing down the sounds of the words we speak. This is known as the alphabetic code. In England, spoken words are made up of approximately 44 different sounds that can be made from the 26 letters of the alphabet by using them alone and in different combinations.

Phonemes are the smallest units of sound in a word. In Year R (the Reception Year), pupils learn one way of representing each of the 44+ sounds that they will need to read and write. In the Reading Framework, this is known as the simple code.

Graphemes are the written representations of the phonemes. As children learn a new phoneme, they also learn to write the letter shape(s) used to represent it in writing. In schools, this is usually referred to as grapheme phone correspondence (GPC) or letter-sound correspondence reinforcing the link between the sound and the letter shapes that represent it.

Children learn both the sound and the letter shape(s) at the same time. Many phonemes are represented by just one letter, for example, s, a, t, p, i, n, m and d.

Some phonemes are represented by more than one letter, for example, sh, ch, oo and igh. These are called digraphs when they represent two letters, and trigraphs when they represent three letters.

The process of blending (or sound-blending) is key to effective phonics practice. This skill enables the children to draw the sounds of a word together so that they can read it. According to the DfE (2023), blending involves a three-step process:

Children:

1. see the written word 'sheep'

2. say the corresponding three phonemes /sh//ee//p/

3. blend the three phonemes to say the word 'sheep'. (p. 7)

When spelling, children need to learn to segment a word. For example, if a child wants to write the word dog, they need to break down the word into each of its sounds in order to write it. According to the DfE (2023), segmenting for spelling also involves a three-step process:

Children:

1. hear the spoken word 'dog'

2. say 'dog' – /d//o//g/

3. write the three corresponding graphemes 'd', 'o', 'g' to spell the word 'dog' (p. 8).

Although many words in the English language are phonically regular (i.e., using the simple alphabetic code like the words hat, lamp and mushroom), there are also many words which contain one or more phonemes that are irregular (e.g., sea and build). Some words don't fully follow the simple code rules but are often used in writing, for example, he, go and when, so children are taught to recognise these by sight. In DfE publications, these are known as common exception words but different schemes may use different terms such as tricky words or red words. This helps children to understand that they will use a sight recognition strategy rather than a phonic decoding strategy to learn, read and spell these words.

Curriculum Continuity and Progression

Children's knowledge and understanding of phonics is underpinned by key visual and auditory skills which enable them to discriminate between letter shapes and sounds and to remember the sequence in which shapes and sounds can be seen and heard. Alongside this, children need to build a vocabulary for talking about sounds, for example, loud, quiet, long, short, high, low, buzzing, cracking and rustling. Developing children's knowledge of different sounds in the environment can be gradually refined. For example, this process may begin with listening to environmental sounds, such as vehicles, weather and animal noises. Subsequently, children can explore more subtle differences, such as those between different percussion instruments which can be played and performed in different ways. Eventually, they may delve into sounds that can be produced with the body, such as popping, clapping and clicking. Oral blending and segmenting games and lots of exposure to alliteration and rhyme all serve to strengthen children's phonological and phonemic development. While these foundations for phonics may not necessarily be an explicit part of an Systematic Synthetic Phonics Programme (SSP) and may have already been developed through the children's pre-school experiences, they form an important part of shared experiences within school. Glazzard and Stokoe (2017) also highlight the importance of children developing a good understanding of key concepts in order to help them comprehend texts, for example, using a story such as *The Three Billy Goats Gruff* to develop the concept of crossing over something (e.g. a bridge or a road.).

Formal phonics teaching usually starts in Year R. Here, children are taught the simple code very soon after starting school, often learning two or three sounds each week, with periods of review, consolidation and assessment built in. The children also begin to explore the complex code, developing their understanding that some phonemes are represented by more than one grapheme, for example, ss, ff and ll, which may sound the same as s, f and l but are written differently. To meet the relevant early learning goals for the end of Year R, children will demonstrate their ability to produce a sound for each letter in the alphabet and know at least 10 digraphs. They read words consistent with their phonic knowledge by sound-blending and read-aloud simple sentences and books that are consistent with their phonic knowledge, including some common exception words. In writing, children will demonstrate their ability to write recognisable letters, most of which are correctly formed. They should be able to spell words by identifying sounds in them and representing the sounds with a letter or letters. Additionally, they will write simple phrases and sentences that can be read by others (DfE, 2021). Writing skills are underpinned by a range of physical development skills which are considered in Chapter 16.

The National Curriculum in England: English Programmes of Study for Key Stage 1 and Key Stage 2 identifies specific expectations for pupils in each year group in the main body of the document. Dedicated phonics teaching time continues into Year 1 with children continuing to learn the complex alphabetic code, with children learning more about phonemes which are represented by more than one grapheme, for example, the long e sound which can be represented by ee, ea, ey (as in donkey), ie (as in piece) and so on. They also learn that some graphemes can represent more than one phoneme, for example, a long a sound which can be represented by ay, ai, ei (as in weigh), ea (as in great) and so on.

Word Reading

In Year 1, pupils learn to apply their phonic knowledge and skills to decode words; read all 40+ letters/groups for 40+ phonemes, including, where applicable, alternative sounds for graphemes; read accurately by blending sounds in unfamiliar words containing GPCs that have been taught; read all of the Reception and Year 1 common exception words; read common suffixes (-s, -es, -ing, -ed, er and est); read words of more than one-syllable containing taught GPCs; read-aloud phonically decodable texts, re-reading them to build fluency and confidence; and read words with contractions.

In Year 2, pupils build on their phonic knowledge, typically learning more through the teaching of spelling rather than phonics, although there is some overlap. Children learn to apply their growing knowledge of root words, prefixes and suffixes, both to read-aloud and to understand the meaning of new words they meet (to include 'dis-', 'mis-', 'in-', 'il-', 'im-', 'ir-' and '-ly'); and read further exception words, noting the unusual correspondences between spelling and sound, and where these occur in the word.

Throughout Key Stage 2, children continue to learn to read the words on the relevant Year 3/ 4 and Year 5/6 word lists; read further exception words, noting any unusual correspondences between spellings and sounds; and apply their growing knowledge of root words, prefixes and suffixes in order to read and understand the meanings of new words.

Writing

In Year 1, pupils learn to spell words containing each of the 40+ phonemes already taught; common exception words; and to write from memory simple sentences dictated by the teacher that include words using the GPCs and common exception words taught so far.

In Year 2, pupils learn to segment spoken words into phonemes and represent these by graphemes, spelling many correctly; new ways of spelling phonemes for which one or more spellings are already known, and learn some words with each spelling, including a few common homophones; spell common exception words; and write from memory simple sentences dictated by the teacher that include words using the GPCs, common exception words and punctuation taught so far.

Children build on these skills throughout Key Stage 2, developing a wider knowledge of how to spell a range of words.

Curriculum and Pedagogy

Effective phonics teaching is underpinned by strong subject knowledge. It will be helpful for you to be able to explain what the alphabetic code is, to be able to identify the number of phonemes in a word and to be able to recognise words which are phonically regular and words which aren't.

Activity Developing your Knowledge of Phonemes and Grapheme-Phoneme Correspondences

Activity 1: Identifying How Many Phonemes There Are in Words

Read each of the words below and identify how many phonemes make up each one.

  pin, lot, jump, drink, shoes, flake, garden, throughout

Extend this activity a little further by using your own words.

(Continued)

Activity 2: Identifying Irregular GPCs in Words

In the word 'mess', most of the phonemes which make up the word are phonically regular, but there is one sound which could be considered to be phonically irregular: – the ss (pronounced s). This is an alternative GPC, i.e., a different way of representing the already known phoneme s that was taught as part of the simple code.

Read each of the words below and decide which parts are phonically irregular:

said, was, do, to, what, they, earth, water, brother, good, listen.

Which already known phoneme is each irregularity an alternative for?

Whether a school uses a commercial phonics programme or their own, there will be resources, terminology, and teaching and learning routines on which good practice is built, and it is essential that you follow the school's approach so as not to confuse the children. The Reading Framework (DfE, 2023) suggests that phonics lessons will vary in length according to the children's experience. These might be ten minutes a day as children start Year R, introducing them systematically to each new GPC. By the end of Year R, phonics work might last up to an hour a day, allowing children to not only engage in new learning but also to consolidate their previous learning and apply their phonics knowledge in meaningful reading and writing activities.

As in any high-quality lesson, the most effective practice typically focuses on a clear learning objective, some explicit teaching and good opportunities for children to practise and apply their learning. Effective lessons are also marked by high levels of pupil participation, well-planned and carefully structured chunks of learning which maximise learning time, skilled use of formative assessment to ascertain what progress is being made and the provision of high-quality feedback.

The DfE identifies the use of dictated sentences as a vital part of effective phonics teaching, allowing the children to focus on transcribing a sentence without having the additional pressure of the compositional elements that are often associated with writing. Dictated sentences should use only those GPCs which the children have already learned, giving them a chance to practise and apply their learning.

To learn a new GPC, children need to be able to:

- Hear the sound (phoneme).
- Pronounce the sound (phoneme).
- Recognise the sound's symbol (grapheme).

When they are ready, they also need to be able to:

- Write the grapheme using correct letter formation.

To apply their knowledge, children need to be able to:

- Identify and read the sound (phoneme) when they come across it in a word.
- Isolate and write the sound (phoneme) when they want to spell a word which uses it.

The goal is for children to build automaticity in their learning so that they apply their phonics knowledge quickly and effortlessly when reading and writing so it is essential that they are given lots of practice at retrieving and applying their knowledge so it is really secure.

Systematic Synthetic Phonics programmes often have a range of resources to support teaching. Each phoneme may well have a character or rhyme/phrase to help children remember it, for example, the 's' phoneme may be linked to a snake which the children are introduced to, giving them a visual prompt through the use of large GPC cards which have the snake on one side of the card and the letter s on the other. This can help the children to differentiate between all the letters' sounds and shapes, making the learning more memorable. They can be used to support recall with the children saying 's' when they see the grapheme, and 'sssssnake' when they see the picture. To help the children write a grapheme, many schemes provide a letter formation script, sometimes called a ditty, which they can repeat to support recall. For example, when learning to write the letter s, the letter formation script may be something like 'round the snake's head, slide down his back and round his tail' (DfE, 2007, p. 52).

Among its recommendations, the Rose Report (2006) highlighted the value of a multisensory approach to the teaching of phonics suggesting activities such as the use of physical movement to copy letter shapes, magnetic letters to build words, and picture cues and actions to embed phoneme knowledge and recall. The Reading Framework guidance does not specifically identify this as part of its principles of high-quality phonics teaching. However, Glazzard and Stokoe (2017) emphasise the value of supporting effective teaching by allowing children to participate practically in phonics learning. This approach also enables the teacher to utilise a variety of teaching strategies to strengthen learning and maintain children's interest and engagement.

Modelling

To teach phonics well, you will need to model effectively. First, you need to be able to model how to enunciate each phoneme accurately and clearly. This can sometimes feel quite daunting, especially if an SSP approach wasn't a significant part of your own learning. There are a number of online sources which demonstrate this effectively; these are identified in the 'Further reading' section of this chapter. Of course, not all phonemes are pronounced in the same way by all people in all parts of the United Kingdom, so it is important to show sensitivity to regional accents. It may be that it is your regional accent which is different from the majority of children in your class (in which case you will need to practise saying it in the way that makes the most sense to them during phonics teaching), or it may be that one or more of the children have different regional accents to those of the majority. Respectfully recognising the different ways we say words will help to foster the children's interest in words and language, and hearing you have a go will help them to develop confidence in having a go themselves.

As well as enunciating the phoneme clearly, you will want to check that the children can do this too so give them plenty of opportunities to echo you, noting that their mouths are forming the sound correctly and that they are saying it right. Call and response routines are often part of phonics schemes. These involve the teacher modelling a particular skill and then asking the children to do it. These routines might be indicated by words, for example, 'my turn, your turn', or non-verbal gestures, for example, cupping a hand behind your ear to indicate that children should repeat what you have just said. These are likely to be built into a validated SSP scheme or be part of a school's approach so observe carefully first.

As well as modelling by showing children, you should also use a think-aloud strategy to explain what you are thinking so that the invisible processes of reading and spelling become visible. To model the process of blending, remember that it is a three-step approach which involves children looking at the word, saying its corresponding phonemes in turn, and then blending them to produce the word. In practice, this is often modelled a number of times by the teacher, saying the phonemes in turn with increasing speed in order to support the blending skill, for example:

c/a/t
c/a/t
c/a/t cat.

The teacher may also use a visual cue to support children's understanding, for example, pointing at each GPC in turn with increasing speed and sweeping their finger underneath the whole word to show the blending.

As well as learning to blend individual words, children need to apply this knowledge within longer chunks of text such as phrases, sentences and whole texts. You will model these first. For example, imagine that the children have already learned the GPCs s, a, t, p i, n, c, and today they are learning h. After some practise with individual words, you will be able to model reading the phrase 'a cat in a hat'. Children build up to reading whole phrases gradually so check with your school whether they are all ready for this.

To model the process of encoding, you will tell the children which word you want to write and then explain what to do. This involves what is often referred to as sound talk where you say each sound in the word clearly.

'I want to write the word cat – cat – c/a/t (you might repeat this more than once and count each sound on your fingers as you say it). There are three phonemes in the word cat. The first sound is c. I know how to write that sound (you might use a letter formation script here if the children know one) c. Next, I can hear an 'a' sound...' (and so on).

To teach common exception words, you will need to model a sight recognition strategy. This usually involves presenting the word clearly to the children, identifying it as a common exception or tricky word (check what term your school uses) and asking them to repeat it.

> Here is the word 'said'. It's a tricky word because the graphemes in the middle don't make their usual sound. We say it like this: said. Now you try.

Get the children to practise a few times and remember to practise recall with them in the coming days and weeks until their automatic recall is secure.

When you are directly teaching phonics, it is essential that all pupils make the most of the practice time. This means they should all join in (unless there is a specific reason why they can't or shouldn't). Make sure they can all see you clearly and are watching you when it is your turn to model, and watch them as closely as possible when it is their turn so that you can check that everyone is joining in. It is also important to ensure that children are not spending their practice time waiting for their turn at something so make sure that when you are directly teaching a class or group, everyone can respond at the same time, for example, 'Everybody get ready to copy me, c, c'.

Choosing a Learning Objective

Prior to planning and teaching your own lessons, you will of course need to find out what the school's approach is; your class teacher will be able to tell you whether you are expected to teach the phonics lesson exactly as it appears in the school's scheme (whether their own or bought in from a commercial publisher), to annotate it with your own prompts in order to ensure it is tailored for your class or to create your own lesson from the school's framework.

The Reading Framework outlines a clear structure for direct phonics teaching. The first part of the lesson involves the children revisiting and reviewing prior learning by practising quick recall of previously learned phonemes, graphemes, blending or segmenting as appropriate. This is often supported by the use of GPC cards or wall friezes. The second part of the lesson is where new teaching happens. This may focus on teaching new phonemes, graphemes, tricky words, blending or segmenting. In the third part of the lesson, the teacher leads the children in focused practice activities using words and then phrases/sentences. It is important that the new GPC is the only new part of the lesson – all words, phrases and sentences which are used in the 'practice' part of the session should use only the new learning focus among otherwise known GPCs and words.

Lesson Plan

Here is one suggestion for what a lesson plan might look like for a Year R class (Table 7.1).

Relevant prior learning: Pupils have learned the following GPCs: s, a, t, p, i

What will children learn: to be able to read and write the GPC n

What will effective learning look like:

- Pronounce the 'n' phoneme clearly.
- Recognise the 'n' GPC.
- Write a 'n' using the correct letter formation.
- Read simple words containing a 'n': nip, tin, pin, pan, nap.

How will learning be assessed:

- Observation of pupils.

Planned next steps to follow this lesson: practise this skill to develop consistent and automatic recall.

Table 7.1 A lesson plan for teaching phonics

Today's lesson sequence/content
9:00 **Revisit and review**: use grapheme cards s, a, t, p, i – children to say the phoneme when they see the corresponding grapheme.
9:02 **Teach**: tell the children that today we are learning a new sound 'n'. Ask them to repeat the sound after me – do this a few times.
Show the children the 'n' card, telling them this is the grapheme for the sound 'n'. Ask children to say it when I show them the card – play a short game where I hide the card and when I reveal it, the children say 'n'.
Show the other side of the card where there is a picture of a net. Tell the children this is a net and you use it to catch things in. Ask the children to say 'n' when they see the grapheme side of the card and 'net' when they see the picture side. Repeat a few times.
Tell the children we are now going to have a go at writing the grapheme ourselves. Show them first, tracing over the letter with my finger three times, then do this again saying 'down to the bottom, back up, over and down' - repeat twice. Ask them to have a go with me. Repeat a few times.
Tell the children we are now going to practise saying some words with the 'n' in using our sound talk skills. Start with n/a/p – the children say it with me three times, each time getting faster and then blending orally into 'nap' - tell the children that a nap means a short sleep. Repeat with n/i/p and t/i/n.
9:05 **Practise reading**: Now tell the children we are going to read some words with the 'n' sound using our decoding skills. Use the GPC cards to make nap, showing the children how to blend the word, pointing to each GPC in turn and saying it. Repeat three times getting faster and then blend the word. Ask the children to repeat this process all together.
Swap the 'a' for an 'i' and repeat the process. After blending, tell the children what nip means. Tell the children we are now going to look at a word with an 'n' at the end. Make the word 'pin' with the cards and repeat the process, then make 'tin' and 'pan'.
Praise the children for their work today. Show them the 'n' GPC and tell them you are going to add it to the phonics board so that they can look at it to help them with their reading and writing.

Introduction to the Lesson – Revisit and Review

In this introduction, the children engage in recall practice, helping them to develop automatic recall of the GPCs or tricky words. If the children have only learned a few, there will be time to revisit all of them. However, as they develop their learning in phonics, you may want to select from the most recent learning with just a few from earlier learning. Use your knowledge of the children's learning to guide your selection – for example, if a few children were struggling to recall a particular GPC in their reading or writing, you could choose to include that one. The same process will apply to practising common exception words.

Teach

The example given is for an early GPC so the lesson is very short and straightforward. The children are relatively new to phonics learning so they practise with only a few GPCs and words, and there is not too much emphasis on writing at this stage (although you could ask them to practise writing the words either on the carpet with their fingers or on paper once they are at their tables). The lesson is quite pacey and you can inject some energy into it by varying your voice and facial expression to keep the children's interest. One commercial SSP, Song of Sounds, uses a host of colourful characters to support the children's learning. The teacher dresses up as a builder to emphasise how the GPCs are used to build words, presenting them on bricks rather than on cards. This shows that there may be creative ideas that you can bring to a lesson once you have made sure that the learning itself is clear and well-structured. As children progress through phonics, you might spend more time teaching the writing part within the lesson itself, or this may be more appropriate for another part of the day when it is easier to make sure that the children are sitting at tables.

Practice

As phonics learning is in the early stages, practice at this point only involves reading words. Once they have learned a few more GPCs, the children will be ready to start reading short phrases so you can introduce those, gradually building up to reading sentences. Check how your school does these things, and make sure you have a good grasp of what the children know and can do as this is key to effective planning. Some practice will take place outside the main phonics lesson and can involve the children in more active games where they have to find a particular phoneme. There are some great ideas for this in *Hands On Phonics* by Liz Webster.

Plenary

The plenary is not identified as a key part of the phonics lesson in the Reading Framework. However, you may wish to return to the learning objective to reinforce this and to praise good learning. You might also indicate to the children what will happen next, for example, by saying when you will practise this some more, or saying that you are looking forward to seeing them use the new learning when they're reading. It is so important to remember that phonics is about helping children learn to read, and reading is a really enjoyable experience. It may be that you can follow up the teaching of a particular GPC with a really good picture book, poem or song which uses it and that you can tantalise them with by saying that later today you'll be sharing a new story/song or game that uses their new sound.

Assessing the Children's Learning

As well as formative assessment, there are likely to be periods of review and assessment that are part of a school's approach to phonics. Some schemes review and assess children's learning weekly, and others at longer intervals (some do both). It is important that you know what each child can do so that you can plan the next steps of their learning. The Reading Framework highlights the importance of using a 'keep up' approach where the children who need further practice get this quickly, rather than waiting for the gaps to become too large so that they have to 'catch up'. The Reading Framework suggests that this can be done daily one to one with a pupil or with a small group of pupils with similar needs and should focus on consolidating the knowledge the children are not yet secure with. Any consolidation needs to be in line with the approach the children are experiencing in their main phonics learning which should continue. As well as assessing children in the phonics session and tracking their knowledge of GPCs through focused assessment tasks, teachers also need to know whether the child is making the link between their phonics lessons and reading and writing. If the children have learned particular GPCs, they should begin to transfer that knowledge so that they can read those GPCs accurately when reading and write them accurately when spelling. It can be useful to make reference to classroom prompts, reminding the children to look at the phonics frieze, for example, and for you to prompt them when you are hearing them read or supporting their writing. Modelling when you are engaging in shared reading and writing with the class will also support this transfer of learning.

Using Resources

Commercial SSPs will have their own resources relevant to the teaching and practice activities they use. Some of the most common resources are as follows. Grapheme cards are used to introduce a new GPC, often with just the grapheme on one side and a picture which acts as a mnemonic on the other. Children can say the phoneme when the grapheme side is shown to them, and recall the prompt word or phrase when they are shown the picture, helping to prompt automatic and speedy recall. Wall friezes or posters are also popular. These often display the grapheme alongside the mnemonic prompt and can be used in the revisit/review section of the lesson, or to promote accurate application in independent, shared and guided reading and writing lessons. Sometimes, there are smaller desktop versions of these which may be called a sound mat or something similar. Children can use these when writing to help them recall phonemes and copy the graphemes and may find these easier to use as they sit alongside whatever they are writing on and remove the need to stop and look elsewhere in the room before looking back at their work and trying to remember. Phonics schemes usually have word cards, smallish cards each with a word that uses a particular GPC for you to use to support practice within words, and perhaps phrase or caption cards too so that children can practise their learning within longer chunks of text. Some schemes make use of a puppet who can only talk in phonemes and so requests the help of the children to 'blend' their messages ('What's that Cat? You want to go out to p/l/a/y? Oh, you want to go out to play!'). It is important that puppets face and talk to the teacher so that the children don't watch and try to copy the puppet's mouth shapes as these are usually quite limited in puppets and don't offer a good model to best support the children's learning.

Adaptive/Responsive Teaching

Some possible ways in which you could adapt the learning for those needing additional scaffolding or stretch and challenge are:

- Make sure the children who are finding it trickier to pick up new phonics learning are sitting near to you or another adult so that additional modelling and focused feedback can be given quickly.
- Use pencil grips or other supports for children who are not yet secure with an appropriate grasp.
- Provided additional short burst reviews throughout the day for children who aren't yet secure with one or more GPCs.
- Consider the use of multisensory resources such as magnetic letters unless letter formation is the specific learning goal – alternative ways of recording or demonstrating their knowledge should always be considered if this is a specific challenge for some pupils.
- Extend the application for pupils who are ready – they might read or write whole words, phrases or sentences while others practise only the isolated GPC, or may be able to generate examples of their own while other learners might require more matching and copying activities.
- Consider whether resources need to be adapted for some pupils, for example, by providing resources on different coloured paper or cards for those who find black and white contrasts difficult.
- Consider whether the learning can be presented in smaller (or longer) chunks and whether everyone needs to start and finish at the same point.
- Monitor the learning carefully to identify whether you might make use of reteaching, additional modelling and pupil discussions.

Providing Feedback

Within the phonics lesson, it's useful to focus your feedback towards the learning goals for the lesson, making sure that children enunciate phonemes accurately and clearly, and form the graphemes accurately using an appropriate pencil grip. When practising reading and spelling, children will need to remember the three-part processes described earlier in this chapter.

Beyond the phonics lesson, it's really important to give children feedback on their attempts to apply their knowledge in reading and writing, for example, in the form of reminder prompts to cue children to use what they have already learned.

Where Am I Going?

You will have primarily pre-empted this through your lesson introduction where you shared the objectives and modelled what success will look like. You may see opportunities where giving children positive feedback to remind children of the key processes would be helpful to them.

How Am I Going?

Remind yourself of the success criteria and give feedback in relation to this. Phonics can be challenging for some pupils to pick up and you won't want to make children feel so self-conscious that they don't want to participate or respond. Highlight what the child is doing well. In addition to supporting motivation, this will help them to understand which bits they have got right and begin to identify specific parts they find tricky. As always, remember to be specific in your use of praise so a child knows exactly what they have done effectively.

Where to Next?

Make sure you are clear and don't overload the learners' working memories. Use reminder prompts or hints so they know exactly what to work on next.

Application of Learning

The Reading Framework places great emphasis on the use of decodable readers as providing valuable opportunities for children to practise their phonics skills. Decodable readers are texts which are composed entirely of a specific set of GPCs which children progress through as they learn new ones. Early decodable readers use just a few GPCs such as s, a, t, p, i and n. The DfE believe that they are useful in providing carefully structured practice for the children to use their phonic decoding skills and experience success. As a teacher, you will need to make sure that each child is reading the right decodable reader to match their knowledge of phonics. Your school will provide guidance on how these are used, for example, whether the pupils read them in small groups, each having their own copy, with guidance from the teacher and when to send them home for more practice.

It is perhaps inevitable that the decodable texts, which are created from a limited number of words chosen purely because of their decodability, can sometimes lack an authentically engaging storyline or rich information. Therefore, providing plentiful opportunities for children to engage meaningfully with a wealth of rich, high-quality texts through which they can reinforce their growing knowledge and understanding alongside their daily phonics teaching is key to supporting reading development.

Using shared reading and read-alouds to explore high-quality texts helps to build positive attitudes towards reading and develop the essential skills of comprehension. Through carefully chosen texts, children can make personal connections and develop inference and under-standing, while the teacher can model and articulate a wide range of reading strategies with children in an authentic way, handing over responsibility to the children in places where they will experience success.

The use of high-quality books with patterned language, repeated refrains and rhyme will support children's ongoing phonic and vocabulary development. For younger children, choose books which make use of sounds such as *What the Ladybird Heard* and *Polar Bear Polar Bear What Do You Hear?* help to support phonological awareness, and joining in by practising and artic-ulating a wide variety of sounds will support their ability to hear and articulate phonemes. Texts which use alliteration and rhyme will reinforce key learning from phonics lessons, and hearing and performing poetry will support children's understanding of syllables and beats.

Re-reading texts and sharing favourites with the children a number of times will help them to deepen their comprehension skills and enable them to build a good mental model of what fluent reading sounds and feels like. Having memorised them, encouraging children to share these well-loved texts together helps to support reader identity as children see themselves as readers by emulating what good readers do. Opportunities to play fun word games will encourage children's playful exploration of language, and a focus on rhythm and rhyme sup-ports children's early phonological development.

Make sure that alongside the teaching of phonics, you read and share a wide variety of reading materials and experiences rooted in both fiction and non-fiction so that children realise how valuable and exciting it is to learn to read.

Summary

Throughout this chapter, the effective teaching of phonics has been explored, and key aspects of a meaningful and high-quality curriculum for teaching this is proposed. The importance of teaching this as one part of a rich and meaningful English curriculum is established, with the need to read and share lots of good age-appropriate real books and rhymes, songs, poems and language play games highlighted. Supporting the application of children's knowledge and skills through teacher modelling, and authentic reading and writing opportunities and focused feedback is also established.

Further reading

1 To develop your subject knowledge for phonics, read *Teaching Systematic Synthetic Phonics in Primary Schools* by Wendy Jolliffe, David Waugh and Angela Gill., or *Teaching Systematic Synthetic Phonics and Early English* by Jonathan Glazzard and Jane Stokoe.

2 Find out about the DfE's latest guidance on the effective teaching of phonics: https://assets.publishing.service.gov.uk/government/uploads/system/uploads/attachment_data/file/1178136/The_Reading_Framework_2023.pdf (pp. 40–49).

3 Extend your knowledge of some of the DfE's validated systematic synthetic phonics schemes by visiting: https://www.gov.uk/government/publications/choosing-a-phonics-teaching-programme/contact-details-for-the-validated-systematic-synthetic-phonics-ssp-programmes

References

Department for Education. (2021). *Statutory framework for the early years foundation stage: Setting the standards for learning, development and care for children from birth to five.* Crown Copyright.

Department for Education. (2023). *The reading framework.* Crown Copyright.

Department for Education and Skills. (2007). *Letters and sounds: Principles and practice of high quality phonics.* Crown Copyright.

Glazzard, J., & Stokoe, J. (2017). *Teaching systematic synthetic phonics and early English* (2nd ed.). Critical Publishing.

Rose, J. (2006). *Independent review of the teaching of early reading: Final report.* Department for Education and Skills.

8

Planning to Teach Reading Comprehension

Chapter Objectives

This chapter will:

- Identify the key elements of a high-quality reading comprehension curriculum.
- Consider what effective pedagogy for teaching reading comprehension might look like.
- Demonstrate one way of approaching the planning of a reading comprehension lesson.

Introduction

Reading comprehension forms one strand of the reading curriculum. In line with the Simple View of Reading presented in Chapter 6, it focuses on developing children's understanding of a wide range of texts by both listening to them and reading them for themselves.

What Is Reading Comprehension?

Reading comprehension differs from language comprehension because of the reliance on print, instead of spoken language, to perceive the words and derive meaning (Hoover & Gough, 1990). The reader's understanding (comprehension) of what they read is underpinned by their word reading (decoding) skills. Kamhi describes decoding as a skill because it 'involves a well-defined scope of knowledge (e.g. letters, sounds, words) and processes (decoding) that can be systematically taught' (2009, p. 175). However, Kamhi states that comprehension 'is not a skill. It is a complex of higher-level mental processes that include thinking, reasoning, imagining and interpreting'. Interestingly, research shows that a reader's understanding of the key content of a text is also underpinned by how much they know about that content in the first place – their background knowledge. In fact, 'familiarity with the content of a passage is in fact so important that poor decoders do better than good decoders when they have more knowledge of a topic' (2009, p. 175).

Bearne and Reedy also note that reading 'comprehension is not a single mental process; it is made up of a range of component parts which work together to help the reader understand the text' (2017, p. 194). Tennent (2015) shows that comprehension relies on the reader's ability to:

- Draw on linguistic processes including understanding of words, phrases and sentences and how these combine to make meaning.
- Utilise knowledge bases including general knowledge.
- Employ cognitive/metacognitive processes including short- and long-term memory, comprehension monitoring, phonic decoding and word recognition, and inference making. (Bearne & Reedy, 2017, p. 194)

Research Focus: What Good Readers Do by Duke and Pearson (2002)

Duke and Pearson define comprehension as a complex but productive activity which offers a sense of satisfaction to the reader.

In their review of research into what good readers do, Duke and Pearson concluded the following:

- Good readers are active; they set clear goals for what they would like to gain from their reading and check in with themselves to see whether they are achieving these.

- Good readers are involved in a continual decision-making process when reading; they choose to read some parts of a text quickly and some more slowly. They may choose to read some parts again, for example, if they recognise that they didn't understand something.
- Good readers take time to process what they have read. Some of their processing occurs while reading, but they often continue to process what they have read after they have finished.

Building a Mental Model

A key idea in the research into effective comprehension is that of the mental model. This puts forward the idea that the reader builds a representation, or mental model of what they have read. This is constructed by the reader as a result of the meaning they have made from the words, sentences, themes and topics in the text along with the reader's own prior/background knowledge. This mental model is not necessarily in the form of pictures – it might be quite abstract and is personal to the reader. There are a number of strategies that good readers use to support them in building a strong mental model such as making connections to background knowledge, making use of text structure, using prediction skills, questioning and clarifying parts of the text and being able to summarise the text. All these strategies need to be modelled by the teacher so that the invisible process of reading becomes visible to the children.

The Role of Background Knowledge

Background knowledge is a key factor in a reader's ability to comprehend a text; readers will have varying levels of background knowledge about the words, topics, events and themes within any text which can impact their comprehension. Background knowledge may have been acquired from the reader's own experiences or developed from other sources such as discussions, films and books. According to Oakhill et al. (2014), early readers are likely to rely more on their own experiences to help them understand texts; this is typically reflected in early reading books which often make use of storylines and characters which are likely to be familiar to the young reader. Reading comprehension is supported by background knowledge, but reading also extends background knowledge. Making connections is, therefore, a key part of effective reading as this enables readers to draw on knowledge they already have, activate it at the right time and assimilate new knowledge acquired from the reading.

Using Text Structure to Support Comprehension

Oakhill et al. (2014) also note how readers can use the structure of a text to support deeper comprehension and recall. In narrative texts, knowledge of where and how elements such as characters, settings, plot, problem and resolution fit in can help the reader to navigate the text.

In non-narrative texts, understanding what the purpose of the text is and how it is laid out can also help the reader. One way to support children's understanding of text structure is to ask them to build visual representations of the text, for example, by creating a story mountain or map or using graphic organisers to record the information they have gathered.

Prediction

Prediction skills begin in Year 1, with pupils learning to predict what might happen based on what has been read so far. In Year 2, this extends so that pupils use a range of clues. In Key Stage 2, pupils learn to predict what might happen from details stated or implied. Duke and Pearson (2002) note that good readers frequently make predictions about what is to come. Before beginning to read the text, the reader activates some of the prior knowledge they might need to help their comprehension. Knowing whether a text is fiction or non-fiction will help them activate their knowledge of likely text structure, and the title will prepare them for possible and likely vocabulary and the kinds of sentence structure that they are likely to encounter. For example, a non-fiction text about frogs is likely to have pictures, captions, headings and subheadings, and be organised by theme such as what frogs eat, where they live and so on. Sentences are likely to be factual, with adjectives used to specify rather than entertain. This helps the reader with fluency, and gives them a sense of context which could well help them to work out any unfamiliar words.

Questioning and Clarifying

In Key Stage 1, pupils learn to check that their reading makes sense to them, developing the skill of self-correcting if it doesn't. In Key Stage 2, this extends to include their ability to discuss their understanding of words they meet in the context of their reading. Alongside this, pupils learn to ask and answer questions in the context of reading during Key Stage 1 and develop these skills across Key Stage 2 to improve their understanding of a text.

According to Duke and Pearson (2002), good readers construct, revise and question the meaning they are making from a text as they read it. The process of questioning allows readers to draw on their background knowledge to help them understand beyond the words on the page. For example, asking themselves why a particular character did something draws on the reader's knowledge of similar situations or what they know about a particular place, experience or feeling. Making these links helps to deepen understanding of a text and may introduce the reader to some new information, for example, by suggesting a new way in which a character might react to an event.

The reader can also use self-questioning to monitor their comprehension, helping them to clarify their understanding either through the activation of background knowledge or prompting them to look back over a part of the text to see if they have missed or misinterpreted something, to read on and see if the answer lies ahead, or to stop and get a dictionary if they have come across a new word whose meaning cannot be reliably inferred from the context.

Summarising

In Year 2, pupils learn to discuss the sequence of events in books and how different information is related. In Key Stage 2, pupils learn to identify the main ideas drawn from more than one paragraph and summarise them, specifying key details which support the main ideas in Year 5/6. Summarising a text enables the reader to work out the main ideas in what is being read, discarding the smaller details. Being able to summarise means that the reader has been able to follow the main content of a text. In this way, it is easier to keep track of the text as a whole which allows the reader to discuss and make evaluations of the text, for example, identifying a text's style or mood.

Inference

Inference skills play a key part in the process of reading comprehension, impacting the reader's ability to understand the text in literal terms as well as to provoke a deeper understanding of a text as a whole. According to Kispal:

> The ability to make inferences is, in simple terms, the ability to use two or more pieces of information from a text to arrive at a third piece of information that is implicit. Inference can be as simple as associating the pronoun 'he' with a previously mentioned male person. Or, it can be as complex as understanding a subtle implicit message, conveyed through the choice of particular vocabulary by the writer and drawing on the reader's own background knowledge. (Kispal, 2008, p. 2)

As is clear from the quotation above, there are different types of inference which can occur at a word, sentence and whole-text level. Kispal's review of evidence on how inference is used by readers and taught most effectively to them showed that to be good at inferencing, pupils need to:

- be an active reader who wants to make sense of the text;
- monitor comprehension and repair misunderstandings;
- have a rich vocabulary;
- have a competent working memory. (Kispal, 2008, p. 3)

The ability to infer accurately was also influenced by the reader's background knowledge of the world and supported when the reader had experience or understanding of the cultural background of the text.

Kispal's literature review showed that children can begin to use inference skills at a young age, even with those who are at pre-reading stage using picture books. She concluded that this suggests that inference skills can also be practised in contexts other than word reading, for example, with images. This offers interesting opportunities for teachers to use a range of visual sources to develop children's inference skills across the curriculum, for example, using historical images to practise inference.

Kispal suggests that teaching strategies, such as the teacher modelling inference-making through a think-aloud approach, emphasising that different interpretations can be drawn from fiction, activating children's background knowledge, making use of questioning, and giving pupils time to think by not interrupting their reading too quickly, can be helpful in supporting children's abilities to develop inference skills.

Although reading comprehension is supported by all the skills identified above, the Department for Education's (DfE) Reading Framework states that as comprehension is an outcome of reading, the elements of skilled reading should not be divided and taught separately. They suggest that reading lessons should instead focus on 'supporting pupils to construct a mental model of a specific text so that they understand its meaning' (DfE, 2023, p. 108). Therefore, the teacher should have good understanding of each of the skills identified so he or she is able to model and cue them in at relevant points thus demonstrating how each skill can be used to support pupils to build an effective mental model of a text which supports their reading comprehension.

In Year 1, pupils learn to discuss the importance of a book's title and key events, building on this in Year 2 to make inferences from the text. In Year 3/4, pupils begin to infer characters' feelings, thoughts and motives with reference to the text, and in Year 5/6 these become more complex, justifying their inferences with reference to at least one specific piece of evidence from the text.

Making Connections

One of the threads of comprehension presented in the National Curriculum is making connections. In Year 1, children should begin to link what they have read or heard read to their own experiences, drawing on what they already know or on background information and vocabulary provided by the teacher. In Year 2, they should be able to draw on what they already know or on background information and vocabulary provided by the teacher. In Year 3/4, pupils learn to recognise and identify themes and conventions, building on this in Year 5/6 through discussion and making comparisons both within and across books.

Activity   Planning to Teach Reading Comprehension

Choose a text that you might want or plan to use to teach reading comprehension. Read it through a few times so you are really familiar with it, then work through the following prompts. Some people prefer to make lists, while others annotate post-it notes and stick them on the relevant pages of the book, or you may have a different way to record your thoughts which you would prefer to use.

Activating and Extending Background and Linguistic Knowledge

Meaningful reading comprehension is dependent on background and linguistic knowledge, as well as word reading skills. Guidance from the DfE (2023) suggests that interrupting reading too often to model the use of reading strategies will break the children's flow and concentration. Therefore, it is really useful to consider what you will do before reading a book to help the children tune in and to activate their background knowledge. This may involve drama and/or discussion, and usually aims to:

- Hook the children in by giving them experiences which help them connect to one or more of the characters, the setting, and/or one or more elements of the plot or the book's themes.
- Activate children's understanding of the world of the text, for example, by asking them to discuss key vocabulary, watch some audio-visual material or images which will initiate recall of prior knowledge or extend this so that events or key ideas will then be known to them when they occur.
- Deepen the children's knowledge and understanding of vocabulary, for example, by exploring tier two words that will come up in the text through games and activities.

What real-life experiences, settings or emotions are relevant to the book which the children could connect to before they start reading?

What background knowledge might be useful to activate (or to teach) to aid the children in understanding the book?

Are there any words which the children might not be familiar with that they need to know?

Identifying Teaching Points

It will also be helpful for you to identify places where you could authentically model the use of specific reading comprehension strategies to show what good readers do. Where might it be useful or interesting to:

- Stop and predict what might happen next?
- Summarise what has happened so far?
- Question or clarify points?
- Use inference skills to fill in the gaps?
- Draw the children's attention to the structure of the text?
- Use visualisation to support the construction of the mental model?

(Continued)

You Will Also Want to Think About

- How the text connects to other texts that the children have read or seen.
- How the text may connect to the children's own lives in terms of what they have seen or experienced – or what it teaches us about others' experiences of the world.
- The big ideas and themes that occur in the book.

Make a note of these things, as they will really support you when it comes to planning individual lessons.

Curriculum Continuity and Progression

There are a number of Early Learning goals Goals which are linked to reading comprehension. Comprehension is identified specifically within 'Literacy'. A child who has met the relevant Early Learning goals (ELGs) for the end of Year R will have:

- Demonstrated understanding of what has been read to them by retelling stories and narratives using their own words and recently introduced vocabulary.
- Anticipated – where appropriate – key events in stories.
- Used and understood recently introduced vocabulary during discussions about stories, non-fiction, rhymes and poems and during role play.

However, comprehension is also key to other ELGs. In Communication and Language, a child who has met the relevant ELGs for the end of Year R will have demonstrated the ability to listen and respond to texts which are read to them, asking questions to clarify their understanding, and using vocabulary which they have heard in stories, non-fiction, rhymes and poems. In Understanding the World, a child will have drawn on texts that they have heard in class to develop their understanding of the past, their environment, the natural environment, and religious and cultural communities. Understanding of texts also underpins children's Expressive Arts and Design development, enabling them to use props and materials in their role play, and adapt and recount narratives and stories.

According to *The National Curriculum in England: English Programmes of study for Key Stage 1 and Key Stage 2,*

> Good comprehension draws from linguistic knowledge (in particular of vocabulary and grammar) and on knowledge of the world. Comprehension skills develop through pupils' experience of high-quality discussion with the teacher, as well as from reading and discussing a range of stories, poems and non-fiction. (DfE, 2013, p. 4)

There are a number of aspects within the comprehension strand which provide a progression framework for pupils from Year 1 to Year 6; although the wording of the objectives does become a little more detailed as pupils progress through Key Stages 1 and 2, much of the progression comes as children read more complex texts. Developing pleasure and building familiarity with a wide range of texts including poetry are discussed elsewhere in this book. Many of the objectives relate to the research on comprehension discussed above.

Curriculum and Pedagogy

Since the 1990s, children's reading comprehension skills have been assessed through the National Curriculum tests at the end of Key Stage 1 and again at the end of Key Stage 2. New reading tests are published every year and are designed to draw on what are known as content domains. These are as follows:

Reading Content domain reference Key Stage 1:

  1a draw on knowledge of vocabulary to understand texts
  1b identify/explain key aspects of fiction and non-fiction texts, such as characters, events, titles and information
  1c identify and explain the sequence of events in texts
  1d make inferences from the text
  1e predict what might happen on the basis of what has been read so far

Reading Content domain reference Key Stage 2:

  2a give/explain the meaning of words in context
  2b retrieve and record information/identify key details from fiction and non-fiction
  2c summarise main ideas from more than one paragraph
  2d make inferences from the text/explain and justify inferences with evidence from the text
  2e predict what might happen from details stated and implied
  2f identify/explain how information/narrative content is related and contributes to meaning as a whole
  2g identify/explain how meaning is enhanced through choice of words and phrases
  2h make comparisons within the text

As a result, many schools adopted approaches to the teaching of reading comprehension which used questions from these content domains. In some cases, this perhaps led to a diet of rather narrow, generic and formulaic questions which could be applied across many texts rather than the use of authentic questions which were relevant to the individual text under exploration and which were, therefore, genuinely meaningful and provoked deep thinking and learning. Nystrand (2006) defines authentic questions as questions which allow various answers including those not anticipated by the teacher. According to Tennent et al.:

> Authentic questions are much more likely to give rise to extended answers because children must include their reasoning. . .This allows the teacher the opportunity to listen to and make a judgement about the current state of the children's understanding and so can respond appropriately building further understanding or dealing with any apparent misconceptions. (2016, p. 51)

Research also shows that using higher order questions as prompts for discussion between pupils is highly beneficial. For example, Wolf (2008) found that pupils showed good comprehension when discussion focused on good understanding of and critical thinking about texts, listening to and linking to others' ideas, and providing evidence to support thinking. Furthermore, pupils who engaged in good conversations about texts developed higher levels of comprehension (Van den Branden, 2000), while participation in collaborative reasoning was shown to provoke deep and long-lasting effects on the quality of pupils' responses (Dong et al., 2008).

Therefore, an authentic approach to the teaching of reading comprehension centres around a focus on how to uncover and develop the children's understanding, helping pupils to make meaning from texts. This can be achieved using carefully planned questions and rich opportunities for collaborative discussion which enable children to both draw on and develop a range of reading strategies and skills to build strong mental models and comprehend a text at a deep level.

The recently updated Reading Framework (2023) will undoubtedly impact the planning of reading comprehension, and schools may well change their practices in response to this, considering how best to enable pupils to achieve the age-related expectations outlined in the National Curriculum. Therefore, it is important to talk to class teachers and the English or Reading subject leader to ascertain how the school is approaching this, understanding that schools will likely be in a period of change as they take account of this new guidance.

Key Document Summary: The Reading Framework (DfE, 2023)

For pupils who can decode well, effective teaching supports pupils to develop as readers through:

- Introducing a wide range of literature and non-fiction that they could not or might not choose to read independently.
- Explanations, modelling and support from the teacher for different aspects of reading, including fluency.
- Allowing pupils to think deeply and discuss a range of rich and challenging texts (p. 107).

Effective reading lessons should:

- Support pupils to become confident readers, able to construct coherent mental models of the texts they encounter.
- Enable children to experience the excitement, wonder and fascination that can come from reading, to feel what it is like to lose themselves in a story.
- Offer rich opportunities for children to see themselves as readers.
- Give children access to all the things that can be learned from great books and stories.
- Allow children to listen to and read beautiful language, encounter profound ideas, engage with a wide range of human experience such as why characters make the choices they make, and why they feel what they feel, consider ideas beyond their own experience, and encounter concepts that might never occurred to them before (pp. 108–109).

Reading in English lessons is likely to feature a combination of:

1 The teacher reading aloud.
2 Pupils reading.
3 The teacher's modelling and explanations.
4 Questioning. (p. 111)

Other key ideas to note:

- Interrupting the reading too often will disturb the flow. The teacher must think carefully about when to stop to give background information, explain unfamiliar vocabulary and to model their own use of a particular reading strategy to show how the reader can construct a coherent mental model of a text.
- The focus should be on rich and challenging texts, broadening the experience of pupils with high prior attainment, and allowing those pupils who cannot yet read such texts on their own to engage with age-appropriate high-quality materials.
- When pupils are reading, the teacher can consider whether they will read independently or in pairs. If pupils are to read in pairs, teachers should clarify the role of the listener (e.g., whether this is to give feedback on their partner's reading or to concentrate on the meaning of the text).

The teacher's role, then, is to engage the children with rich, high-quality, engaging texts which expand their knowledge of language, text elements (e.g., setting, character and plot in the case of fiction texts) and the world, provoking them to think deeply and discuss their thoughts within (and perhaps beyond) the classroom community. To support the children to develop their comprehension skills, the teacher needs to understand what sense the children have made of what they have read and consider how to scaffold or stretch and challenge from that point.

The following teaching strategies typically form the basis of effective lessons in reading comprehension.

Teacher Modelling With Think-Aloud

This teaching strategy involves talking your thoughts out loud while you are reading. It has been shown to improve pupils' comprehension when teachers model it so that children learn to do it themselves. This helps them to understand a text, summarise it effectively and monitor their comprehension when they are reading for themselves, supporting metacognition. The most recent guidance from the DfE highlights the importance of using modelling with think-aloud to help children to see exactly how mental models of a text are created. They suggest that teachers might choose one supporting strategy to focus on in a lesson, for example:

- Model how ideas in the text and ideas from pupils' background knowledge are combined to make meaning.
- Show how to decode the unfamiliar word and then explain its meaning.
- Comment on and consider the impact of specific words or phrases.
- Model how a skilled reader fills in the gaps as they read. (DfE, 2023, p. 113)

It is important to be authentic here – model a supporting strategy when it is relevant to the text, for example, ask children to imagine or visualise a character or setting after a description comes up in the text. Try not to interrupt the reading too frequently as this disturbs its flow.

Shared Reading

Shared reading is a teaching strategy which involves the teacher and children reading a text together. This is the second stage in the gradual release of responsibility model where responsibility or control over the reading is shared between teacher and pupils. The children might follow the text as the teacher reads, or read-aloud together with the teacher.

Shared reading enables teachers to:

- Build a collection of shared texts with the class.
- Engage the children with age-appropriate reading material.
- Model the reading process.
- Share their expertise as a reader.
- Offer an externalised model of expressive reading, enabling children to access texts beyond their current reading ability.

According to Heisey and Kucan (2010), reading aloud to children enables them to process challenging content, text features and vocabulary, even in subjects not normally associated with reading aloud. Therefore, it is also useful to share the reading of different kinds of texts across a wide range of curriculum subjects so that children develop the knowledge and skills needed to tackle both fiction and non-fiction texts with confidence.

Guided Reading

In my experience, the term 'guided reading' has become muddled in recent years; some teachers conflate it with a specific classroom organisation strategy known as a carousel in which the class is divided into small groups of children who rotate between different reading activities. However, guided reading as a teaching strategy is not this. Guided reading is a teaching strategy which was specifically designed to enable comprehension strategies to be taught systematically in which the teacher works closely with a small group of pupils (it is up to the teacher to decide what the rest of the class should do while he or she is engaged with this group – they may all work on an task independently or otherwise as the teacher sees fit). This is part of the gradual release of responsibility model, allowing the teacher to transfer more control over to the learners while he or she observes and intervenes to scaffold their learning when needed.

Guided reading enables teachers to:

- Tailor teaching to learners' needs.
- Provide greater support to children while they are building skills and independence.
- Interact with quieter or less confident pupils.
- Monitor each pupil's processing of texts and adjust further teaching and text selection in the light of their responses.

A guided reading session typically has five parts:

- Book introduction.
- Strategy check.
- Independent reading.
- Returning to the text.
- Responding to the text.

In the book introduction, the teacher introduces the text to be explored in the session. This allows children time to activate some relevant prior knowledge and tune in to the text. It might also be helpful to identify any potentially tricky vocabulary in the text so that when the children meet it, this does not disrupt their comprehension too greatly.

Next, the teacher models or reminds the children of a specific strategy which is likely to be particularly helpful to them. This may be the decoding of a particular grapheme-phoneme correspondence, or a comprehension skill.

Next, the pupils read the text independently. The emphasis here should be on each child reading the text silently as this is more authentic and relevant to real life than reading aloud. Each pupil should have their own copy of a text and read it to themselves, using all the strategies but particularly the ones highlighted as relevant for the session, and monitoring their own reading. The teacher might want to listen in to the reading of one or more of the pupils in this part of the session. To do this, the teacher moves to the child and asks them to read-aloud (in a voice which does not unduly disturb the other readers). This allows the teacher to check the child's reading and pause to check their understanding or use of a strategy as needed. When the teacher is ready, they can move on to another child.

In the fourth part of the session, the group returns to the text, discussing it together and reviewing their mental models and any strategies they used, with a particular focus on the ones the teacher modelled at the beginning. This time offers all the readers a chance to ask questions about the text and talk about its meaning.

Finally, the children respond to the text. This allows them some time just to talk about the impact of the text, perhaps sharing their opinions on it or the ideas within it.

Questioning

Questioning is a key strategy for supporting children's ability to make meaning from texts they read and hear. As is stated in The Reading Framework:

> effective questioning can deepen pupils' understanding, prompting them to think about the ideas and language used in the texts they read and hear, driving productive discussion and thus improving attainment. Questioning that promotes elaboration and flexible thinking will support pupils to integrate new ideas and knowledge into their existing schema. (DfE, 2023, p. 115)

Questions operate at different levels and can take children deeper into texts. They are also useful in helping children to make connections between what they read and their own lives, between different texts they have read, and to the wider world. Furthermore, careful use of questions can scaffold children's understanding of challenging texts as teachers assess children's understanding to identify where support may be needed, and use questions to direct the children's attention to critical content (Blything et al., 2020). This enables them to see the power and purpose of reading, and to gain satisfaction from it. Our choice of questions is key to effective teaching as these will result in different cognitive demand for our learners. Blything et al. (2020) highlight the use of interrogative why questions asked by teachers during reading comprehension instruction to foster deeper understanding.

One way of thinking about questions is in terms of developing children's understanding of the text to promote thinking at three levels:

- Literal questions involve simple retrieval, designed to help children recall/revise material already covered as well as simple comprehension questions to elicit their understanding of main points. This can be thought of as 'reading the text'. These are usually quite straightforward and can be useful in cueing the children in to thinking about a particular section of the text before their thinking is extended through deeper questions.

- Inferential questions ask children to become text detectives, using inference to fill in the gaps that are not explicitly stated by the author. This can be thought of as 'reading between the lines of the text'.
- Evaluative questions ask children to evaluate a text, thinking about whether a text achieves its purpose, and to make connections with other texts. This can be thought of as 'reading beyond the text'.

According to Blything et al. (2020):

> the primary purpose of teacher-led questions in comprehension instruction...is to stimulate meaningful discussion that goes beyond basic assessment of memory or understanding of the text to instead scaffold the higher level thinking, reasoning, and inferential processes involved in constructing meaning from text. (p. 5)

Therefore, questions should be carefully planned to ensure that a good balance is achieved between literal, inferential and evaluative questions so that they achieve these benefits. Murphy et al. (2009) note that the use of higher order questions during discussions about texts promotes greater levels of active participation for readers.

These learning and teaching strategies form the basis of effective reading comprehension lessons. It may also be useful to draw on some of the teaching strategies identified for teaching reading fluency which were presented in Chapter 6.

Lesson Plan

Here is a suggestion for a lesson plan for a Year 1 class using the picture book *Stanley's Stick* by John Hegley, illustrated by Neal Layton (Table 8.1). In this book, Stanley has a stick which he imagines could be lots of different things such as a rocket and a dinosaur. When Stanley goes on holiday to the seaside, he decides that it is time for someone else to enjoy the stick and so he lets the sea carry it away. To give more context, I have included my initial planning notes from the activity earlier in this chapter. You might like to find a reading of the story on YouTube.

Over a series of lessons, the children will develop their ability to:

- Listen to and discuss a wide range of poems, stories and non-fiction at a level beyond that at which they can read independently.
- Predict what might happen based on what has been read so far, e.g., titles, blurb, characters, and plot.
- Check that the text makes sense to them.
- Begin to link what they have read or heard read to their own experiences.
- Draw on what they already know or on background information and vocabulary provided by the teacher.
- Discuss word meanings, linking new meanings to those already known.
- Begin to discuss the significance of the title and events.

- Participate in discussions about what is read to them, taking turns and listening to what others say.
- Explain clearly their understanding of what is read to them.

While a number of these objectives could be relevant to many teaching sessions, it is probably most helpful to stick to choosing just one or two for any individual lesson as this will help to provide a clear focus for learning and feedback.

Initial Planning

Real-life experiences, settings/emotions relevant to the book:

- Imaginative play where the children have pretended one object was something else or used an imaginary object
- Going on holiday and/or going somewhere on a train
- Having a special toy or object
- Hobbies and interests

What background knowledge might be useful to activate (or to teach) to aid the children in understanding the book:

- The natural world, especially trees and sticks, and the sea with its tides
- Holidays and trains

Are there any words which the children might not be familiar with that they need to know:

- aflame;
- extinct;
- fate;
- station;
- tide.

Other words to discuss in context (the children possibly know them but they may be used in a different context here): whistle, sticky, stay, at the side of, pulls in, hurls, splosh, tucks it into itself, spot, treads, stumbles, wonky, and blurt.

Language play to highlight: stickless, twiggy-back, fantastic.

Where might it be good to:

- Stop and predict what might happen next.
  - P16 Why is Stanley standing at the edge of the sea with the stick? What might he do next?

- Summarise what has happened so far.
  - The story will be read over several days so the children will be asked to summarise it at the beginning and end of each reading session.
- Question or clarify points.
  - P5 What does it mean that 'You don't have to be Great to be great'?
  - P6 What does 'aflame' mean? What does 'game after sticky game' mean?
- Use inference skills to fill in the gaps.
  - P1 Why does Stanley always carry his stick with him?
  - P3 Why will the stick never return – is it still tall and grand?
  - P9 Why can't Stanley think of a name for his stick? Does the stick need a name? Why might it bother Stanley that he can't think of one?
  - P13/14 What kind of person is Bertie? What makes you think that? Is Stanley ever this kind of person too? What makes you think that?
  - P18 Why does the author say that the stick has been so big in Stanley's days?
  - P19 How does the sea pick up the stick?
- Draw the children's attention to the structure of the text.
  - Typical story structure
  - Pictures support words by showing what Stanley is doing, often adding extra detail.
  - Language – alliteration, play with 'osaurus' ending to make our own 'stickosaurus' words using objects in the role play area and outside classroom
- Use visualisation to support the construction of the mental model:
  - Ask the children to remember some of the things that Stanley does with his stick and the key points of the story-they could draw some pictures of 'Stanley's Sticky Adventures'/their favourite part of the story.

You will also want to think about:

- How the text connects to other texts that the children have read or seen:
  - *Not a box* by Antoinette Portis
  - *Bonting* and *Dogger* by Shirley Hughes
  - Other alliterative texts (e.g., Julia Donaldson)
- How the text may connect to the children's own lives in terms of what they have seen or experienced – or what it teaches us about others' experiences of the world:
  - Nature and the concept of change, playing outdoors
  - Dinosaurs, slugs and fish
  - The sea and its tides
- The big ideas and themes that occur in the book:
  - The concept of change in nature
  - Is Stanley right to give us his stick? Why might he do this? Why does he get a new one?
  - Friendship

Relevant prior learning: The children have had lots of experience in Year R of listening to stories in small groups and as a whole class, responding by sharing their thoughts about what they liked and didn't like, and asking questions. They have been introduced to some of the ideas in *Stanley's Stick* by talking about what toys they like to play with. In small groups (with an adult), they have been outside to watch clouds, talking about what they remind them of from their shapes. The role play area has been deconstructed (see https://abcdoes.com/abc-does-a-blog/2011/02/14/amazing-role-play-deconstruct-it/) to allow imaginative play. They have looked at the cover of the picture book and made some predictions about what they think might happen from the images and title. We have discussed key vocabulary which the children needed to know in advance (listed earlier).

What will children learn: To check that the text makes sense to them.

Planned next steps: Read on in the story and continue to check that the story makes sense.

Assessment – What will effective learning look like?: Children will show that they are listening carefully to the read-aloud and think-aloud and checking that the story makes sense to them. By the end of the session, they will be able to explain the story accurately and confidently.

How will learning be assessed (and what are the opportunities for effective feedback)?:

- Observing the children during the echo reading part of the lesson to make sure they are joining in with good pace, intonation and emphasis
- Listening in to paired discussions and checking that children are focused on making sense of what they have heard, questioning aloud when they don't.

Table 8.1 A lesson plan for teaching reading comprehension

Today's lesson sequence/content
1.00 p.m.
Recap what we have done so far with the story *Stanley's Stick* • Show the front cover again and remind the children of what we can see. • Ask some of the children to remind us of what some of our predictions were. • Remind the children that we have been being imaginative in our play and some of the indoor/outdoor activities we have done such as looking at clouds and making our role play area into anything we like plus anything noticed during child-initiated learning, etc.
1.05 p.m. • Begin to read the story up to p6. Read it straight through. • Reread this part. This time, stop to explain the words 'grand' and 'return' as they come up. • Ask the children to turn to their talk partner and say what they think of the story so far – do they like any parts so far/Do they dislike any parts so far? Does it all make sense? • Listen in so that you can share interesting thoughts and ideas.

Today's lesson sequence/content

- Ask the children to share their thoughts so far, recording them on some poster paper to make a list of their likes 😋, dislikes ☹, and any bits that didn't make sense to them 😕.
- Keep this so it can be added to over the next few lessons.

1.15 p.m.

- Shared reading – share a copy of the text with the children (this might be copies of the books for them to use in pairs or an electronic version of the text if you have one). Read-aloud again, this time stopping at 'it will never return' and use a think-aloud strategy to show that you are not sure what this bit means so you are going to reread it and think about it. For example, 'Stanley's stick was once part of something tall and grand and it will never return'. Hmm, I wonder what that part means. I'm going to reread it and see if I can work it out. The story says that the stick was once part of something tall and grand. Well I know that a stick is part of a tree, and trees are usually tall and grand (remember we talked about the word grand earlier) so I think that it means that the stick used to be part of the tree but now it's not. It has broken off and fallen to the ground. The second part of that sentence says 'and it will never return'. So I think 'it' means the stick and the story is saying that because the stick has broken off the tree, it can never be part of the tree again so it won't return (go back) to the tree. When I look at the picture, I think that shows I am right – look at the way Stanley is looking at the stick on the ground. On the next page, the story says 'But it can still be a stick as best it can' so I think this means that even though it is not part of the tall and grand tree anymore, the stick is still going to be really good.' Continue to reread until the end of p6.

1.20 p.m.

- Fluency development – now ask the children to do some echo reading – reread each page, one sentence at a time, asking the children to echo your reading using the same pace, intonation and emphasis (the children could stand up if you prefer and add an action or two if it doesn't distract them from the reading).

1.25 p.m.

- Responding to the text – now shut the book (get the children to shut theirs/stop sharing the electronic version) and ask the children to talk together to discuss (you might need to break this up so that the children discuss one question at a time):
- What games has Stanley played so far with his stick (this is a literal question which asks them to recall and supports the building of the mental model)?
- What might happen next (prediction skills)?
- Finally, return to the first page and ask the children 'Why does Stanley always carry his stick with him?'

1.30 p.m.

- Share some ideas from the children, showing enthusiasm for their thinking. Reinforce any key points from the lesson through focused feedback (in relation to fluency and checking that the story made sense to them) and say you are looking forward to the next lesson when you can find out what Stanley does next with his stick.

NB Whenever the children are talking together, listen out for other parts of the story that have been read so far that you haven't yet talked about (e.g. 'You don't have to be Great to be great', 'Like pretending the stick is a match to catch the world aflame' and 'There is game after sticky game'); alternatively, they may ask you directly what these parts mean. If they do come up, praise this. You could add them to the 'bits that didn't make sense' list for discussion later, or talk about them now, perhaps asking the children if anyone has any ideas about what they mean and identifying this as a good place to use the think-aloud idea you showed them earlier).

Adaptive/Responsive Teaching

Some ways in which you could adapt the learning for those needing additional scaffolding or stretch and challenge are:

- Ensuring that children can join in easily with the shared reading activities – some might need an enlarged copy of the text, a coloured overlay, a ruler/pointer to follow the words or their own copy.
- Pairing children carefully for discussions; consider the use of adults (including the teacher) to support individuals or pairs as needed.
- Consider whether pre-reading the text with an individual or small group will enhance familiarisation and allow greater or more confident participation (as well as another opportunity to build fluency and word recognition).
- Consider preteaching of vocabulary – would any pupils benefit from longer discussion, matching games and activities or visual prompts to help them to understand keywords?
- Check for cultural assumptions that may be underpinning the text that may need further explanation and/or that pupils would benefit from first-hand experience with.
- Consider the use of challenge questions for some pupils when engaging with paired discussions. These could aim to pick up on the points outlined in the planning that have not yet been addressed, or could prompt the children to think about a particular line or page to deepen their thinking.

Summary

This chapter has considered what research tells us about how to teach reading comprehension effectively. The key strategies for teaching comprehension effectively have been established, with suggestions as to how these might be enacted in the classroom.

Further Reading

1   Read about Blything's study on the use of questions in reading comprehension available at: https://ila.onlinelibrary.wiley.com/doi/epdf/10.1002/rrq.279.
2   Read the latest guidance from the DfE on teaching reading comprehension available at: https://assets.publishing.service.gov.uk/government/uploads/system/uploads/attachment_data/file/1178136/The_Reading_Framework_2023.pdf (pp. 107–119).
3   Develop your understanding of reading comprehension and see some examples of planning by Tennent et al. in *Guiding Readers – Layers of Meaning: A handbook for teaching reading comprehension to 7–11-year-olds*, published by UCL IoE Press.

References

Bearne, E., & Reedy, D. (2017). *Teaching primary English: Subject knowledge and classroom practice.* Routledge.

Blything, L., Hardie, A., & Cain, K. (2020). Question asking during reading comprehension instruction: A corpus study of how question type influences the linguistic complexity of primary school students' responses. *Reading Research Quarterly, 55*(3), 443–472.

Department for Education. (2013). *The national curriculum in England: Key stages 1 and 2 framework document.* https://www.gov.uk/government/publications/national-curriculum-in-england-primary-curriculum. Accessed on May 16, 2022.

Department for Education. (2023). *The reading framework.* Crown Copyright.

Dong, T., Anderson, R. C., Kim, I., & Li, Y. (2008). Collaborative reasoning in China and Korea. *Reading Research Quarterly, 43*, 400–424.

Duke, N., & Pearson, P. (2002). Effective practices for developing reading comprehension. In A. E. Farstrup & S. Jay Samuels (Eds.), *What research has to say about reading instruction* (3rd ed., pp. 205–242). International Reading Association, Inc.

Heisey, N., & Kucan, L. (2010). Introducing science concepts to primary students through read-alouds: Interactions and multiple texts make the difference. *The Reading Teacher, 63*(8), 666–676.

Hoover, W., & Gough, P. (1990). The simple view of reading. *Reading and Writing: An Interdisciplinary Journal, 2*, 127–160.

Kamhi, A. (2009). The case for the narrow view of reading. *Language, Speech, and Hearing Services in Schools, 40*, 174–177.

Kispal, A. (2008). *Effective teaching of inference skills for reading: Literature review.* Department for Children, Schools and Families (DCSF).

Murphy, P. K., Wilkinson, I., Soter, A., Hennessey, M., & Alexander, J. (2009). Examining the effects of classroom discussion on students' high-level comprehension of text: A meta analysis. *Journal of Educational Psychology, 101*, 740–764.

Nystrand, M. (2006). Research on the role of classroom discourse as it affects reading comprehension. *Research into the Teaching of Reading, 40*.

Oakhill, J., Cain, K. and Elbro, C. (2014) *Understanding and teaching reading comprehension: A handbook.* Routledge.

Tennent, W., Reedy, D., Hobsbaum, A., & Gamble, N. (Eds.), (2016) *Guiding readers – Layers of meaning: A handbook for teaching reading comprehension to 7–11 year-olds.* UCL IOE Press.

Van den Branden, K. (2000). Does negotiation of meaning promote reading comprehension? A study of multilingual primary school classes. *Reading Research Quarterly, 35*(3), 426–443.

Wolf, M. (2008). *Proust and the squid: The story and science of the reading brain.* Icon Books Ltd.

9

Planning to Teach Reading for Pleasure

Chapter Objectives

This chapter will:

- Identify the key elements of classroom provision to promote reading for pleasure.
- Consider what effective pedagogy for fostering reading for pleasure might look like.
- Demonstrate one way to plan a reading for pleasure session.

Introduction

In recent years, research has highlighted the impact of reading for pleasure (R4P) on children's attainment. Sullivan and Brown's analysis of pupil progress and attainment at ages 10 and 16 found that:

- Children who read for pleasure are likely to do significantly better at school than their peers.
- R4P was more important for children's cognitive development between the ages of 10 and 16 than their parents' level of education.
- R4P had the strongest effect on children's vocabulary development, but the impact on spelling (and maths) was still significant.

The Organisation for Economic Co-operation and Development (OECD) is an international organisation which analyses practices and outcomes in order to identify the factors that promote prosperity, equality, opportunity and well-being, identifying that pupils who were highly engaged in reading typically attained higher literacy scores, regardless of a family's occupational status. A conclusion from their 2002 analysis emphasises that reading practices have the potential to reduce the gap between pupils from different socio-economic backgrounds. In addition, the results of the 2016 Progress in International Reading Literacy Study (PIRLS) assessment showed that Year 5 pupils from the UK who enjoyed reading the most achieved higher scores than those who reported not enjoying it. The Department for Education highlights the importance of promoting R4P because 'making sure that children become engaged with reading from the beginning is, therefore, one of the most important ways to make a difference to their life chances, whatever their socio-economic background' (DfE, 2023, p. 12).

However, R4P doesn't just bring academic benefits. Through its research into the relationship between children's reading, writing and mental well-being, Clark and Teravainen-Goff found that through high levels of engagement with literacy, pupils were three times more likely to have higher levels of mental well-being than those who were the least engaged (2018).

So, what is R4P? In their review of research, Clark and Rumbold define it as 'reading that we do of our own free will, anticipating the satisfaction that we will get from the act of reading. It also refers to reading that having begun at someone else's request, we continue because we are interested in it' (2006, p. 5).

In an article on independent reading, Raleigh suggests that independently chosen reading offers the following benefits:

- Pleasure: The pleasure of reading easy and entertaining material effortlessly, as well as the more strenuous pleasure which comes from understanding difficult material.
- Personal enrichment: As a source of experience and knowledge, reading extends your horizons, broadens your vision and enlarges your perspective.

- Practical value: Being able to apply reading skills maximises your chances of benefiting from schooling and enables you to discover information in print, both now and in the future.
- Power: Reading means access and enables you to find out things about your history and the society you live in. (1996, p. 118).

Readers have different preferences and different motivations for reading. As teachers, our role is to try to support each child in our classes to find a meaningful purpose which really engages them in reading.

The whole notion of whether R4P should be part of the formal lesson-planning process is an interesting one! It is quite possible that you won't need to produce formal plans but you will certainly need to think carefully about how to foster this crucial interest in your pupils.

Curriculum Continuity and Progression

Whilst the concept of R4P does not feature explicitly in the Early Learning Goals, there are some clear connections within the Year R curriculum which will support children's enjoyment of reading.

In Expressive Arts and Design, children will:

- Make use of props and materials when role-playing characters in narratives and stories, and invent, adapt and recount narratives and stories with peers and their teacher.
- Sing a range of well-known nursery rhymes and songs.
- Perform songs, rhymes, poems and stories with others.

In Understanding the World, children will:

- Know some similarities and differences between things in the past and now, drawing on their experiences and what has been read in class.
- Understand the past through settings, characters and events encountered in books read in class and storytelling.
- Describe their immediate environment using knowledge from observation, discussion, stories, non-fiction texts and maps.
- Know some similarities and differences between different religious and cultural communities in this country, drawing on their experiences and what has been read in class.
- Explain some similarities and differences between life in this country and life in other countries, drawing on knowledge from stories, non-fiction texts and – when appropriate – maps.

In Communication and Language, children will:

- Listen attentively and respond to what they hear with relevant questions, comments and actions when being read to and during whole class discussions and small group interactions.
- Hold a conversation when engaged in back-and-forth exchanges with their teacher and peers.

In Reading, children will:

- Demonstrate understanding of what has been read to them by retelling stories and narratives using their own words and recently introduced vocabulary.
- Anticipate – where appropriate – key events in stories.
- Use and understand recently introduced vocabulary during discussions about stories, non-fiction, rhymes and poems and during role-play. (DfE, 2021)

The National Curriculum in England: English Programmes of Study for Key Stage 1 and Key Stage 2 identifies specific expectations for pupils in each year group in the main body of the document. For each year group, there is a set of expectations which aim to support children in developing pleasure in and motivation for reading. These goals are combined with expectations that children will also develop vocabulary and understanding, linking pleasure to the sharing and discussion of texts. In Year 1 and Year 2, while pupils are still developing their knowledge, understanding and skills in decoding, such texts are typically above the independent reading levels of the children with the range of texts expanding from stories and non-fiction in Year 1 to include a wide range of contemporary and classic poetry, stories and non-fiction in Year 2. In Key Stage 2, this range expands further to include plays and references or textbooks and encompasses books that are structured in different ways and read for different purposes.

Children may also find a sense of pleasure through the experience of book talk. National Curriculum expectations involve engaging in discussions and listening to others, including discussions on their favourite words and phrases. It also includes the practice of recommending books, particularly in Year 5/6. Pupils may also find pleasure in developing their familiarity with a range of texts, joining in with and/or orally retelling some, drawing connections to their own lives and other texts, and enhancing their experiences with poetry (see Chapter 14).

Curriculum and Pedagogy

A joint project between the Open University and the United Kingdom Literacy Association (OU/UKLA) explored practice in 27 schools to analyse key factors in high-quality pedagogical practice to support R4P (see https://ourfp.org). Their conclusions are summarised into three key areas. The first relates to teacher knowledge. To be able to foster children's enjoyment in reading, it is critical that teachers' knowledge of high-quality texts is both wide and deep. This allows teachers to make really well-informed choices regarding what to share with a class and what to recommend to an individual reader.

Three Ways to Extend Your Knowledge of Children's Texts

There are many excellent ways to develop your knowledge which include the following:

1   Be a regular visitor to the Open University Reading for Pleasure website (https://ourfp.org/) which is rich with details about underpinning research and examples of excellent classroom practice.
2   Tune in to Nikki Gamble's monthly Book Blasts and visit her YouTube channel which has excellent interviews with authors and fantastic presentations on what to look for when choosing books for each year group.
3   Find some R4P champions to follow online; there are many great teachers and schools, and a host of children's librarians, authors and publishers.

Teachers also need to make sure that they really know about the children in their class, finding out how and what they like to read at home as well as in school, and to what extent they see themselves as readers. Information can be gathered through discussions, observations of the children reading, displays for children to share what they had been reading at home and pupil-friendly surveys. If you do this with your children, you will likely find out some interesting things about their digital reading practices too as they engage with various devices and platforms in their own time.

The second key area of effective practice identified by the OU/UKLA is the need for a robust pedagogy. This comprises four key elements which include building social reading environments, reading aloud, independent reading and informal book talk.

A social reading environment is one into which children are drawn physically, allowing them to browse and choose books, read comfortably and interact with others through key strategies such as book talk and sharing recommended reads with each other. Time and space for reading, and sharing and discussion are considered carefully, and the children's agency to make their own choices about what to read next is key. Getting to know each individual as a reader, finding out what they like and don't like to read about, and how they choose books is really important. The OURfP research showed that successful teachers often encouraged children to bring in texts (such as comics and magazines) that they enjoyed at home. Other interesting strategies to consider are the use of reading-related role-play areas (no matter the age of the children!), and the use of story bags and boxes to encourage deeper engagement with characters, themes and plots. Displays can also be used effectively to inspire and intrigue children, and to encourage them to share their thoughts on books they have read.

Reading aloud has already been explored as a key aspect of effective practice (Chapter 6). As well as daily read-alouds, the idea of a weekly read-aloud is proposed. This aims to mix things up a bit, for example, by sharing an extract of text from a new author, a prize-winning author, thinking about a specific theme and so on. Other strategies include giving time and space for children to engage with read-alouds from time to time, for example, through the use of drama strategies such as freeze frames or role-play, or inviting the children to draw while you read.

Independent reading is a feature of the school day in many schools. Its impact is realised as a result of the extent to which it is valued. It can be challenging, as in its early stages, you may find that some children really enjoy it while others are restless and struggle to focus. The OURfP's findings on this are really interesting: when teachers really valued this time and thought about it in conjunction with the other elements of effective practice outlined in this chapter, it was productive and engaging for the pupils. It is worth considering the messages that you send in how you make use of any independent reading time too; are you showing that you really value having the time to read, or are you busy with other jobs? This will reflect on how the children perceive and value it.

Book Talk

Although teachers often initiate conversations about books, the teachers in the OURfP research project found that providing time for pupils to discuss their current reading with each other was really valuable. Sometimes pupils talked to teachers but as a reader-to-reader rather than teacher-to-reader. They discussed particular texts, the characters and the events, and they discussed themselves as readers, sharing their preferences for what and how to read. There are many excellent ideas for developing this aspect of practice through the OURfP's web resource.

Book talk is:

> the extended opportunity to use talk to explore children's personal and collective responses to a text as readers...After careful reading of a shared text, the teacher often...initiates 'book-talk' with open invitations such as, 'Tell me what you thought/felt about...', 'What came into your mind when you read...', or 'Have you come across anything like this before?' and then focuses on extending the children's responses with prompts such as, 'Tell me more about...', 'What led you to think that?' or 'Can you extend that idea a bit for us?'...In this way rich exchanges often occur, helping children to develop and extend their own responses. (DCSF, 2008, p. 8)

Note that these questions are open and authentic; the teacher does not have a predetermined answer in mind and they cue in extended responses from the children as they explain their responses.

The final area identified is the creation of inclusive communities of readers which involve reading teachers and reading communities.

Reading Teachers

It is worth thinking about who you are as a reader–teacher; what is your own identity as a reader and to what extent do you really share this with the children? How do you share what it means authentically to be a reader – for example, do you talk to the children about what readers do when they start a book and find out they don't like it, or what to do when you like the book but find a bit of it boring? If these things aren't shared with children, they won't know what to do when they meet challenges like this or have good strategies to overcome them.

Reading Communities

Finally, it is worth thinking about the reading community beyond your classroom. For example, are there ways to connect with parents and carers about R4P and the children as readers? How might school and local librarians become involved in your reading community? How might you engage with authors? Finding ways to include others to celebrate reading is a worthwhile investment.

Research Focus: Reading for Pleasure

You will see that the features of effective practice identified through the OURfP study reflect other research into R4P. For example, Guthrie et al. (1996) argued that classroom contexts which promote pleasure and engagement are:

- Self-directing, featuring student autonomy and choice of topics, books and peers.
- Metacognitive, containing explicit teaching of reading strategies and problem-solving.
- Collaborative, involving the social construction of meaning.

Along with the ideas explored in Chapters 6, 7 and 8 of this book, the OURfP's findings also reflect the ten principles for teaching for pleasure published by the Centre for Literacy in Primary Education (CLPE) (2018):

1   Developing an ethos and an environment that excites, enthuses, inspires and values.
2   High-quality texts with depth and interest in story, character, illustration, vocabulary, structure and subject matter.
3   A read-aloud programme.
4   Teachers who are knowledgeable about children's literature.
5   Creating a community of readers with opportunities to share responses and opinions.
6   Planning for talking about books and stories, providing structures within which to do this.
7   Understanding the importance of illustration in reading both in terms of creating a text and responding to a text.

(Continued)

8   Using drama and role-play to help children understand and access texts.
9   Working with authors and illustrators to understand the process of creating books.
10   Using literature beyond the literacy lesson – cross-curricular planning with quality literature as the starting point.

Research presented by Farshore, publisher of children's books and researchers of children's reading practices, in 2023 showed that:

- While R4P among 8–13s continues to grow, this is driven more by girls than boys.
- While R4P among 5–7s and 14–17s continues to decline, this is driven more by boys than girls.
- Reading to children at home remains low.
- Many parents were unaware of the positive impact that reading for pleasure brings their children.
- Many parents were unaware that reading aloud to children motivates them to read.
- Pre-school boys were read to significantly less than girls.
- Boys read for pleasure less than girls do.
- Fathers read to children less than mothers do.

Recent research by Farshore involved fathers who agreed to read with their children every day for six weeks. Books were chosen by the children and the fathers agreed that they could either read books the children already owned or a new book, whichever the children chose. The fathers completed a survey about their children before and after the six weeks. The study showed that the children's enjoyment, well-being, learning, feelings of togetherness and behaviour all increased regardless of age and gender. A wide and free choice of what to read was found to promote children's engagement with reading. and the study concluded that 'the dads' diaries revealed the positive effect of children being able to select their own books: this gave the children a valued sense of agency and control and, hence, enjoyment' (2023, p. 9). This also highlights the importance of working with parents for whom reading and sharing books may not be instinctive. Teachers need to talk to parents about why this matters so much, show them how to do it and enthuse them about doing it at home. Events such as a bedtime story evening can be really engaging. In one school, it worked like this:

- The parents and children arrived at school early one winter evening in their pyjamas. They went into the school hall where there were lots of beanbags, cushions and books. Some books were there for people to read, and there were lots of teachers and school governors (also in their pyjamas) ready to read to small groups.
- Suddenly, a white rabbit ran through the hall, muttering 'I'm late, I'm late'. The children were encouraged to follow (the corridors were adorned with fairy lights to give a cosy, magical glow), while the parents stayed behind for a ten-minute talk about why R4P is so important.
- The parents then went to join their children. Each age group listened to two different people read them a story and had one timetabled session in the school kitchen for hot chocolate and biscuits. Each of the rooms with readers in them was laid out with a bed and bedside

lamp, and the readers were teachers, governors, local children's literature authors, and children's librarians from the school and local libraries. After the children had engaged in all the activities, everyone went home.

- The same sort of idea could be repeated in the summer but outdoors with solar lights and logs for sitting on, centred around a fire pit (this need not be real!). If budget allows, you could get a professional storyteller in, or there may be a local storytelling group who would be happy to volunteer their time. If not, members of the school community might be persuaded to volunteer.

Supporting Diversity and Inclusion

As highlighted in other chapters, there is a real need for teachers to consider the extent to which the texts, authors and illustrators they share with children truly represent the rich diversity found within society and the wider world. According to Sims-Bishop (1990, p. ix):

> Books are sometimes windows, offering views of worlds that may be real or imagined, familiar or strange... However, a window can also be a mirror. Literature transforms human experience and reflects it back to us, and in that reflection we can see our own lives and experiences as part of a larger human experience. Reading, then, becomes a means of self-affirmation, and readers often seek their mirrors in books.

As explored in Chapter 3, avoiding stereotypical portrayals in regard to characteristics such as race, gender, sexuality, learning need and disability, family background, religion – while including positive representations, sometimes as the main character and other times as fully integrated background characters (rather than as tokenistic representations) – is critical. This enables all children to see themselves reflected in the curriculum and expands every child's understanding of the world. A useful list of resources can be found at https://www.book trust.org.uk/news-and-features/features/2022/july/creating-inclusive-bookshelves-why-diversity-matters/. Consider accessibility of the texts too – have you provided a good range of audio texts, texts with larger print, visual texts, comics and graphic novels, shorter and longer texts, dyslexia friendly texts, multimodal texts, texts with high interest and good accessibility, and dual language texts where possible so that the learning needs of all the children in your class are met?

Planning to Foster a Reading-for-Pleasure Mindset

As you will see from what has been explored up until this point in this chapter, R4P is fostered through a wide range of classroom routines and curriculum experiences which may not look much like formal lessons. Formalising learning too much or too often will quite possibly be counteractive in terms of developing children's pleasure in reading. However, the National Curriculum highlights the role of discussion as a way in which children can develop pleasure and this principle is clearly supported by R4P theory and research, emphasising the social element of book talk in building communities of readers. The majority of the time, opportunities which enable pupils and adults to talk freely about their reading preferences and recent reading are likely to be of most benefit. However, there may be times when you (or the children) want to focus on extending the range of their reading in a specific way and to experience a more structured discussion which will enhance and underpin their skills in discussing texts more generally. Therefore, the following plan offers one way in which you might achieve this.

Lesson plan

Here is one suggestion for what a lesson plan might look like for a Year 6 class (Table 9.1). It focuses on the concept of book talk, adapting an idea from Aidan Chambers's 'Tell Me' approach which uses authentic, open questions to stimulate reader talk, using an activity called 'The Sentence Game' (2011, p. 210).

Relevant prior learning: Over the last few weeks, pupils have been reading books by the same author (this is in addition to their personal choice reading). They have also been developing their talk skills, learning to work effectively in a group using the class's agreed ground rules (see Chapter 4).

What will children learn:

- To participate confidently in discussions about books, building on their own and others' ideas and challenging views courteously.
- To be able to confidently explain and discuss their understanding of what they have read, including through formal presentations and debates, maintaining a focus on the topic and using notes where necessary.

The suggested lesson that follows also has the potential to contribute to other end-of-year expectations for Year 6, depending on the texts/author chosen, for example, widening their familiarity with texts that are structured in different ways and for a range of purposes, or with a wider range of books, including myths, legends and traditional stories, modern fiction, fiction from our literary heritage, and books from other cultures and traditions. Children may also ask questions to improve their understanding, discuss themes and conventions, summarise main ideas, discuss and justify inferences they have made, refer to evidence and discuss how authors have used language, including figurative language, considering the impact on the reader.

What will effective learning look like: Pupils will participate well in discussions, listen to others, make contributions and work together to create a presentation on their book.

How will learning be assessed: Observation of pupils. Give specific positive praise to pupils to show they have listened carefully to someone else's ideas, and to those who extend the discussion or introduce points of their own, encouraging the children to take ownership of the conversation.

Planned next steps to follow this lesson: Make comparisons within and across books by reflecting on the presentations of the different groups and identifying any similarities and differences that they have noted (you may therefore wish to record the presentations in the lesson outline above, or keep the written notes prepared by the groups to aide subsequent lessons).

Table 9.1 A lesson plan to develop book talk

Today's lesson sequence /content
2.00 p.m.
• Sort the children into small groups, each group having read a different book by the author.
• Ask the children to start by discussing the book they have read, starting with what they liked, didn't like, any puzzles or questions they have (or had), and any patterns or connections that they made to their own lives, to other texts they have read, and to the world (i.e. people, places, animals, nature, themes and so on).
2.10 p.m.
• Stop the talk and ask each child to write down one sentence about the book that they would say to someone who hasn't read it.
2.15 p.m.
• Ask each pupil to share their sentence with the rest of their small group, asking the group members to help each pupil revise it until it is expressed really clearly and effectively.
• Now ask the group to order the sentences they have.
2.30 p.m.
• Now ask each group in turn to come to the front of the room and sit together as an expert panel.
• Each group has a specified time (e.g. five minutes) to introduce the book, its author and illustrator (if relevant), and then read their sentences in the order agreed. Now the rest of the class can question them about the book. The panel can confer over the answers and/or refuse to give away any information that they think might spoil it for anyone who wants to read it.
• You might want to check in to see who is interested in reading the book after each panel's presentation, perhaps asking any child interested to give their reasons (offering the teacher the opportunity to learn more about the individual reader).
2.50 p.m.
• Highlight and praise aspects of effective group work demonstrated by the pupils, and how this impacted their presentations. Explain how the class will build on this session.

Adaptive/Responsive Teaching

Considerations could include:

• Checking that pupils with specific learning needs can participate comfortably in all R4P activities and understand any rules that are different from those expected in more typical learning contexts. Check that sensory demands are manageable and won't be over-stimulating for any pupil. You might consider making use of visual prompts, or think about how to plan for pupils to transition between activities if they are less formal than usual teaching and some pupils find it hard to adjust quickly.

- Thinking about how you could make use of audiobooks and multimodal (e.g., animated tales) resources for children who might benefit from having stories read-aloud to them or engaging interactively with them.
- If pupils are sharing recommendations in written form, think about how to provide scaffolding (such as sentence stems or writing frames) for pupils who would benefit.
- If any pupils aren't engaged, talk to them to find out why. Consider providing a wider range of text forms including comics and graphic novels, supporting children to learn how to choose a new text to read, and whether the content of the books they can choose from matches the children's interests and reading profiles.

Summary

In this chapter, the principles of promoting R4P have been explored, with practical suggestions given as to how these might be enacted in the primary classroom, with a particular focus on the development of book talk.

Further Reading

1 Find out about more about how to promote R4P in the primary classroom at https://ourfp.org/
2 See the findings of the CLPE's R4P research at https://clpe.org.uk/research.
3 Track down and read Aidan Chamber's excellent text on book talk: *Tell Me: Children, Reading and Talk.*

References

Bishop, R. S. (1990). Mirrors, windows, and sliding glass doors. *Perspectives: Choosing and Using Books for the Classroom, 6*(3).

Chambers, A. (2011). *Tell me: Children, reading and talk with the reading environment.* The Thimble Press.

Clark, C., & Teravainen-Goff, A. (2018). *Mental wellbeing, reading and writing: How children and young people's mental wellbeing is related to their reading and writing experiences.* National Literacy Trust.

CLPE. (2018). *Reading for pleasure: What we know works.* Centre for Literacy in Primary Education.

Department for Children, Schools and Families (DCSF). (2008). *Talk for writing.* Crown Copyright.

Department for Education. (2021). *Statutory framework for the early years foundation stage: Setting the standards for learning, development and care for children from birth to five.* Crown Copyright.

Department for Education. (2023). *The reading framework*. Crown Copyright.

Farshore and Harper Collins Children's Books. (2023). *Children's reading for pleasure: Progress, problems and practical solutions*. https://www.farshore.co.uk/wp-content/uploads/sites/46/2023/06/E6722-2023-Farshore-Insight-Day-Research-Paper.pdf. Accessed on August 20, 2023.

Guthrie, J., Van Meter, P., & McCann, A. (1996). Growth of literacy engagement: Changes in motivations and strategies during concept-oriented reading instruction. *Reading Research Quarterly*, *31*(3), 306–331.

Raleigh, M. (1996). Independent reading. In M. Simons (Ed.), Where We've Been: Articles from The English & Media Magazine. English and Media Centre.

10

Planning Lessons That Develop Children as Writers

Chapter Objectives

This chapter will:

- Consider what writing is and what knowledge and skills children need to develop.
- Explore the key components of writing which underpin the structure of the National Curriculum.
- Explore what the effective teaching of writing looks like, highlighting what effective teachers of writing do.
- Consider how to support children whose progress may not keep pace with age-related expectations.

Introduction

Writing is a complex process which is underpinned by knowledge (Ofsted, 2022), and involves the orchestration of a number of skills (Dombey, 2013). In a review of research that shows what practices underpin the effective literacy development of pupils, Breadmore et al. (2019) define writing as 'the process of translating thoughts or ideas into text' (p. 26). However,

> learning to write is more than the mastery of the range of technical skills and transcriptional conventions that determine how words should be set down on the page or screen. Composition - the construction of meaning through words - is central....if we are to teach our children to write most effectively, we need to be fully aware of what writing is and what it can do. (Dombey, 2013)

Activity   Reflecting on the Knowledge and Skills Involved in Writing

If you could visit any place in the world, where would you go?

Take some time to think about how you might answer this question, and then write your answer, giving as much detail as you can so that your writing extends over at least a couple of paragraphs

Now take some time to reflect on the process. Were any aspects of the task easy or hard for you? What did you need to know in order to produce that text? What skills did you demonstrate? How did you feel during the experience? How do you feel about the finished draft?

This activity is inspired by the fantastic book *You Choose!* in which author Pippa Goodhart poses a number of questions which invite children to think about where and how they might choose to live. Each question is accompanied by Nick Sharratt's great illustrations which suggest a plethora of possibilities to spark the children's imagination. You might like to use this resource in school.

As you read on through this chapter, continue to reflect on the ideas that are presented and consider the extent to which they match your experiences of writing.

Knowledge for Writing

To compose a piece of writing, the writer must first know what writing is and how it differs from spoken language. When we are speaking, our audience is usually present; this means we are afforded the luxury of speaking in utterances rather than complete sentences, and our observation of verbal and non-verbal signals from our listener(s) can prompt us to revise or elaborate on our words to ensure that we communicate our intentions with some degree of success. However, when we are writing, our audience is typically not present, and so we must learn that different conventions are required, for example packaging our thoughts in complete sentences with punctuation that defines and enhances our meaning, and choosing our words with precision and care so that our reader(s), who may be unknown to us and who may receive our writing in a different space and at a different time, fully understands what we want to tell them. Knowledge of what writing is and how it differs from spoken language is therefore a key concept for our pupils to understand.

The writer also needs to know what to write about, drawing on content knowledge which has been gathered through: first-hand experiences, for example if writing about our first day at school; second-hand sources such as books and films, for example if writing about frogs; or a combination of both, for example if in addition to knowledge gained from books and films, the author also visited a local pond to observe frogs. This content knowledge needs to be sufficiently secure in order for it to be readily available to the writer; it is usually much harder to write about something in the early stages of learning the content than it is when the relevant knowledge has been deepened and rehearsed a number of times, for example through recalling and discussing it.

In addition, the writer must have secure knowledge of the type of text they are going to produce, understanding the purpose of such texts as 'to describe, narrate, explain, instruct, give and respond to information, and argue' (Ofsted, 2022), how they are structured, and the style of language used. Suggested text types include:

> ... well-structured formal expository and narrative essays; stories, scripts, poetry and other imaginative writing; notes and polished scripts for talks and presentations; and a range of other narrative and non-narrative texts, including arguments, and personal and formal letters. (DfE, 2013)

Both familiarity with the content and with texts will support the reader to develop a secure knowledge and understanding of the language that will be used for composition. This includes any relevant vocabulary such as the use of technical terms in non-fiction texts, and the use of grammatical features such as expanded noun phrases to describe in the case of fiction writing or to specify in the case of non-fiction writing. Knowledge of the intended audience will influence the choices the writer makes; a story written to entertain younger pupils will be written very differently to a formal letter intended to persuade a member of the local council to implement or halt a course of action such as replacing the local park with new housing. Thus the writer will make decisions about the words they include and the register, the level of formality, of the writing.

Knowledge of the process through which a piece of writing is produced is also key. This involves a number of stages; it would be unusual for anyone to sit down and produce one perfect draft of any piece of writing – even a simple shopping list written for the author themselves so that they don't forget what to buy when they get to the shops – may have revisions and corrections. Thus it is helpful for writers to know that writing often starts with a plan which is followed by a first draft which is then revised to improve it, clarifying the writer's intentions in line with the writer's intended purpose, for example, deciding that writing 'you MUST' rather than 'you could' is more compelling in a persuasive piece. When the writer is happy with the revised version of the text, the writer then edits the piece to ensure that it their meaning is transcribed with accuracy and proofreads it to check for any mistakes. The final stage of the writing process is the sharing stage which is key to supporting children's development as writers. Through sharing their writing with an audience, children experience the satisfaction of knowing that they have successfully communicated their ideas and knowledge to someone else, entertaining, informing or aiming to persuade them depending on their purpose. If the writing is shared in such a way as to allow the writer to watch the audience's reaction, they have the opportunity to reflect on the extent to which they achieved their goals which is highly useful feedback that they can use to inform their next piece. It is important to note that the idea of an audience could involve people outside the school environment, such as a local councillor or staff or visitors of a place the children have visited or could involve people from within the school community, such as one or two pupils from another class, staff, parents or governors. Ideas for possible audiences are explored further in Chapter 12 and Chapter 13.

Finally, to produce the writing, the writer will also need to draw on their knowledge of spelling and letter formation. Research demonstrates that children should be taught these transcription skills discretely, through short and frequent focused teaching which aims to build automaticity, thus freeing the writer to focus on the creation and sharing of meaning. These aspects of writing are considered in more depth in Chapters 15 and 16.

Of course, building such knowledge takes time. It is developed through children's spoken language experiences, which increase the number of words that they know, and deepen their understanding of words they already know, and their experiences as a reader, through the books that they read for themselves and through the books that are read to them which enable them to hear and absorb the language and conventions of different text types. Each component is supported through ongoing, carefully crafted engagement with high-quality texts and through meaningful experiences which show children how writing works, highlighting the role of the author in composing the text, selecting form, language and style according to his or her intention and audience. Writing, then, is developed over time through a high-quality writing curriculum constructed from carefully designed sequences of learning which allow them to explore, investigate and play with new ideas and language.

Skills for Writing

This knowledge on its own is of no help to writers unless they develop the necessary skills which allow them to make good use of this knowledge in order to produce a written text. The writer, therefore, needs to develop the following skills:

- The ability to frame their ideas in written form so that the reader can follow them.
- The ability to learn and recall content knowledge so that their writing has something interesting to say.
- The ability to structure and style their writing in a reasonably conventional form that the reader will find easy to follow.
- The ability to use language to achieve their intended effect.
- The ability to sustain the momentum required to engage with the writing process at all stages.
- The ability to write legibly and produce phonically plausible or accurate spellings.

In addition, research has shown that writers must also employ metacognitive skills which allow them to identify the goals for their writing, monitor their output and take action when it is going off course.

Document Summary: Ofsted's Research and Analysis: Curriculum Research Review Series: English, Published 23 May 2022

In 2022, Ofsted published a curriculum research review which aimed to identify what research evidence underpinning a high-quality education in the teaching of English. This review drew on a range of published research and documentation, concluding that a high-quality writing curriculum may focus on developing the following:

- Proficiency in spelling and handwriting as the 'foundations of writing'.
- A secure knowledge of grammar.
- A broad and deep vocabulary.
- Knowledge of the world so that the child has things to write about.
- Knowledge of the different stages of the writing process.
- Knowledge of different text types and genres of writing created for specific purposes and audiences through the provision and sharing of models of effective writing.

The report also suggests that developing both a school and classroom environment that promote motivation for writing correlates strongly with pupils' attitudes to writing and their skill as writers. It proposes that motivation can be experienced through the sense of pride that follows the creation of a piece of writing, through overcoming challenges, and through recognition of writing as a key life skill, for example, in building readiness for the workplace.
Factors associated with motivation include:

- Writing for real audiences and purposes.
- Writing collaboratively with peers.
- A choice of topic.
- The desire to share ideas with an audience. (Ofsted, 2022)

The Writing Process

The term writing process has been used frequently in this chapter so far. This approach emphasises the process of creating the piece of writing, allowing children to develop their understanding of how ideas and language can be crafted through a sequence of planning, drafting, revising and editing in order to produce the final piece which is then shared with an audience. Teachers who use the process approach understand that writing is not simply the production of a piece of text, but an undertaking that demands careful thought to shape meaning (Graham & Kelly, 2010).

Slavin et al. (2019) note that a focus on the process supports more reluctant writers, allowing them to revise and improve their writing and thus alleviating the pressure of having to produce something perfect at the first attempt. This approach is endorsed by published author Richard Osman who advises 'first get it done, then get it good' (2020, p. 380). The process approach is widely attributed to American researcher and teacher Donald Graves whose book *Writing: Teachers and Children at* Work (1983) championed the idea of engaging children as writers, giving them ownership over their writing and guiding them through the use of a workshop approach which aimed to support them as they composed their texts, using the teacher's formative assessment strategies (although these were not termed as such) to indicate when and how the teacher could provide short bursts of input to teach the child necessary skills and knowledge. Other principles which were key to this approach were the provision of sufficient time to produce the finished product, and the need for children to choose what they wished to write about (Clements & Tobin, 2021). It is important to note that the plan, draft, revise and edit, and share process is not necessarily linear but may well involve the writer in revisiting different elements of the sequence at different points (Clements & Tobin, 2021).

This process approach to teaching writing underpins the National Curriculum in England and is evident in the end-of-year expectations presented for pupils in Key Stages 1 and 2, following a plan, draft, evaluate and edit, and share sequence.

Curriculum Continuity and Progression

If a child has met the relevant early learning goals for the end of Year R, they will be able to write recognisable letters, with the majority correctly formed, spell words by identifying sounds in them and representing the sounds with a letter or letters, and write simple phrases and sentences that can be ready by others (DFE, 2021).

From Year 1 onwards, the end-of-year expectations specified in the National Curriculum for English composition strand centre around five key ideas, aiming to build children's knowledge, understanding and ability to:

- Compose sentences accurately, extending their knowledge of vocabulary and grammar so that meaning is communicated with increasing precision (these ideas are explored more fully in Chapter 11).

- Plan their writing.
- Draft their writing.
- Evaluate and edit their writing.
- Share their texts with an audience.

Planning Their Writing

In Year 1, pupils begin to develop their understanding of the planning process by saying what they are going to write about. In Year 2, pupils should continue to plan what they will write about, writing down key ideas including vocabulary. In Years 3 and 4, pupils develop their planning skills by discussing writing similar to that which they are planning to write about in order to understand and learn from its structure vocabulary and grammar, and discussing and recording their ideas. In Years 5 and 6, pupils learn to plan their writing by identifying the audience, form and purpose of their writing, using similar writing as models for their own. They use their reading and research to note and develop their initial ideas.

Drafting Their Writing

In Year 1, pupils use the strategy of oral rehearsal to compose each sentence before transcribing it. They will sequence their sentences to form a short narrative. In Year 2, pupils create longer pieces, writing sentence by sentence. In Years 3 and 4, pupils learn to draft and write, composing and rehearsing sentences orally with an increasingly varied and rich vocabulary and range of sentence structures, organising paragraphs, creating settings, characters and plots in narratives. In Years 5 and 6, pupils extend their knowledge and understanding of the drafting stage of the writing process, for example, by selecting appropriate grammar and vocabulary to ensure that their meaning is clear. In narrative writing, they learn to describe settings, characters and atmosphere, integrating dialogue to convey character and advance the action.

Evaluating and Editing Their Writing

In Year 1, pupils are taught to re-read their work to check it makes sense and to discuss what they have written with the teacher or peers. In Year 2, pupils learn how to make simple additions, revisions and corrections to their writing. They will evaluate their writing with the teacher and/or their peers, re-read to check it makes sense and proofread to check for errors. The National Curriculum identifies a particular focus on the accuracy of verb tenses as these are specified in *Appendix 2* which outlines the vocabulary, grammar and punctuation foci for Year 2. In Years 3 and 4, pupils extend their revision skills, evaluating and editing their writing by assessing the effectiveness of their own and others' writing, and suggesting improvements and proposing changes which improve consistency. They should then proofread for spelling and punctuation errors. In Years 5 and 6, pupils further develop their evaluation skills, assessing the effectiveness of their own and others' writing, proposing changes to vocabulary, grammar and punctuation to enhance the impact and clarify their meaning, ensuring consistent and correct use of tense and subject and verb agreement. Pupils should also learn to proofread for spelling and punctuation errors.

Sharing Their Texts With an Audience

In Year 1, pupils learn to read their writing aloud in a voice that is clear enough to be heard. In Year 2, pupils learn to read their work aloud with appropriate intonation. In Years 3 and 4, pupils learn how to read aloud their own writing using appropriate intonation and controlling tone and volume so that the meaning is clear. In Years 5 and 6, pupils learn how to share their own compositions using appropriate intonation, volume and movement.

You will notice that these objectives are very broad, aiming to develop the children's knowledge, understanding and skills which can then be applied in different contexts. These are developed through children's encounters with an increasingly wide range of text types. In Year 1, pupils compose short narratives, and in Year 2, pupils begin to widen their knowledge of purposes for writing and develop the stamina needed to create real and fictional narratives, write about real events, write poems and write for other purposes. In Years 3 and 4, non-statutory guidance states that pupils should continue to have opportunities to write for a range of real audiences and purposes as part of their work across the curriculum.

When planning a sequence of writing lessons, the teacher will design a meaningful and authentic context in which pupils will apply what they have learned through contexts previously explored as well as engaging with newer learning which has been developed in this context.

Effective Teachers of Writing

A number of authors have aimed to identify what effective teachers of writing do (e.g., Parr and Limbrick (2010), Young (2019) and Dombey (2013)). These reviews offer useful insights into the practices of effective teachers and highlight the importance of providing meaningful opportunities for pupils to practise different elements of the writing process and authentic contexts through which pupils can apply their learning and experience the satisfaction of crafting their own compositions.

Research Focus: Key Principles of the Effective Teaching of Writing

Research on the effective teaching of writing carried out by Young and Ferguson (2021, 2023), the CLPE (2017), Dombey (2013) and the UKLA (n.d.) broadly identifies three key strands to effective practice: laying the foundations for writing, approaches to the teaching of writing and providing the conditions that support writing.

Laying the Foundations for Writing

Research shows that children typically tackle the composition of a piece of writing with confidence and enthusiasm when they are ready to write and know what they want to say. This readiness is primarily built through:

- Making extensive use of drama and other teaching approaches to help children become immersed in scenarios and try out language and ideas for structure as a form of oral rehearsal.
- Rich experiences of reading and text study through immersion in high-quality literature which includes visual and digital texts, making links between texts they read and texts they write by using such texts as models for their own writing, as a springboard for ideas to take into their own writing, and/or learning from the language and style of writing.
- Good opportunities to play with language and language techniques such as rhyme and alliteration so that they become flexible and adept in their word choices.
- Providing rich opportunities for children to respond to writing (composed by published authors, themselves and their peers) as readers, noting and sharing the effect a particular piece of writing has had on them and considering how the author might have achieved this.

Approaches to the Teaching of Writing

An effective teaching approach centres around the teaching of writing as a craft. The craft of writing is defined by Myhill et al. (2021) as knowing how to compose and shape a text including:

- Knowledge about the strategies and processes involved in writing, from pre-writing activities to final proofreading
- Knowledge about structural and text-level features and their effects
- Knowledge about language choices and their effects
- Knowledge about the personal resources and intentions that authors bring to their writing
- Knowledge about the interaction between reader and writer, and the ways in which readers become engaged in or affected by writing (p. 7).

In teaching this craft knowledge, effective teachers engage in writing themselves, sharing their experiences of writing, and modelling the process authentically for the children. Young and Ferguson

(Continued)

(2021, 2023) suggest that providing daily mini lessons which focus on different aspects of the craft of writing support the children's learning. Adults also dedicate quality time to supporting the young writers in their classrooms, focusing their responses and feedback first on the meaning the writer has tried to communicate and then on how the writer's use of technical aspects has affected this. They work alongside young writers at every stage of the process as needed, acting as scribes, response partners, editors and advisors. The teaching of composition and transcription is well-balanced with discrete teaching which ensures that the teaching of spelling and grammar (including punctuation) is embedded in the context of purposeful and authentic writing. Children have plentiful opportunities to develop their knowledge about words and spelling, and to develop accurate and efficient hand-writing. When composing, invented spelling is supported, allowing children to use their existing spelling knowledge to represent a word during the drafting stage of the writing process and revisiting this at the appropriate editing stage.

Providing the Conditions That Support Writing

Fundamental to our teaching of writing is the idea that writing is about making sense of the world and our lives within it. Writing should, therefore, be presented as a purposeful and engaging activity where mastering the techniques of writing makes a difference to what you say and how you say it. Therefore, children should be treated as and supported to identify as writers them-selves, developing their own writers' voices. Children will develop an understanding of the craft of writing in a number of ways including engaging with professional authors and finding out about how they go about the process of writing, as well as through talking about their own and others' writing, and engaging in collaborative writing activities. This helps to build a community of writers who can share their writing and think and learn together. Opportunities for the children to write are rich and meaningful, aiming to:

- Foster choice and independence
- Provide a range of real purposes and audiences
- Publish, celebrate and share the children's writing with an audience beyond the teacher
- Often build on the children's personal interests and concerns
- Provide enough time and space for the writing to develop fully

The Teacher as a Writer

Following their own extensive analysis of research into the effective teaching of writing, Young and Ferguson have built on the writer's workshop and process approach to develop a writing for pleasure manifesto in which teachers recognise the power of harnessing children's ownership of and engagement in what they term real-world writing. This approach to writing curriculum design seeks to build a community of writers in the classroom, highlighting the teacher's role in posi-tioning themselves as a writer. Research studies conducted by Grainger (2005) and Ings (2009) also explored the value of teachers developing themselves as writers. Both studies concluded that this supported teachers to develop a deeper understanding of the writing process which influenced their teaching as they talked to their pupils as one writer to another, subsequently impacting positively on their children's enjoyment of and engagement in writing in the classroom and their depth of understanding, increasing the quality of the writing the children produced.

Franks (2020) notes that a teacher's confidence in regarding him or herself as a writer may well prompt the teacher to produce model texts in advance of the lesson for discussion with pupils. However, being willing to model writing 'live' is much more authentic and likely to support children's writing development more effectively. It is always helpful to have a go at any writing task you will ask your children to achieve as this will help you to understand exactly what knowledge they will need to draw on and thus design a sequence of learning which is focused and effective. However, where possible, try to avoid the temptation simply to share that piece of writing with the children once it is already completed, although you could always save this piece and use it later in the sequence as an additional model for some or all children to discuss. Instead, use that experience to develop your skills in live modelling with the children by composing a similar text in front of them.

Activity   Reflecting on Yourself as a Writer

Think about your own practices as a writer. Do you still produce for yourself the kinds of writing that you ask your children to produce? How do you feel about modelling the writing process in front of the children? Do you feel the same about all aspects of the writing process or do you prefer some parts to others? Would all writers approach the writing process in the same way as you or might there be some differences, for example, do you like to plan your ideas thoroughly first and if so, how? Do you always create a paragraph plan or do you use drawing, imagining and/or drama? It is worth finding out what the children in your class are used to so compile a list of questions to ask the class teacher.

Think about a recent or upcoming piece of writing that you will ask the children to produce and have a go at producing this yourself. As you do so, or when you've finished – think about the knowledge that the children will draw on under the following headings:

What knowledge will the children need to build on in order to ensure:

- They have relevant and sufficiently detailed content to write about.
- They understand the structure and style of the text type.
- They can use appropriate vocabulary and grammatical features which fit the purpose of the text.
- They understand the needs of their intended audience.

These principles can all be supported through carefully planned writing lessons. Specific teaching strategies which reflect these principles of effective teaching are explored in Chapter 12.

Curriculum Design for Writing

Because children's knowledge of texts they have shared and read and their understanding of language are key aspects of children's development as writers, a high-quality writing curriculum offers rich opportunities for children to refresh and enhance their knowledge of the related genre and of how they could express their ideas, linking this to the programmes of study for each year group in relation to vocabulary and grammar. This reinforces children's understanding of the interconnected nature of the language modes, spoken language, reading and writing, in English, and offers meaningful contexts for them to apply their learning from one mode in another.

To achieve this, high-quality texts are chosen as models for children's writing from which they can deepen their knowledge and understanding, and begin to experiment and play with new ways of structuring writing and using language for effect. Not all texts offer rich potential for learning in this way. Some texts are just fun or interesting for a particular class or year group to share and should definitely be included in the teacher's read-alouds from time to time. However, to ensure that the writing curriculum is rich and meaningful, texts to be used here must be carefully selected to ensure that they offer good potential to deepen the children's knowledge and understanding of structure and language. It is worthwhile spending time on this as the better you know the text and understand its potential as a context for children's learning, the more purposeful and engaging your lessons are likely to be.

The National Curriculum in England: English Programmes of Study for Key Stage 1 and Key Stage 2 identifies specific expectations for pupils in each year group in the main body of the document through the 'composition' strand of writing.

> Effective composition involves articulating and communicating ideas, and then organizing them coherently for a reader. This requires clarity, awareness of the audience, purpose and context, and an increasingly wide knowledge of vocabulary and grammar. (DfE, 2013, p. 15)

The other strand of the writing aspect is transcription which encompasses spelling and handwriting. Of course, the writer's transcription skills support the composition process, allowing pupils to transcribe their ideas with sufficient fluency to allow them to focus on communicating their ideas in a way that the reader will understand. As research shows that these are best taught discretely, transcription skills are explored in fully in Chapter 15 and Chapter 16.

Curriculum and Pedagogy

So far, we have established that children must draw on knowledge about texts, readers, content and language as well as their understanding of the process of creating written texts and knowledge of and skills in aspects of transcription (spelling and handwriting). The wealth of knowledge that underpins writing is developed over time as children encounter and re-encounter a range of different styles of text and explore increasingly complex language features such as the use of expanded noun phrases (Years 2 and 4), the impact of fronted adverbials (Year 4) and the use of relative clauses (Year 5) which enable them to communicate their ideas in increasingly sophisticated ways. To embed this knowledge and understanding, and to hone these language skills, children need to engage in meaningful writing opportunities which allow them to practise and refine their use in order to build the secure learning that successfully underpins what follows. The act of writing exerts a high level of demand on the writer's skills, requiring them to simultaneously juggle a number of complex tasks at any one time and sustain this level of effort until the job is done. As a result, 'writing places far greater demands on other cognitive processes such as planning, goal maintenance, and working memory' (Breadmore et al., 2019, p. 31).

You will see from the National Curriculum that once children have begun drafting, the different stages of the writing process typically unfold one at a time so that pupils are focusing only on drafting, evaluating the impact of their writing in order to make revisions, editing it to check it makes sense or sharing with an audience. This staged approach seeks to support the writer in managing the cognitive load of the writing task by reducing the number of elements which are the focus of the writer at any one time. However, before the drafting process can begin, children must engage in planning so that they know what they are going to write about and who they are going to write for. This helps them to identify what knowledge about texts, readers and language they are likely to draw on, again supporting the management of cognitive load within the writing process. One useful model which proposes a clear sequence to support the planning stage of the writing process is Bearne and Reedy's planning and teaching sequence (2017). This outlines a way of structuring children's learning over a sequence of learning (often referred to in schools as a unit of work), building and consolidating the children's knowledge and enabling them to develop the skills needed to write successfully with independence and in a way which reduces cognitive load as far as possible within the writing process.

Research Focus: Bearne and Reedy's Planning and Teaching Sequence (2017)

Bearne and Reedy present an approach to the planning and teaching of effective writing lessons which describe three overlapping stages during which children:

- Read, investigate and explore a text type, building their knowledge of its purpose, structure and conventions, and language. The aim here is for children to 'become familiar with the features of the text and how to make sense of it; for example, by studying the writer's craft' (2017, p. 7).
- Capture ideas for their own writing which may take many forms, for example, using discussion and drama activities to explore ideas suggested by the text and exploring

(Continued)

language features through the teacher's use of explicit teaching and modelling. This stage of the planning process may engage in collaborative activities to try out the ideas and uses of language that the teacher has introduced them to.

- Are supported by the teacher through the use of shared and supported writing activities which prepare them for the drafting stage in which they will compose a piece of writing independently.

Therefore, the aims of an effective sequence of learning to compose texts are to:

- Deepen children's knowledge of a particular style of writing and the writing process through which such texts are composed.
- Extend children's knowledge of how language can be shaped and used to communicate meaning and impact on the reader, thus developing their ability to use language for effect.
- Develop children's experience as writers through meaningful and authentic contexts for writing.

This is achieved by careful design of a sequence of lessons which provide time for pupils to:

- Read to build their knowledge of a text type.
- Understand the writing process.
- Explore the language and structure of texts.
- Generate ideas for their own writing.
- Draft their writing.
- Revise their writing.
- Edit and proofread their writing.
- Share their writing with an audience.

The first four of the above bullet points form the planning phase, through which children capture ideas and inspiration for the writing that follows. In a study of Year 5 pupils, Barrs and Cork (2001) identified the value of what they termed indirect planning, preparing for writing through opportunities for rich engagement with texts, and in peer discussions, drama and collaborative writing, as more effective in supporting pupils' planning that the use of more direct strategies such as the use of graphic organisers or writing frames.

This is not to say that explicit (direct) planning opportunities should not take place, but that they should be in addition to rather than instead of indirect strategies which allow pupils to engage more fully with the content and language of what they will be writing about. When direct planning processes are included in a sequence of learning, it is important that these are modelled clearly for pupils unless they have already built sufficient knowledge and experience of different ways of planning to be able to achieve this independently.

Effective Teaching Strategies

Pupils' ability to make good progress in writing rests on the extent to which they successfully develop their knowledge, understanding and skills, and are able to bring these together in order to produce increasingly sophisticated texts with independence. This concept is underpinned by the gradual release of responsibility model which was explored in previous chapters.

Shared Writing: Teacher Demonstration (Also Referred to as Teacher Modelling)

Research shows that leading the pupils in shared writing is key to teaching writing effectively. Wyse et al. (2018) define shared writing as 'a term used to describe a whole class writing experience designed to form a bridge between the teacher demonstrating the writing process to pupils and independent writing by children' (p. 222).

As an experienced writer, the teacher demonstrates (or models) the writing process, effectively showing children how writers draw on their knowledge of how spoken language differs from written language, of the purpose and conventions of different text types and the needs of different audiences, and of the writing process. The use of the think-aloud strategy which involves the teacher in articulating what is happening in the writer's head shows children how to formulate content knowledge into sentences, one at a time, constructing these accurately to communicate meaning in line with the purpose of the text.

> For example, the teacher might explain 'in my next sentence I want to move the action of the story on and I want to show the reader that Lucy feels really nervous about walking into those woods all alone so I'm going to write 'The woods loomed before her causing her heart to pound wildly but she knew that Jack's safety rested entirely on her shoulders and so she swallowed down her fear and stepped forward.'

Through the use of this strategy, the teacher can show the children how grammatical features can be used meaningfully in context, for example, 'I've used a noun phrase here, 'the woods', but if I expand it, it will give the reader a much better picture of why Lucy feels so scared. Perhaps I could add an adjective so that it reads 'The foreboding woods'. Does that help the reader to understand?'.

Shared Writing: Teacher Scribing

The teacher scribing strategy also involves the teacher in composing with the children. The teacher maintains control of the writing but invites the children to contribute. For example, the teacher might say:

> The next thing I want to write about is what frogs eat, and that's a new idea so I am going to start a new paragraph here. My first sentence will be an introduction to this idea so

that the reader understands what this paragraph is about. We know that frogs eat lots of different things. How could we write this first sentence? Yes, James, that's a clear sentence opener – Frogs eat a wide diet which includes.... What would come next? Yes, Hannah, we could list some examples.

It is up to the teacher to decide which parts of the process would be most beneficial to involve the children in, for example, the choice of words, how to construct or punctuate the sentence, what to include next and so on. The teacher may develop the children's understanding by reframing their ideas in conventional written language. For example,

> 'I was jaw-dropped' - that's a great idea, Maisie. It would be really good to let the reader know what a shock it was. We can write that idea in two ways, we could write 'My jaw dropped' or we could write 'It was jaw dropping'. Which do you think sounds better?

Shared Writing: Supported Writing

Supported writing involves the children in taking more of the responsibility. This could be done through a collaborative approach, for example,

> Have a go at writing the next sentence now. We have opened our new paragraph with a clear topic sentence which tells the reader that this section is about what frogs eat. With your partner, have a go at composing the next sentence.

This allows the teacher to see which children are confident with the writing style and ready to work with more independence. It also offers the children an opportunity to have a go with the style, articulating their thinking as they work together to craft the next sentence.

Guided Writing

In the gradual release of responsibility model, the stage of guided writing follows within supported writing and precedes the independence stage. In guided writing, the teacher typically works with a small group of pupils while they develop their own writing as an additional step to support independent writing. Waugh and Jolliffe (2017) note that the guided group context provides valuable opportunities for the teacher to focus in on a particular aspect of the writing or writing process, for example, helping them to generate initial ideas, to plan or produce a first draft, or to revise or edit their work. They offer excellent opportunities for meaningful dialogue, helping pupils to see directly how to use ideas discussed through the class's shared writing experiences in their own work, and for the teacher to assess the children's knowledge and understanding so that future teaching can be tailored directly to their needs.

In practice, it may be that the teacher decides to use the guided writing strategy with only some pupils, for example, with pupils who he or she has identified through formative assessment strategies as requiring further support such as reteaching or benefiting from engagement with more examples to consolidate one or more key aspects of learning before they are ready to write with independence. However, it is worth remembering that this strategy is helpful to support small groups of pupils with any aspect of learning, for example, it can also be extremely effective when working with pupils with high prior attainment to extend their knowledge and skills, perhaps by exploring an author's use of a particular language feature, or teaching them to analyse a wider range of texts or more complex texts in order to deepen or broaden their learning.

Writing Conferences

An additional teaching strategy is the use of writing conferences. Writing conferences are opportunities 'to spend time with a knowledgeable other in one-on-one conversations tailored to students' unique writing needs' (Hawkins, 2019, p. 22). Graves highlights the role of the pupil here: 'the purpose of the writing conference is to help children teach you about what they know so that you can help them more effectively with their writing' (1994, p. 59).

One challenge for teachers is to identify how best to ensure that the conference really does allow the pupil to demonstrate their knowledge and understanding. Some teachers may approach writing conferences as an opportunity for further teacher-led instruction, for example, by identifying errors for the child to fix. However, their real power is felt when the teacher approaches the writing conference as an opportunity to be the audience for a pupil's writing, responding as one writer to another.

The use of writing conferences is suggested in Young and Ferguson's Writing for Pleasure approach, emphasising the value of these as an opportunity to give constructive feedback which responds to the child's needs. Both guided writing and writing conferences can be effective strategies for supporting children whose learning does not always keep pace with age-related expectations, allowing these pupils more time to explore and apply new knowledge and skills with closer support from the teacher.

Using Talk Effectively as Part of All Teaching Strategies

Just as in reading, the use of shared and guided strategies for teaching writing supports pupils' readiness to compose a text within a new context with independence and confidence. Within each stage of the gradual release of responsibility model, the use of talk is key to enabling pupils to build their knowledge and understanding. The Department for Schools, Children and Families (DCSF, 2008) identifies that talk should be developed as pupils generate, explore and plan ideas before they write, and during the different stages of the writing process. This includes:

- Teacher talk – The verbalisation of the reader's or writer's thought processes as the teacher is demonstrating, modelling and discussing.
- Supported pupil talk – Structured and scaffolded opportunities for children to develop and practise talk for writing through class and group conversations and activities.
- Independent pupil talk – Opportunities for children to develop and practise talk for writing in pairs and small groups, independent of the teacher (p. 5).

The use of shared and guided writing as teaching strategies offer excellent opportunities to reinforce key aspects of the children's learning within the transcription element of the English curriculum. The teacher can model the application of skills learned in spelling and handwriting at an appropriate time, showing children how to make connections between patterns and rules explored in their discrete sessions.

Adaptive/Responsive Teaching

Considerations could include:

- Making use of resources such as word banks, models of writing, sentence banks and stems, graphic organisers and planning sheets (it is far better to develop these with the children in the context of each piece of writing than simply giving them prepopulated lists of words and so on).
- Making full use of the gradual release of responsibility framework starting with teacher modelling and progressing through shared and guided writing before children write independently.
- Using visual prompts and planning a sequence of learning carefully so that the ideas for a piece of writing are encountered in concrete contexts initially and move in stages towards abstract ones.
- Giving children some choices in their writing. This could be as broad as giving them free reign as to what each would like to write about (see Lynda Graham's excellent *Children's Writing Journals* for ideas to make this as successful part of your practice) to the whole class writing their own stories in which they can choose one or more elements such as characters, plot, settings and so on.

Summary

This chapter has considered an evidence-informed approach to the teaching of writing. A consideration of the place of individual lessons within an overall sequence of learning which builds children's knowledge of texts, readers, language and the writing process has been considered, along with the need for the teacher to provide meaningful and authentic opportunities for writing for a range of specific purposes and audiences. The importance of making connections across the English curriculum more widely, drawing on children's developing proficiency in spelling and handwriting, and developing children's spoken language, and reading skills is emphasised as key to effective practice.

Further Reading

1   Find out more about Young and Ferguson's work on promoting a writing for pleasure philosophy in the classroom along with many excellent examples of classroom practice shared by primary teachers who use this approach at https://writing4pleasure.com/.
2   Read about Bearne and Reedy's planning and teaching sequence in *Teaching Primary English: Subject Knowledge and Classroom Practice*, published by Routledge.
3   Develop your modelling skills by reading Bushnell et al.'s *Modelling Exciting Writing: A guide for primary teaching*, published by Corwin.

References

Barrs, M., & Cork, V. (2001). *The reader in the writer: The links between the study of literature and writing development at Key Stage 2.* CLPE.

Bearne, E., & Reedy, D. (2017). *Teaching primary English.* Routledge.

Breadmore, H., Vardy, E., Cunningham, A., Kwok, R., & Carroll, J. (2019). *Literacy development: Evidence review.* Education Endowment Foundation.

Clements, J., & Tobin, M. (2021). *Understanding and teaching primary English: Theory into practice.* SAGE.

CLPE. (2017). *Writing in primary schools – What we know works.* CLPE.

DCSF. (2008). *Talk for writing.* Crown Publications.

Department for Education. (2013). *The national curriculum in England: Key stages 1 and 2 framework document.* https://www.gov.uk/government/publications/national-curriculum-in-england-primary-curriculum. Accessed on May 16, 2022.

Department for Education. (2021). *Statutory framework for the early years foundation stage.* https://www.gov.uk/government/publications/early-years-foundation-stage-framework–2. Accessed on November 22, 2022.

Dombey, H. (2013). *Teaching writing: What the evidence says.* UKLA.

Graham, J., & Kelly, A. (2010). *Writing under control* (3rd ed.). Routledge.

Grainger, T (2005). Teachers as writers: Learning together. *English in Education, 39*(1), 75–87.

Graves, D. (1994). *A fresh look at writing.* Heinemann.

Hawkins, L. K. (2019). Writing conference purpose and how it positions primary-grade children as authoritative agents or passive observers. *Reading Horizons: A Journal of Literacy and Language Arts, 58*(1).

Ings, R. (2009). *Writing is primary.* Esmee Fairbairn Foundation. www.esmeefairbairn.org.uk/grants_reports.html. Accessed on May 21, 2023.

Myhill, D., Cremin, T., & Oliver, L. (2021). Writing as a craft: Reconsidering teacher subject content knowledge for teaching writing. *Research Papers in Education, 38*(3), 403–425.

Ofsted. (2022). *Curriculum research reviews series: English.* https://www.gov.uk/government/publications/curriculum-research-review-series-english/curriculum-research-review-series-english. Accessed on September 5, 2022.

Osman, R. (2020). *The Thursday Murder Club.* Viking.

Parr, J., & Limbrick, L. (2010). Contextualising practice: Hallmarks of effective teachers of writing. *Teaching and Teacher Education, 26*(3), 583–590.

Slavin, R., Lake, C., Inns, A., Baye, A., Dachet, D., & Haslam, J. (2019). *A quantitative synthesis of research on writing approaches in grades 2 to 12.* Psychology.

UKLA. (n.d.). *UKLA fact cards on teaching writing.* https://ukla.org/ukla_resources/reading-and-writing-fact-cards-professional-development-activities/. Accessed on March 31, 2024.

Waugh, D., & Joliffe, W. (2017). *English 5–11: A guide for teachers.* Routledge.

Wyse, D., Jones, R., Bradford, H., & Wolpert, M. (2018). *Teaching English, language and literacy.* Routledge.

Young, R. (2019). *What is it writing for pleasure teachers do that makes the difference?* The Goldsmiths' Company & The University of Sussex. http://writing4pleasure.com

Young, R., & Ferguson, F. (2021). *Effective writing teaching: What the research says.* writing4pleasure.com. Accessed on August 9, 2023.

Young, R., & Ferguson, F. (2023). *Handbook of research on teaching young writers* (2nd ed.). The Writing for Pleasure Centre.

11

Planning to Teach Grammar

Chapter Objectives

This chapter will:

- Explore the role of grammar within a high-quality writing curriculum.
- Consider what effective pedagogy for teaching grammar might look like.
- Demonstrate one way of approaching the planning of a grammar lesson.

Introduction

The Cambridge English Dictionary defines grammar as 'the study or use of the rules about how words change their form and combine with other words to express meaning'. Grammar is, therefore, the study of how we use language to share meaning with others (Reedy & Bearne, 2013). Just as we aim to develop children's interest in and knowledge of a wide range of vocabulary, we also aim to develop their knowledge of different ways to combine and sequence words in order to express their ideas effectively in a range of situations when using spoken or written language and to understand a text more fully when reading. Grammar is an integral part of the English curriculum; to develop children's language is to develop their ability to engage fully and with increasing skill in speaking, listening, reading and writing.

Activity   Reflecting on Your Knowledge of Grammar

Think about your knowledge of grammar. How does the mention of the word grammar make you feel, and what words do you associate with it?

Write a list of any grammar terms that you know. Can you give an example of how each is used in a sentence?

Curriculum Continuity and Progression

If a child has met the relevant early learning goals for the end of Year R, they will already be proficient in their understanding and use of a number of grammatical forms which have enabled them to listen and respond to what they hear, participate in small group, class and one-to-one discussions, and offer their own ideas and explanations.

Children who have achieved the expected level of development will also be able to use language effectively across the Early Years Foundation Stage curriculum. This will be demonstrated in their ability to follow instructions involving several ideas or actions, explain the reasons for rules, work and play co-operatively, retell stories and narratives in their own words, and write phrases and sentences that can be read by others.

They will also be able to express their ideas and feelings about their experiences using full sentences, including the use of past, present and future tenses and making use of conjunctions, with modelling and support from their teacher. In addition, they will have used language effectively to develop an understanding of the past, be able to describe their environment, be able to explain some similarities and differences between life in their own and other countries and be able to use language to invent, adapt and recount narratives and stories with peers and their teacher.

To achieve all of these expectations, children must have learned to use language effectively. However, links to what we might more consider formally as grammar can be found in the

Communication and Language: Speaking aspect which states that by the end of Year R, pupils achieving the expected level of development should be able to:

> express their ideas and feelings about their experiences using full sentences, including use of past, present and future tenses and making use of conjunctions, with modelling and support from their teacher. (DfE, 2013, p. 11)

Building on this foundation, *The National Curriculum in England: English Programmes of Study for Key Stage 1 and Key Stage 2* identifies specific expectations for pupils in each year group in both the main body of the document and in *Appendix 2*. These outline specific ways in which children's knowledge and understanding of the structure of words (these are linked to the spelling requirements), sentences and texts as they encounter and explore different ways to structure and sequence language to achieve different effects.

Developing Children's Knowledge and Understanding of Sentence Structure

In Year 1, pupils focus on developing their knowledge and understanding of how words combine to form a sentence. This includes an exploration of the use of the conjunction 'and' to join additional words and clauses.

In Year 2, children expand their knowledge and understanding of how to join ideas within a sentence by using a wider range of co-ordinating conjunctions' such as 'but' and 'or', and some subordinating conjunctions, such as 'because' and 'when'. They also learn how to expand noun phrases to develop description, for example, expanding 'the cat' to 'the sleek, black cat', or specification, for example, expanding 'the flour' to 'the plain flour'. Children also learn about four key sentence forms: the statement (I like cats), the question (Do you like cats?), an exclamation (What a beautiful cat that is!) and commands (Go away, Cat.).

In Year 3, children build on the development of the basic sentence by exploring how and where the meaning can be expanded by telling the reader when, where or why something happened. This is developed through the use of:

- Conjunctions (which join or link ideas, e.g., 'James went outside after he had eaten his tea,' or 'James played with his phone because he was bored').
- Adverbs (which give more meaning to a verb, e.g., 'and then he ran' or 'Soon he arrived at the cottage').
- Prepositions (which show the relationship between one thing and another, linking them in time, space, position or distance, e.g., 'she stumbled towards the finish line', or 'they slept under the stars').

In Year 4, children build on their knowledge of how to expand noun phrases starting with a determiner (a word such as a, the, some, any, my or your) that comes before a noun and is used to show which thing is being referred to. They do this by adding adjectives, nouns and preposition phrases, for example, expanding 'the cat' to 'the sleek, black cat with glittering green eyes'. Children also learn about fronted adverbials. An adverbial is a term for a phrase or clause that adds more meaning within a sentence, for example, 'later that day'. An adverbial can usually go in different places within a sentence, for example, 'she left later that day' or 'she left, later that day, taking the cat with her'. However, in a fronted adverbial, the adverbial goes before the main clause, for example, 'later that day, she left'.

In Year 5, the children learn to use relative clauses to drop more information into the sentence. A relative clause is a group of words which contains a verb (that's the clause part) and a relative pronoun such as 'who, which, where, when, whose', or 'that', for example, 'Mr Greedy, who loved to eat, was feeling hungry' or 'The book that I read is on the table'. Sometimes, the relative pronoun is implied but not actually there, for example, 'The book I read is on the table'. In this example, the relative pronoun 'that' has been omitted. Pupils also learn to indicate the possibility or likelihood of something happening through their use of adverbs, such as 'perhaps' or 'surely', or modal verbs. Modal verbs are a particular group of verbs which indicate possibility or likelihood. There are only a few modal verbs: shall, should, can, could, might, may, must, will and would. They work with another verb (and are therefore known as auxiliary or helping verbs), for example, in the sentence 'I might go to the fair', the modal verb 'might' works with the verb 'go' to indicate the level of possibility.

In Year 6, children learn to change the order in which ideas can be presented in a sentence by using the passive voice. Passive voice can be useful when you want to:

- Make the action more of a focus than the agent who performed it ('The dog was followed by the cat').
- Create a detached voice ('The parachutes were dropped from the top of the climbing frame').
- Withhold information about who did the action, perhaps because they are unknown or for dramatic effect ('Jackson was cornered').
- Maintain cohesion ('The children stared with surprise at the strange giant. The giant was distressed by so many eyes upon him').

Children also explore levels of formality in language use, understanding how speech conventions in informal situations differs from the use of speech and writing conventions for formal situations. Examples given include the use of question tags which tag onto the end of a sentence, for example, 'You're coming too, aren't you?' and the use of the subjunctive form of the verb 'to be', for example 'If I were you...'

Developing Children's Knowledge and Understanding of Text Structure

In Year 1, pupils learn to sequence sentences to form short narratives.

In Year 2, children learn to use the present and past tense accurately and consistently within their writing. They also learn to use the progressive aspect of verbs in both the present and past tense, helping them to expand the ways in which they signify actions in their writing. The progressive (also known as the continuous form) generally describes events in progress. It is formed by combining the verb's present participle (e.g., singing) with a form of the verb 'be' (e.g., 'he was singing'), for example, 'Michael is singing in the store' (present progressive) and 'Amanda was making a patchwork quilt' (past progressive). Using these different forms of verbs allows writers to order events in time and reveal interesting details about characters by showing what they do (rather than telling).

In Year 3, children learn to use paragraphs to group related material and to use headings and subheadings to help the presentation of their ideas. They also expand their knowledge of verb aspects by learning to use the perfect form of verbs. The perfect aspect typically describes an event or action that happened or started happening earlier. It is formed by using the auxiliary verb 'to have' in front of the main verb. When using the present perfect form, this involves putting 'I have, you have, he/she has, they have' in front of the main verb ('I have finished eating my tea'), and 'I had, you had, he/she had' when using the past perfect form ('I had finished eating my tea'). As you can see with this second example, these main clauses could well be followed by more information, for example, 'I had finished eating my tea when the doorbell rang'.

In Year 4, pupils further develop their understanding of the use of paragraphs to organise their ideas and learn to use nouns and pronouns (words that stand in the place of nouns such as he, she, it or they) across their sentences to support the text's cohesion. Cohesion is the term which describes how a writer uses vocabulary and grammatical structures to support the connections between the ideas in a text, for example, rather than writing 'The giant had big eyes. The giant wore black boots', the writer can use pronouns to avoid repetition, for example, 'The giant had big eyes. He wore black boots'.

In Year 5, children learn a wider range of cohesive devices to help the reader navigate a text easily, for example, using words and phrases such as 'after that' or 'First' within a paragraph, and linking ideas across paragraphs using adverbials of time (e.g., 'later'), place (e.g., 'nearby') and number (e.g., 'secondly') or drawing on their knowledge of verb tense and aspect (e.g., 'he had seen her before').

In Year 6, children learn more ways to link their ideas across paragraphs using a wider range of cohesive devices such as the repetition of a word or phrase, making grammatical connections through the use of forms such as adverbials, and using ellipsis where the writer intentionally omits one or more words for effect. Children also learn to use a wider range of devices which enhance layouts such as bullet points, tables and columns to structure their texts.

Developing Children's Knowledge and Understanding of Punctuation

To enhance the children's knowledge, understanding and ability to communicate meaning effectively, they also develop their knowledge of punctuation.

In Year 1, pupils learn to separate words with spaces and are introduced to the use of capital letters, full stops, questions and exclamation marks to demarcate sentences. They also learned to use capital letters for names and the personal pronoun I.

In Year 2, pupils learn to use capital letters, full stops, question marks and exclamation marks to demarcate sentences. They also learn to use commas to separate items in a list, and apostrophes to mark where letters are missing in spelling and singular possession in nouns.

In Year 3, pupils are introduced to the use of inverted commas to punctuate direct speech.

In Year 4, pupils learn to use inverted commas and other punctuation to indicate direct speech, apostrophes to mark plural possession, and how to use commas after fronted adverbials.

In Year 5, pupils learn to use brackets, dashes or commas to indicate parenthesis and commas to clarify meaning or avoid ambiguity.

In Year 6, pupils learn the use of the semi-colon, colon and dash to mark the boundary between independent clauses. They also learn to use a colon to introduce a list and use semi-colons within lists. They learn how to punctuate bullet points to list information, and how hyphens can be used to avoid ambiguity.

Curriculum and Pedagogy

Research into the most effective way of teaching grammar shows us unequivocally that embedding learning and teaching within the context of real writing has the most powerful impact on children's knowledge, understanding and ability to use new ideas (Barrs & Cork, 2001; Cremin & Myhill, 2012). The United Kingdom Literacy Association states that 'if grammatical knowledge, spelling and punctuation are to make positive contributions to children's writing, they need to be taught and assessed in the context of writing meaningful texts, not as sets of "facts" or "rules"' (UKLA, n.d.). This is supported in *The National Curriculum in England: English Programmes of Study for Key Stage 1 and Key Stage 2* which states clearly that pupils in each year group should use and understand the relevant grammatical terminology in English *Appendix 2* when discussing their writing. This can be described as a contextualised and descriptive approach in which grammar is explored within the context of authentic high-quality texts, including both professionally published texts and the children's own, rather than a decontextualised, prescriptive approach in which children learn the rules of grammar through isolated exercises.

Research Focus: The University of Exeter's Centre for Research in Writing

Based on research, including a number of studies conducted by the centre's director, Debra Myhill, and her colleagues, the Centre for Research in Writing promotes a pedagogy of 'Grammar as Choice'. This involves the explicit teaching of grammar by exploring how language works in different kinds of writing, and how choices made by authors enable them to communicate meaning effectively. The focus is very much on how writers craft and shape text for particular effects rather than teaching grammar as a set of rules to be learned. The correct terminology is taught, but the overall focus on the writing and its impact is maintained. As a result of their learning about language, the children have a wider range of choices on which to draw as they compose their own texts.

Children need to build grammatical knowledge, knowing what words do and how they work together to communicate meaning within sentences and texts. They also need to develop grammatical skills, supporting their ability to choose and craft words and phrases carefully to construct sentences and compose a range of cohesive texts.

Teaching grammar can be a daunting concept. However, you already have an excellent implicit knowledge of grammar which allows you to communicate effectively using spoken and written language, and to derive meaning from a very wide range of books. The biggest challenge for teachers is usually to extend this excellent implicit knowledge base, making it explicit by recognising how to use grammatical terminology with accuracy and knowing how to articulate this knowledge in the classroom. There are a couple of key concepts which can initially challenge our thinking as we learn grammar. The first concerns word classes.

In your list of the grammar terminology you know, you possibly listed one or more word classes. The term 'word class' refers to the idea that words can be grouped according to what they do in a sentence. The most well-known word classes are possibly: nouns (cat, dog and London), verbs (run, love and be) and adjectives (small, red and smelly). You may also have included any of these: pronouns (I, you and me), prepositions (at, in and under), adverbs (slowly, happily and next), conjunctions (and, but and because) or determiners (a, the and this).

Some words belong to more than one word class. For example, the word pig would belong to the noun word class when it means an animal but to the verb class when it means to eat a lot. So, to determine which word class a specific word belongs to, you have to look at the context in which it appears.

The other key concept which can confuse learners sometimes is the use of the word 'modify' which appears often in texts about grammar, including the National Curriculum. In the context of grammar, modify means to give more meaning to. As children build their knowledge of grammar (language) and how it works, they extend their understanding of how grammatical forms can be used to give more meaning to a particular idea. For example, 'The owl sat on the branch' can be modified by adding adjectives ('the small, feathery owl sat on the branch'), a fronted adverbial ('in the middle of the deep, dark forest, the small, feathery owl sat on a branch') or an adverb ('in the middle of the deep, dark forest, the small, feathery owl sat precariously on a branch').

There are some excellent texts which aim to develop your subject knowledge of grammar; these are identified in the further reading section of this chapter.

Using authentic, high-quality texts in the classroom allows children to explore how experienced writers have chosen and crafted language to create a particular effect, and these can be used models for the children's own explorations, encouraging them to play with new ideas and analyse their impact before making deliberate choices in their own independent writing (Bearne & Reedy, 2017).

Research Focus: Principles of Effective Practice in Teaching Grammar

Reedy and Bearne (2013) highlight the following as principles of highly effective practice in teaching grammar:

- Always link a grammar feature to its effect on writing (in published texts and using a think-aloud strategy when modelling writing).
- Explain terms through examples (build collections).
- Plan high-quality discussions about language and its effects.
- Use authentic examples from authentic texts.
- Use model patterns for children to imitate.
- Support children in designing their writing by making deliberate language choices.
- Encourage language play, experimentation and risk-taking.
- Use working walls to help embed concepts.

Another approach you could try is Young and Ferguson's use of mini-lessons (2021). This approach is also built on a recognition of the importance of function in teaching grammar: children learn best when they learn grammar from and through meaningful, authentic texts which show them how a language form works in action. In this approach, the teacher introduces the grammar focus explicitly and tells the children its purpose. Examples from authentic texts are shared (including the children's own – perhaps from a previous year group, or when the teacher notices that a couple of children are beginning to use it already). The teacher then invites the children to try it out in their next writing lesson. This approach supports the children's autonomy as writers, allowing them to make their own choices about how to craft their writing. This forms part of Young and Ferguson's Writing for Pleasure pedagogy in which the teacher and children together create a community of writers, allowing them to develop a strong sense of agency and enjoyment in their writing.

Through meaningful interactions and their engagement with high-quality texts which they have read, had read to them and discussed, children will already be building their implicit knowledge of how language is formed and used for effect. Reedy and Bearne (2013) propose that effective contextualised teaching and learning of grammar can be taught through a sequence of reading, explicit teaching, discussion and experimentation, and making choices (REDM) as follows:

Reading and Investigating the Language Form

Starting with the children's reading enables them to build on their prior and implicit knowledge of grammar. Using a high-quality text as a starting point, the teacher focuses the children on one or more models of a particular language form from the text. It can be helpful to use sentence strips, lengths of (usually coloured) cards or paper, to write specific examples phrases, clauses or sentences so that children can see them clearly and learn from their structure.

The children's understanding can be extended by investigating whether more examples can be found, for example, by hunting through shared and guided reading texts and the children's own independent reading texts. A collection of examples can be built on a working wall. The children could also undertake a text detective task in which they have a text with some words highlighted for them to discuss and see if they can work out what the words have in common (Corbett & Strong, 2014). Key questions to support the children's understanding at this stage are:

- What examples of this language can we find in our reading?
- Where does it occur in the story/sentence?
- What effect does it have on the reader?

Explicit Teaching

When children's implicit knowledge is activated, and they are using this to recognise examples of the grammatical form in use, explicit teaching, which names the grammatical form and explains what it is is helpful. This enables children to begin to learn the correct terminology and extend their understanding of when and why to use it. Key questions to support the children's understanding at this stage are:

- What is this language form called?
- What effect does it have on the reader?
- Where does it come in a sentence?
- How is it constructed?

Definitions, preferably written in your own words so they are easy to understand, and annotations can be made to the working wall, and the children might at this stage engage with activities that help them to spot it. For example, when working on adverbs of probability, we might explicit identify the following:

Definition: Some adverbs enable us to communicate the possibility that an event might happen. We use adverbs of probability to show how certain we are about something.

Our collection includes:

rarely, occasionally, possibly, probably, certainly, definitely, unquestionably, absolutely, perhaps, maybe, undoubtedly

'Maybe' and 'perhaps' usually come at the beginning of the clause:

> Perhaps the weather will be fine.
> Maybe it won't rain.

Other adverbs of possibility usually come in front of the main verb:

> He is certainly enjoying the party.
> We will possibly visit England next year.

but after 'am', 'is', 'are', 'was', 'were':

> They are definitely at home.
> She was obviously very surprised.

Discussion and Experimentation

In the third stage, the teacher models how to construct the form in demonstrated writing, gradually releasing the responsibility to the children through shared and supported writing. Then, children have a go at constructing their own examples, perhaps working in pairs or small groups at first. A key part of this process is to evaluate the effect on the reader – children can do this by sharing their examples with each other and responding to each other's attempts. It will be helpful if this is modelled by the teacher too so that the children know what makes a constructive and helpful response. The children could link this to their prior learning by trying out examples in different genres. Useful questions at this stage are:

- How could we have a go at doing this using our own ideas/context for writing?
- What impact do our creations have on a reader?
- What else could we try?

Making Controlled Choices in Independent Writing

The final step is to support the children to apply this learning within their own writing, thus demonstrating their ability to make controlled writing choices. Depending on the children's confidence levels, they may remember to use this form when drafting. However, as discussed in the previous chapter, cognitive demand is heavy in any writing task. This can be supported by:

- Getting the children to annotate their planning in advance with words/phrases that use the new form.
- Focusing on it during one of the revision stages of the writing process, looking specifically to see where it could be included for best effect.
- Asking children to work with response partners to identify and/or have a go at including it.

Key questions to use in this stage include:

- How could you include this idea in your current piece of writing?
- Did you do it?
- Would you want to improve/change it?
- What effect do you think it will have on your reader?
- Did it have the effect you intended?

Developing a Sequence of Learning

Here is one example of how a sequence of learning can be planned using the REDM model outlined above. This example expands the idea of how a teacher could teach Year 5 children how to indicate degrees of possibility using adverbs (e.g., 'perhaps', 'surely') or modal verbs (e.g., 'might', 'should', 'will', 'must').

Reading and Investigation

Work with the children to create a scale of language to indicate the level of possibility that any event will happen (you could create this visually using a washing line). Words such as 'definitely, certainly, clearly, obviously, possibly, perhaps, probably' and 'maybe' should be helpful. You could use real events or events from stories/films and/or link this to relevant maths work. You could also share some models from real high-quality texts with the children. Here are two examples, the first is from a narrative text, *The Kraken*, written by Gary Crew and Illustrated by Marc McBride.

'Find your sight? That's silly,' she sneered. 'I hate it when you're silly.'

'You could come with me…' he coaxed.

'Come with you? How could we?'

'I could make a boat.'

'A boat? That's even sillier'

'You're the one who told me that I could make whatever I wanted,' he reminded her. 'I could imagine a boat that could sail…sail *and* fly. Then we could go.'

'Really? And what would this boat be made of?'

'A pearl shell. Its lower half would be the boat, its upper half the sail. And in our shell would be pearls. Giant pillows that we could lean against, with the salty sea wind in our hair'.

This second one is from a non-narrative text, *The Oceanology Handbook: A Course for Underwater Explorers*, written by Clint Twist.

> Although ships are a fairly safe means of transport, it would be foolish to ignore the perils of ocean travel. As well as the hazard of treacherous rocks that could dash a ship to splinters, the greatest danger is that a huge wave might roll across the ocean surface, swamping the ship with water and dragging it down, along with its crew, to a final resting place on the seabed. The ship's hull may appear strong, but it is easily damaged, especially if burrowing sea worms have weakened its timbers. Submerged rocks and coral reefs, floating icebergs, or even collisions with other vessels can break through a hull and let the sea water flood in. If the damage is not too grave, the crew may have time to escape in lifeboats, although their chances of being picked up by another vessel are quite slim.

Read the text aloud to the children or get them to read it for themselves. Linger on the richest parts of the text, asking children to discuss the author's use of language and what impact this has on the reader. Encourage the children to read key passages aloud to hear how they sound.

Explicit Teaching

The National Curriculum tells us that modal verbs are used to modify (give more meaning to) the meaning of other verbs. They can express meanings such as certainty, ability or obligation. The main modal verbs are 'will', 'would', 'can', 'could', 'may', 'might', 'shall', 'should', 'must' and 'ought'.

Examples From the National Curriculum

- 'I can do this maths work by myself'.
- 'This ride may be too scary for you!'
- 'You should help your little brother'.
- 'Is it going to rain? Yes, it might'.

These inform the reader of the likelihood of something and can reveal interesting insights into characters or to add a sense of danger, prompting the reader to speculate on events that may unfold.

Discussion and Experimentation

Ask the children to explore the effect of the examples you have gathered. What difference do the modal verbs make?

You could explore the inner lives of some characters through drama work, exploring what they might, could or should do. The use of conscience alley might be good here (a useful technique for exploring any kind of dilemma faced by a character, providing an opportunity to analyse a decisive moment in greater detail). The class forms two lines facing each other. One person (the teacher or a participant) walks between the lines as each person in the line shares their advice. For non-narrative writing, the children could work in small groups as news reporters, presenting a breaking story on a disaster that might unfold in different ways.

The teacher should then model how to use these ideas in a piece of writing before gradually releasing responsibility to the children. They could then work in groups to write letters in role to another character, exploring the character's options in relation to a dilemma they're facing, or in the case of non-narrative writing, the children could compose a collaborative text using the *Oceanology* text as a model. Collaborative writing offers good opportunities for assessment so that the teacher can listen in and see which groups are confident in the use of the style (taking careful note of whether small group members are equally involved and demonstrating similar levels of knowledge and confidence). Once the children are confidently applying their knowledge in writing, they can move to independent writing. Further reading, discussion and experimentation will be needed for any that are not.

Making Controlled Writing Choices

In this stage of the sequence, the children apply these ideas independently in their own writing. To achieve this, they will need a carefully designed task which offers the opportunity to do this. This should reflect one or more of the models explored, for example, extending a scene within a story to reveal more about the inner thoughts of the characters as in *The Kraken* example or as the author to introduce some tension ('Would James be brave enough? Could he really find the courage to tiptoe through the dark and silent house, go through the door and into the forest beyond?').

In subsequent learning, you will need to look for opportunities to model the use of this idea when possible so that pupils remember it, continuing to show them how to apply it in different pieces of writing and inviting them to try it out in their own pieces.

To support cognitive load, it can be helpful to get children to annotate their planning with specific examples they could use in the planning stages of their writing, or to give it a specific focus time when revising their work. By making it a focus of peer and self-assessment, you will support the expectation that pupils should be taught to:

- Develop their understanding of the concepts set out in *Appendix 2* by:
  - Using modal verbs or adverbs to indicate degrees of possibility.
  - Learning the grammar for years 5 and 6 in *Appendix 2*.

- Use and understand the grammatical terminology in *Appendix 2* accurately and appropriately in discussing their writing and reading. (DfE, 2013, p. 38)

> **Activity   Building Your Knowledge of Texts**
>
> Using *The National Curriculum in England: English Programmes of Study for Key Stage 1 and Key Stage 2 Appendix 2*, look at the expectations. This could be just for the year group(s) you are currently working with, or could be more general if you are not currently on a school placement. Reflect on your knowledge of high-quality narrative and non-narrative texts to see if you can create a list of great texts which you could use to teach each of the terms or ideas. Decide how you could build your knowledge of any gaps. You could do an internet search for recommendations but nothing beats knowing a wide range of high-quality literature yourself. Teachers are also likely to be an excellent source of knowledge so ask those you know and see if any networks you belong to can help.

Throughout any sequence of learning, it is really important to plan lots of opportunities for pupils to discuss their thinking. As Burrows says:

> We learn far more from what we discuss and do rather than what we just hear and see – children need to be engaged in their own learning and not be passive recipients. . . . The importance of talk in developing children's grammar cannot be underestimated. (2014, p. 19)

This can be achieved by planning activities which allow children to discuss the effect of language forms within texts, collaborate to find and discuss examples of language forms in authentic texts, explain what a particular term means, experiment with new language forms in paired and small group writing, and work with a response partner to identify and analyse the effect of language forms in their own writing.

Lesson Plan

Here is a suggestion for a lesson plan for a Year 2 class (Table 11.1).

Relevant Prior Learning: The children are familiar with all the terminology from *The National Curriculum in England: English Programmes of Study for Key Stage 1 and Key Stage 2* shown in *Appendix 2*. From their learning in Year 2 so far, they know what a verb is and have been using this term confidently. They have spent some time working on making the correct choice and consistent use of present tense and past tense throughout their writing.

The children have been reading *Traction Man is Here!* by Mini Grey. They have heard the teacher read the story aloud several times, and have discussed their responses to it in small groups.

What will children learn: To use the progressive form of verbs in the present tense to mark actions in progress.

Planned next steps: The children could create a cartoon storyboard for their own story in which a toy has an adventure. They should annotate their pictures with sentences which use the present progressive aspect.

It would also be helpful to find other texts where this verb aspect is used so that the children can see how to incorporate it into different styles of writing. When you find examples, take some time to explore these and give the children opportunities to write their own sentences using this form in the different writing styles. It may be helpful to link this to some non-fiction information writing.

What will effective learning look like?: Children will be able to give an example of a sentence that uses the present progressive form of a verb.

How will learning be assessed (and what are the opportunities for effective feedback?):

- Observe pupils' writing to check they understand.
- Ask pupils to explain their understanding.

Table 11.1   A lesson plan for teaching grammar

Today's lesson sequence/content
SPECIFIC RESOURCES NEEDED: *Traction Man is Here!* (a version which all the children can see or follow), blank sentence cards/strips for writing on, clipboards, paper and pencils.
10:45: Read the first two pages of the story. Stop and ask the children what is happening so far. Write down each action on a different sentence strip, e.g., • Traction Man is zooming down. • Traction Man jumps on the pillows. • He is wearing his Rocket Boots. Ask the children to look at the cards carefully. Can the children see that even though the author is telling us what is happening each time, she has written her sentences in two different ways? Draw attention to the differences between the two verb forms and underline all the verbs in each sentence.
10:55: Ask the children to stand up and follow your instructions. Ask them to imagine they are Traction Man and they jump on the pillows. Now ask them to imagine they are jumping on the pillows. How are they different? In the pictures, we can see that Traction Man jumps once and lands in his rocket. The author has written the verbs in different ways so that the reader knows which actions happened only once, and which actions lasted longer. Check this with the other examples you have gathered, e.g., 'Yes, the author used "is zooming" to show this happened for a little while and "is wearing" because he has his boots on the whole time'. Write 'Traction Man is jumping on the pillows' on another card and play a quick game where

(Continued)

Table 11.1 A lesson plan for teaching grammar

Today's lesson sequence/content
when you show 'Traction Man jumps on the pillows' the children jump once, and when you show 'Traction Man is jumping on the pillows' they keep jumping.
11:05: Read on together and see if you can find any more examples where the author has written any verbs using 'is' and an 'ing' ending. Write them on cards to add to the display. Each time, ask the children to perform the action when they see the verb form.
11:10: Take the children to the hall or the playground (you could of course do a quieter version of this next activity in any school space). Half the children are going to be active while the others take a clipboard and some paper and write down what they see happening (e.g., Megan is skipping). The children could work in pairs to spot the actions and write about them. When the children have written a certain number (e.g., three each), get them to swap roles so that those who were being active are now writing and vice versa.
11:20: Come back to the classroom and display the sentences. Tell the children the correct name for using verbs in this way – the present progressive. Add this to the display. Ask the children what would happen if two people were performing an action – how would we write that? Ask two children to secretly agree on an action to perform and then do so in front of the class. Ask the children to tell their partner what is happening. Write an example and add this to the display.
Ask the children to keep a look out in their independent reading books over the next few days and to add any sentences they find to the display.

Adaptive/Responsive Teaching

Considerations could include:

- The use of preteaching so that less confident pupils are really familiar with the text.
- Giving some children more time to sort sentences either before, during or after the lesson. You might prepare more sentence strips for this activity.
- Making use of first-hand (concrete) experiences prior to the lesson, as an alternative to one of the later activities, or after the lesson. For example, you could ask an adult to work with a small group performing their own actions ('Libby is climbing up the ladder') and recording their sentences (perhaps taking a photo of actions to accompany these and aid recall). Some children might benefit from rehearsing the key verbs to be used in the lesson (e.g., jumping, etc.) beforehand – this could be in the form of a game with the verbs on cards that they respond to so that they understand these words quickly in the main lesson.
- Extending any children's learning by exploring a wider range of verb forms from the book, or drawing on sentences from other texts as a comparison. Some children may also develop their ideas into short adventures by composing a series of sentences and taking photos to make a double-sided spread.
- Making use of any teaching support – would any children benefit from close working with an adult (this could be you while a teaching assistant works with the rest of the class) to scaffold the learning dialogue?

- Making sure that all the resources are a good size for the children to work with, for example, that they can grip pens or pencils easily, see the marks they make, have tables to write at if that is better for them, and have appropriately sized/coloured paper.

Summary

This chapter has considered what research tells us about how to teach grammar effectively. The importance of using authentic high-quality texts is established. Pupils should have opportunities to read, discuss and play with language, trying out different ways of putting words together in different styles of writing.

Further Reading

1   For many more practical ideas on ways of teaching grammar, read Reedy and Bearne's *Teaching Grammar Effectively in Primary Schools*, published by the UKLA.
2   For more on Myhill and her colleagues' approach, visit The Centre for Research in Writing at: https://education.exeter.ac.uk/research/centres/writing/grammar-teacher-resources/ grammaraschoice/thegrammarforwritingpedagogy/
3   For clear definitions and examples of all the terminology that must be taught in the primary phase, read the Oxford Primary Grammar, Punctuation and Spelling Dictionary published by the Oxford University Press, or use their free glossary which starts at: https://home.oxfordowl.co.uk/at-school/education-glossary/grammar-literacy-glossary-a-c/

References

Barrs, M., & Cork, V. (2001). *The reader in the writer: The links between the study of literature and writing development at Key Stage 2*. CLPE.

Bearne, E., & Reedy, D. (2017). *Teaching primary English*. Routledge.

Burrows, P. (2014). *A creative approach to teaching grammar*. Bloomsbury Education.

Corbett, P., & Strong, J. (2014). *Jumpstart! Grammar: Games and activities for ages 6–14*. Routledge.

Cremin, T., & Myhill, D. (2012). *Writing voices: Creating communities of writers*. Routledge.

Department For Education. (2013). *The National Curriculum for England: Key stages 1 and 2 framework document*. Crown Publishing.

Reedy, D., & Bearne, E. (2013). *Teaching grammar effectively in primary schools*. UKLA.

UKLA Viewpoints: Grammar. (n.d.). https://ukla.org/wp-content/uploads/View_Grammar.pdf. Accessed on May 10, 2023.

Young, R., & Ferguson, F. (2021). *The writing for pleasure centre's grammar mini-lessons* (3rd ed.). https://writing4pleasure.com/the-writing-for-pleasure-centres-grammar-mini-lessons/. Accessed on February 10, 2023.

12

Planning to Teach Narrative Fiction Writing

Chapter Objectives

This chapter will:

- Identify the key elements of a high-quality writing curriculum, focusing on the composition of narrative fiction.
- Consider what effective pedagogy for teaching composition of narrative fiction might look like.
- Demonstrate ways in which you could plan lessons at different stages of the composition process.

Introduction

As established in Chapter 10, individual writing lessons form part of a sequence designed to build children's knowledge and understanding of writing and the writing process through meaningful contexts in which they compose authentic texts. This provides purposeful practice opportunities for children to steadily acquire the knowledge and skills they need to develop effectively as writers. Before you read this chapter, it is recommended that you read Chapter 10 if you have not already done so as this provides essential background knowledge that will help you to understand key elements of effective practice in the teaching of writing.

Curriculum Continuity and Progression

The majority of the end-of-year expectations outlined for each year group in the writing strand of the National Curriculum relate to writing in general, rather than identifying specific genres. However, there are just a few expectations which are specific to narrative fiction writing. While the term 'fiction' is commonly used to talk about writing, the National Curriculum uses the term 'narrative' which means a spoken or written account of events such as a story.

- In Year 1, pupils will learn to sequence sentences to form short narratives.
- In Year 2, pupils will learn to write narratives about personal experiences and those of others (real and fictional).
- In Years 3 and 4, pupils will learn to create settings, characters and plots.
- In Years 5 and 6, pupils will learn to consider how authors have developed characters and settings and to describe settings, characters and atmosphere, integrating dialogue to convey character and advance the action. (DfE, 2013)

Curriculum and Pedagogy for Narrative Fiction Writing

Effective sequences of learning both build and build on the knowledge of texts and of language that children acquire through their reading, spoken language, and vocabulary and grammar learning. As established in Chapter 10, effective sequences involve the following elements:

1 **Reading to build children's knowledge of a text type**

   NC Objectives (any of the following may be considered, depending on the high-quality text chosen as the context for learning):
   - identifying themes and conventions in a wide range of books
   - discussing words and phrases that capture the reader's interest and imagination
   - checking that the text makes sense to them, discussing their understanding and explaining the meaning of words in context
   - asking questions to improve their understanding of a text

- drawing inferences such as inferring characters' feelings, thoughts and motives from their actions and justifying inferences with evidence
- predicting what might happen from details stated and implied.

NB: This will typically take place through the use of teacher read-alouds and reading-teaching sessions. It is important to think carefully about when these lessons need to take place so that children are ready for the next part of the sequence, but they may be taught alongside other ideas such as exploring the author's use of language and structure and/or generating ideas for their own writing.

2   **Understanding the writing process**.

NB: Note that this crucial aspect of the teaching of writing does not have its own learning objectives but will be developed through the use of the shared and guided writing teaching strategies which support the children's learning of the specified learning objectives. Shared writing strategies are identified at various points in the sample lesson plans which follow. Look for opportunities to find out how published children's authors go about the process of writing. There are a number of good websites that you and your class can engage with which will prompt good discussions about writing.

3   **Exploring the language and structure of texts**

NC Objectives:
- Generate ideas for the content and structure of their own writing – plan their writing by discussing writing similar to what they are planning to write in order to understand and learn from its structure, vocabulary and grammar
- discussing and recording ideas.

NB: Aspects of the author's language use will be chosen as the focus for the teaching of vocabulary and grammar. One or more aspects of punctuation may also be chosen for explicit exploration. See Chapter 11 for practical ideas.

4   **Drafting their own writing**

NC Objectives:
- Composing and rehearsing sentences orally (including dialogue), progressively building a varied and rich vocabulary and an increasing range of sentence structures (*Appendix 2*)
- organising paragraphs around a theme
- in narratives, creating settings, characters and plot.

NB: You may wish to use short parts of the children's writing lessons to revisit some key ideas explored earlier in the sequence, but writing lesson time will typically be focused on the children drafting their own writing. You might choose to plan short inputs in response to your set of formative assessment strategies which identify aspects of the writing task which a number of pupils are finding challenging, for example, if you have previously explored the use of fronted adverbials to establish place and time to the reader in your linked grammar sessions but have identified that children are not yet making effective use of this idea in the context of the writing task.

5   **Revising their writing**

NC Objective: Evaluate and edit by assessing the effectiveness of their own and others' writing and suggesting improvements.
NB: You could plan short plenaries which allow children to reconsider one key idea (e.g., describing the setting effectively or using fronted adverbials to establish place or time for the reader) as a focus for revising their writing with a partner, or you may choose to give time for this once children have finished their first drafts.

6   **Editing and proofreading their writing**

NC Objectives:
- Proposing changes to grammar and vocabulary to improve consistency, including the accurate use of pronouns in sentences
- proofread for spelling and punctuation errors.

NB: Again, you may choose to build editing time into the end of each session for this or to spend more time later on (or both). Talk to the class teacher and see if there are already routines in place which you can build on.

7   **Sharing their writing with an audience**

NC Objective: Read-aloud their own writing, to a group or the whole class, using appropriate intonation and controlling the tone and volume so that the meaning is clear.
NB: Ensure you make time for this as it is a key skill for children to learn which will support their development as readers and writers. Some possible audiences include another class (of the same age, younger or older pupils), parents, members of the school community such as governors, the wider public (e.g., through the school's website), education teams based on places that support school trips and visits, and relevant members of society such as the local MP or councillors and celebrities (who sometimes even respond!).

The most effective sequences of learning are often based around one or more excellent models of published writing, typically referred to as high-quality or model texts. Through rich engagement with such models, children consolidate their previous knowledge and encounter new ideas, enriching their understanding of how language can be crafted to communicate meaning with increasing precision and flair.

Activity Choosing a High-Quality Text for Narrative Fiction Writing

This activity can be carried out with any text you have read. Gamble (2022) notes that she reads a new children's book to herself several times, using her re-readings to reflect in more depth on the language, design and pictures to see how these have been crafted and to identify the most powerful spaces where children can be invited to respond to the story.

As you re-read the text, consider the following questions (based on Wilson & Scanlon, 2011):

- What kind of text is it? Does it have a classic story structure? Does it begin in a typical way by introducing one or more of the main characters? Where and when is it set? Is it a story in which any of the characters have magical powers or in which animals have anthropomorphic (human-like) abilities?
- What is the narrative perspective? Is it narrated in the first, second or third person? Is this perspective consistent or does it move between one or more characters? Does the writer ever address the reader directly and if so, how? Does the author make use of asides to the reader at any point?
- What is the plot structure? Is the story told chronologically? Does it story use one of Booker's (2004) seven plots (e.g., is it a quest story or a rags to riches tale?)
- How are the characters portrayed? How are they described? How does the author use dialogue or action to show the reader more about the characters?
- How is the language used? Do the characters always speak in full sentences, or just partial ones? Does the author always write in full sentences? Does the author present text in different ways, for example, through the use of italics, bold or capital letters? Are there places where the language seems to be presented differently? Has the author used figurative language, words or phrases that convey meaning but are not literally true, like idioms, metaphors, similes, hyperbole or personification?
- How is punctuation used? Is additional information demarcated by the use of brackets, dashes or commas? Does the author use ellipsis? How are speech marks presented? Are exclamation marks used to emphasise particular emotions such as surprise or fear?
- How are pictures used? Do they tell any parts of the story?

Reading to Build Children's Knowledge of Narrative Fiction

Familiarity with the text or text type through reading and investigation allows pupils to develop their knowledge of texts. Through reading examples of the kinds of narrative fiction texts they will write, children develop their knowledge and understanding of story structure and language, and the specific elements of the creation of plot, setting and character.

Through children's engagement with stories that they hear, read and retell, they begin to uncover the concept of story structure. In the classroom, story structure often follows a five-step chronological model which Corbett (2013, p. 5) describes as:

> the simplest plot pattern is the story mountain's 'problem/resolution'. In this plot, it is typical to begin with everything ok. We meet a character who is doing something enjoyable. Then a problem happens. This is eventually overcome and the tale ends with everything fine again – though perhaps the main character is a little wiser or stronger.

Corbett identifies the five stages as:

- The beginning which introduces the characters.
- The build-up where the story gets going.
- The problem where something goes wrong.
- The resolution where the problem is resolved.
- The ending where everything is peaceful once more.

Of course not all stories follow this structure. As children become exposed to a wider range of stories, they will also encounter a wide range of structures such as those which use flashbacks or flashforwards. The same five-step structure may be used in different types of plot, for example, one which involves a quest or journey for the main character, or a rebirth in which the main character changes their ways and becomes quite a different sort of person. Many stories for younger children follow this clear five-step structure. Its simplicity and familiarity for both reader and writer make it a useful tool to support success in the earlier stages of storytelling and writing.

Familiarity with the text and text type also supports children's understanding of language. Through exposure to high-quality fiction, children will uncover ways that different authors use language to create interesting characters, describe settings and move the story on. Initially, this understanding is implicit, developed through children's experience with such texts through which they build a sense of how such stories are written.

When developing children's familiarity with texts or text types, it is important to allow time for them to engage fully with the text(s) story or stories before moving on too quickly to the next part of the sequence. It is useful to design high-quality activities which support children to develop a deeper comprehension of the text, aiming to support their development as readers and begin to prepare for writing through the use of open-ended discussion questions which support rich exchanges between pupils as they share their responses. Corbett (2008) suggests that:

> for the text to be well and truly internalised, the children must 'loiter' with it for some time – rereading, dramatising, discussing, focusing on aspects until the text has entered the long-term working memory – until they almost 'own' the text because they are so familiar with it. (p. 2)

There may be specific elements of the story that you want children to focus on, for example, the presentation of a character. Again, rich responses can be developed through high-quality comprehension activities such as asking children to plot a character's emotions at different points in the story as a graph or engage in some drama work involving the creation of freeze frames from different points in the story. You may also want children to learn to retell a story, or key part of it, allowing them to absorb and internalise key story language which becomes a rich resource for their later writing. As the Department for Schools, Children and Families (DCSF) noted in a publication on the impact of embedding high-quality talk opportunities within the writing sequence:

> the learning and development of stories through oral retelling builds up in children enormously valuable banks of language and narrative patterning that can be incorporated into later writing. (2008, p. 7)

The use of engaging, interactive resources such as masks, props, story maps and story strings can all aid retelling and will support children to internalise both the structure and language of stories.

Exploring the Language and Structure of Narrative Fiction

The next stage of the sequence is a phase of capturing ideas. This begins to move children from thinking as a reader to thinking as a writer, building on the children's implicit learning to explicitly consider the model text as a writer and enabling children to begin to gather ideas for use in their own writing.

There is the potential for the teacher to be creative in the use of teaching strategies here, for example, by providing opportunities for children to engage in story-making activities, using resources such as masks, props, drama and drawing to imagine a new story.

Bearne and Reedy (2017) note that to make good progress in narrative writing, children must develop their sense of themselves as a writer, increasing their understanding of how to shape texts to suit their intentions, how to engage and hold a reader's attention, how to become more skilled in choosing the language to create particular effects, and how to handle the conventions of different kinds of narrative. In this part of the learning sequence, children usually revisit the model text to focus on the author's craft with the aim of learning new ways of structuring their own writing or expressing their ideas. This may be termed as 'reading like a writer'. Corbett (2008) asserts that reading as a writer prompts children to develop a writer's eye and writer's curiosity, building their knowledge of how a writer has crafted language for a particular effect. Readers begin to look more carefully at the text's structure or the writer's choice of words, phrases or sentence structures, noticing what the author has done and what impact it has on the reader. Cohesion, how the text hangs together, can also be explored through reading as a writer, noticing how the author uses words and phrases such as 'suddenly' or 'Later that day' to help the reader understand the chronology of the text. Corbett (2008) also suggests that pacing can be explored through this approach, useful for writers who move too quickly through the action and specific objectives such as the Year 5/6 use of dialogue to convey character can be addressed. It is important to choose carefully which elements of a model text will be studied. Exploring too many elements is likely to overwhelm children, so focusing on a couple of things and taking time to explore these in some depth is usually most effective for developing writers.

The second part of capturing ideas enables children to generate ideas for their own writing. In their study of Year 5 pupils, Barrs and Cork (2001) concluded that indirect planning, involving activities which encouraged children to explore and think about ideas they might use in their own writing, prepared children for writing more effectively than planning with a writing frame or model. It is, therefore, helpful to think about capturing ideas as a form of planning. This accords with Clements and Tobin's view that 'in its broadest sense the planning phase is about furnishing children with ideas and giving them something to write about' (p. 210). Indirect planning can involve children's engagement with visits and visitors, with first-hand experiences, with texts and films, and with drama and drawing. All of these can help children to formulate ideas for their own writing. Drama, and in particular, writing in role as a precursor to writing, has been noted by both Cremin (2006) and Barrs and Cork (2001) as being especially beneficial, enabling children to write with more depth and in more detail.

The remaining stages of the writing sequence are the drafting stage, the revision stage, the editing and proofreading stage, and the sharing stage.

Lesson Plans

Here are suggestions for two different lessons within one sequence of learning (or unit of work) for a narrative fiction text (Table 12.1 and Table 12.2). It is important to note that the different elements of the sequence may be ordered differently and/or revisited. This may well depend on the opportunities presented by the choice of high-quality model text itself, and it is important that teachers plan sequences of learning carefully so that they unfold logically to meet the needs of the learners. When choosing your own text, you might it helpful to revisit the ideas presented in Chapter 10.

Planning a Context for Writing

High-quality text: *The Snow Dragon* by Vivian French.

Purpose and audience: Write an entertaining story about Fire Dragons to be shared with other pupils in the class library or with younger pupils to be read to them during story time. It is worth taking time to think about the audience and discuss what children think the agreed audience will want from the story. Of course, the audience could be asked in advance to share what they would like from the story, and these ideas could then be displayed for reference in the classroom.

In this chapter, I have presented the lesson plans as chunks of learning to correspond with different stages of the sequence of learning rather than as individual lessons. When you are planning your own lessons, you will want to make sure your lesson fits the time span you have agreed with your class teacher, so that good time is given to each part of the lesson. Therefore, each chunk of learning may be broken down further as it is organised to fit a specific timetable.

Lesson Plan 1: Exploring the Language and Structure of Texts and Generating Ideas for Their Own Writing

Relevant prior learning: Prior to the lesson, children have shared *The Snow Dragon* by Vivian French through a teacher read-aloud. This was developed over several days with the teacher using a variety of engaging teaching strategies through guided reading sessions to develop the children's comprehension of the story.

The pupils have worked in small groups to create a timeline of key events in the story.

Key vocabulary was identified and discussed with children.

What will children learn:

- To discuss writing similar to that which they are planning to write in order to understand and learn from its structure, vocabulary and grammar.

Planned next steps: For children to try out some of the ideas in their own writing (this will need to be modelled in one or more future sessions and children encouraged to have a go)

What will effective learning look like:
Children will be able to:

- Explain that *The Snow Dragon* is told in a chronological order.
- Explain some ways in which the author uses language to create an impact on the reader.
- Identify at least one idea they are going to try out in their own writing.

How will learning be assessed:

- Listening in to children's discussions to gauge their understanding.
- Use feedback questions to check children understand where they are going and how they are going.
- Observe children's flip chart sheets to see what they have noticed about the author's craft.

Table 12.1 A lesson plan for teaching writing composition

Today's lesson sequence/content
SPECIFIC RESOURCES NEEDED: Flip Chart paper, pens, copies of *The Snow Dragon*, at least one per group
10.45: Tell children that as we have been enjoying reading the story of *The Snow Dragon*, today we are going to read like writers to investigate how the author has managed to tell the story so well. Share the learning objective with children.
10.47: Look at some of the timelines that children created in small groups during their reading sessions, recapping the key events in the story. Using flip chart paper, write one key event at the top of each and display chronologically across a working wall washing line or similar – explicitly note the chronological structure of the story as each is added.
11.05: Ask them to discuss whether they think about the events in the story and what the author did to tell the story so well. Share their thoughts, value their ideas and reinforce any connections made to other learning (e.g., the use of reasoning phrases developed through spoken language learning or giving examples from the text to connect to their reading learning).
11.10: Look at one event together, for example, the First Happening. Ask children to discuss what the author wanted to say in this part of the story, and how they felt after reading this part. What did authors do to make sure readers understand what has happened in the past, and how they made sure that readers had a really clear picture in their mind. Scribe some notes, for example identifying the use of words and phrases which were particularly descriptive or helped the reader to picture the scene clearly. They may also note that the author uses language to show what a character is like – for example, the character of a book.
11.15: Organise small groups to take one event (flip chart sheet) and use the text to answer the questions (display the questions on the board):   • What did the author do to make sure the reader understands what has happened?   • How does the author make sure the reader has a really clear picture in his or her mind?   • Is there anything else the author does well?
11.25: Mid-lesson plenary – revisit the key questions and ask children to check they are on track. Could share some good examples noted through circulating around the class.
11.40: Children bring their flip chart sheets back to display. Look at them all together and draw out interesting points.
Returning to the learning objective, ask children to think in pairs about what we have learned from the structure, vocabulary and language of *The Snow Dragon* that might help us with our own writing (could create a list of ideas for later reference).

To extend the children's knowledge of this genre further, you may want to explore a wider range of texts to broaden and deepen the children's understanding. For example, in *The Snow Dragon* by Vivian French, the story starts in an unusual way. The children could discuss this and think about other stories they have read. They could look at the opening of one or more other stories, for example, *The Snow Dragon* by Abi Elphinstone, *The Ice Palace* by Robert Swindells or *Pugs of the Frozen North* by Philip Reeve and Sarah McIntyre, to compare how these have been written, thus building their knowledge of ways in which a story opening might be crafted.

There are a number of language features used effectively in *The Snow Dragon* by Vivian French, including the use of fronted adverbials which help to orientate the reader's sense of time and place, although these are not always demarcated with a comma. This is one possible choice of a grammar focus within this sequence of learning (unit of work) and could, therefore, be used as a basis for planning to teach grammar (such lessons are explored in Chapter 11).

Lesson Plan 2: Planning Narrative Fiction

Relevant prior learning: Children have developed good comprehension of *The Snow Dragon* and read the text like writers in order to learn from its structure, vocabulary and grammar. Children have previously used story mountains to plan their stories, so they are very familiar with the concept (if this is not the case, I might plan a series of 10–15 minute sessions where I take each part in turn so that children aren't sitting listening for too long – this could be over one or two days or over a week and could have been done alongside their prior reading of the story).

What will children learn:

- To plan their writing by discussing and recording ideas.

Planned next steps: For children to develop these ideas in their writing

What will effective learning look like:
Children will be able to:

- Explain their story mountain.
- Talk about their plans for how their writing will start, develop and conclude.

How will learning be assessed? (and what are the opportunities for effective feedback?)

- Listening in to children's discussions and ideas to gauge their understanding – are they warmed up to the planning process and do they have ideas which develop logically?
- Observe how successful they are in recording their ideas, i.e., are they using note form and/or recording their ideas clearly?

Table 12.2 A lesson plan for teaching a different stage of the composition process

---

Today's lesson sequence/content

SPECIFIC RESOURCES NEEDED: Flip chart paper and pens for shared writing

1:00: Share the learning objective with children, reminding them briefly of the sequence of learning so far. Now share this with children: At the start of *The Snow Dragon*, it is thought that no Snow Dragons are alive but this is wrong. At the end of *The Snow Dragon*, it is thought that there are no Fire Dragons left. What if this is also wrong?

Ask the class to work in pairs to discuss what might happen if there was just one Fire Dragon left alive.

1:10: Act as a scribe (shared writing strategy) for the pupils, composing a list of possible plot ideas which is left up for display (could focus on just quest-type stories (i.e., the plot of *The Snow Dragon*) to help them, e.g., there's just one Fire Dragon and he doesn't have a home – where might he have to go so he can find a place to be happy?). Children may have more good ideas over the next few days, and so it might be good to let them add to it over the week (I might be tempted to do this part of the lesson in a short space earlier in the week before what follows, or on a Friday ready for Monday morning).

1:20: Demonstrate (shared writing strategy) how a writer might look at the list and make decisions about choosing one of the ideas to develop, explaining what you are thinking and why you have chosen the one you have. Show children how to use a story mountain framework to identify the five key parts of the story (opening, build-up, problem, resolution and ending). Model the use of 'note form' language (i.e., not necessarily full sentences and you could use bullet points). You could ask them to share their ideas for some of the parts to help you out but for at least two of the parts model the process of thinking alone, making sure they understand the aim of each part of the story.

Opening – In the opening, I need to decide on who the main characters are (or at least the ones we will meet at the start of the story) and then decide on what I want them to be doing to set the scene for the reader. Perhaps I will just start with the Fire Dragon all alone somewhere, maybe in a small cave where he has no one to live with, or maybe I could start with Little Tuft playing happily. As you model how to make notes about each part, ask one or more children to help you create a freeze frame for the start of that part. Work out whether you can begin to transfer responsibility to children (e.g., after the second stage, could they work in small groups to have a go at the third?)

Build-up – In the build-up, I need to get the story going so maybe Little Tuft is on his own one day and he wanders off to explore a part of the land he has never been to before. While he is there, he hears a strange noise, and when he investigates, he finds a small Fire Dragon all alone in a small cave.

Problem – So now Little Tuft will have to help the Fire Dragon as he lives all alone. But remember that the Fire Dragons weren't all that great to the Two Legs. … What might Little Tuft do? Maybe he will have to teach the Fire Dragon some things or maybe because the Fire Dragon has been on his own all this time, he isn't like the others so maybe Little Tuft will need to convince the other Two Legs to give the dragon a chance. Yes, I'm going to choose that idea.

Resolution – In this part of the story, the problem is resolved. Little Tuft finally convinces the others to let the dragon live with them.

Ending – So now the Fire Dragon is living happily with all the Two Legs –maybe they'll have a feast to welcome him.

Demonstrate how to re-read the plan to check it makes sense, getting children to create the freeze frames as you visit each scene.

1: 35: Ask children to have a go at the process of planning their own stories, choosing a different idea from the list. This could be done collaboratively if you think children need that support (supported writing strategy), or you could use yourself and additional adults to work with small groups (guided writing strategy) while those who are confident work alone or in pairs. Stop children to share ideas or encourage them to look at each other's mountains to help them with ideas.

1:55: Return to the learning objective and ask children to consider where they are in the planning process. What do they need next? (This may mean that extra time needs to be found for some pupils as they will not all necessarily be at the same point).

The next part of the sequence is to model how to use your notes to write the story. To avoid overwhelming children, each of the five sections could be taken on a different day, with the teacher modelling how to approach the writing of each one. The gradual release of responsibility model is key here – the teacher needs to start with the shared writing strategy of demonstration so that children can see the process clearly and listen to the teacher explaining his or her thinking process out loud.

After some demonstration, the teacher could develop his or her use of shared writing strategies by acting as a scribe and/or asking children to confer and suggest ideas for the next sentence, using this assessment opportunity to see who has tuned in to the process of story writing and is ready to begin independent writing. It is important that this bit is quite pacey to keep the children's interest, and that the teacher considers the length of writing children are aiming to compose, e.g., is it a sentence (for Year 1), a series of sentences (for Year 2) or one or more paragraphs per section for pupils in Key Stage 2 who have begun to extend their writing further.

At some point in the sequence of learning, you will want to make links to the aspects of the author's craft that were explored in your grammar teaching so that children can see how to apply the knowledge and skills they have learned. However, specific features can be considered at the revision stage and it is often better to do this rather than overload children with too many things to remember while they are composing a first draft. Success criteria (which may have been co-constructed with children through earlier sessions) for a first draft may, therefore, focus on the content of the writing, for example:

Writing a story opening:

- Describe the setting.
- Introduce one or more key characters.

Criteria which support high-quality writing in line with the children's prior learning (again co-constructed with children where possible) can, therefore, be introduced once the content of the section is largely drafted, for example:

- Use expanded noun phrases to describe the setting so the reader can imagine the place where the story starts.
- Use adjectives to describe the appearance of the main character(s) so the reader can picture them.
- Use powerful verbs to show the reader a little bit about the main character's personality.

Children should then be ready to write their own stories, using their planning notes to support them. It is important that they have plenty of time to develop their own writing. At this stage, pupils should not worry about spelling too much, as this is the focus of the editing/proofreading stage. During the drafting stage, a useful strategy is for pupils to attempt the word as best they can and to put a wiggly line underneath it to indicate that this is a spelling they are unsure of

(Martin, 2014; Clements & Tobin, 2021). Pupils may adapt their plans slightly – through creating their own version of the story, they will be allowed full authorial licence to develop the story as they wish.

Schools may hold different views on the level of independence they want children to demonstrate. It may be that only one or two sentences need to be modelled to get children started or to show them how to tackle a particular part of the section. This all depends on the assessment of the children's prior learning, the understanding they demonstrate in response to any questions or short tasks or supported writing tasks you give them, and how well they achieve the writing goals of each of the sessions, and it is important to be guided by that rather than to slavishly follow each step of the sequence.

The drafting, evaluating and editing stages could then be repeated over several days as children develop the various sections of their stories, with the teacher demonstrating any key teaching points and establishing the goals for the lesson clearly so that children know what to do and where to focus their attention. While pupils are drafting, the teacher can act as a response partner for the pupils, giving high-quality feedback which responds to the content of their writing. Pupils could also support each other's learning by acting as response partners for each other. It is really important that, children understand the role of the response partner. They will learn this through modelling which can come from the teacher's own actions when being a response partner for the children or from the teacher's use of any additional adults who could undertake this role. This is a particularly structured approach; the teacher may of course choose to remove or shorten the use of some of these scaffolds if children are writing confidently and successfully.

It is often helpful to give children some review time at the end of their writing to allow them to re-read their work and check whether they have communicated their meaning effectively. Children could either revise some elements of their writing there and then, or use some indicator to remind them they've noticed something that could be better and will want to come back to it at a later stage. This can be linked to the success criteria set up at the start of the lesson or in a previous lesson and might take account of any ideas about the reader's wishes that were identified at the start of the sequence.

The pupils will need some time to edit and proofread their writing, checking that their sentences make sense and that they have addressed spelling queries.

Finally, the pupils need opportunities to read their writing aloud. This may take place naturally if the context for learning includes a specific audience such as another class of pupils. This can usually be arranged very easily, by agreeing on a time with the other class's teacher and finding a space where children will quickly link up with one or two pupils from the audience class and share their work. It can also be achieved by getting children to read-aloud drafts of one or more sections to each other as part of the response partner process, or just to hear how it sounds.

Adaptive/Responsive Teaching

Considerations could include whether:

- Any pupils might need support to record their ideas such as specific writing implements or paper, writing frames or sentence strips. Some children might benefit from using resources to help them separate the composition and transcription processes more clearly, for example, using a talk tin or other recording device so that they can think about their ideas first and transcribe them afterwards.
- All pupils are ready to write at each stage of the sequence, or whether some need more time for indirect planning such as talk, drama or drawing to think through their ideas. They may also find it helpful to create a visual plan.
- Some pupils might find it hard to sustain their focus and so need extended periods of writing chunked into smaller units.
- Pupils can access models of writing, word banks, dictionaries and thesauri at the right time for them – some pupils may prefer to use these in the initial drafting stages while others may find them more helpful (and less disruptive to the flow of their writing) if they access them at the revision stage.

Summary

This chapter has considered how a teacher could plan the teaching of narrative fiction writing. The importance of considering the place of individual lessons within a carefully planned sequence of learning which builds children's knowledge of texts, readers, language and the writing process has been considered, along with the need for the teacher to provide meaningful and authentic opportunities for writing for a range of specific purposes and audiences. The importance of making connections across the English curriculum more widely, drawing on children's developing proficiency in spelling and handwriting, and developing children's spoken language, and reading skills is emphasised as key to effective practice.

Further Reading

1   There are more examples of planning and teaching sequences in Bearne and Reedy's *Teaching Primary English: Subject Knowledge and Classroom Practice,* published by Routledge.
2   There are examples of case studies which explore possible sequences in Chapter 12 of Clements and Tobin's *Understanding and Teaching Primary English: Theory into Practice,* published by Sage Publications Ltd.
3   For more on identifying the potential of a text, see Chapter 9 of Wilson and Scanlon's *Language Knowledge for Primary Teachers.*

References

Barrs, M., & Cork, V. (2001). *The reader in the writer: The links between the study of literature and writing development at key stage 2*. CLPE.

Bearne, E., & Reedy, D. (2017). *Teaching primary English*. Routledge.

Booker, C. (2004). *The seven basic plots: Why we tell stories*. Continuum.

Clements, J., & Tobin, M. (2021). *Understanding and teaching primary English: Theory into practice*. SAGE.

Corbett, P. (2008). *Primary 'Writer-talk'*. The National Strategies. https://foundationyears.org.uk/wp-content/uploads/2011/10/Writer_Talk1.pdf. Accessed on October 20, 2022.

Corbett, P. (2013). *How to teach story writing at key stage 1*. David Fulton Publishers.

Cremin, T. (2006). Creativity, uncertainty and discomfort: Teachers as writers. *Cambridge Journal of Education, 36*(3), 415–433.

DCSF. (2008). *Talk for writing*. Crown Publications.

Department For Education. (2013). *The National Curriculum for England: Key stages 1 and 2 framework document*. Crown Publishing.

Gamble, N. (2022). *Interview with Nikki Gamble. English 4-11*. United Kingdom Literacy Association and English Association.

Martin, T. (2014). *Talk for spelling*. UKLA.

Wilson, A., & Scanlon, J. (2011). *Language knowledge for primary teachers* (4th ed.). Routledge.

13

Planning to Teach Non-narrative Writing

Chapter Objectives

This chapter will:

- Identify the key elements of a high-quality writing curriculum, focusing on the composition of non-narrative texts.
- Consider what effective pedagogy for teaching the composition of non-narrative texts might look like.
- Demonstrate ways in which you could plan lessons at different stages of the composition process.

Introduction

As established in Chapter 10, individual writing lessons form part of a sequence designed to build children's knowledge and understanding of writing and the writing process through meaningful contexts in which they compose authentic texts. This provides purposeful practice opportunities for children to steadily acquire the knowledge and skills they need to develop effectively as writers. Before you read this chapter, it is recommended that you read Chapter 10 if you have not already done so, as it provides background knowledge that will help you to understand key elements of effective practice in the teaching of writing.

Curriculum Continuity and Progression

The majority of the end-of-year expectations outlined for each year group in the writing strand of *The National Curriculum in England: English Programmes of Study for Key Stage 1 and Key Stage 2* relate to writing in general rather than to specific genres. Genre is a term used to denote different styles of written, visual or spoken texts, for example, romantic, horror and adventure, with each genre having particular characteristics that make it so. Each of these genres falls into one of two much broader genres: fiction and non-fiction. The term 'fiction' signifies texts that are grounded in imagination while the term 'non-fiction' signifies texts that aim to communicate factual information and real events.

The National Curriculum in England: English Programmes of Study for Key Stage 1 and Key Stage 2 uses the terms 'narrative' and 'non-narrative' rather than fiction and non-fiction. We might think of the word 'narrative' as another word for a story, a spoken or written telling of a series of connected events. Such stories may made up from the author's imagination, known as narrative fiction, or they may retell real events in a similar story style, known as narrative non-fiction. Linguistic and structural features of both types of narrative are similar – the content changes depend on whether it is based on real or imagined events. There are a number of historical recount (retelling) texts which may make use of diaries and letters to present factual information in a narrative or story style. This style may also be used in texts from different curriculum areas, for example, *The Pebble in My Pocket* by Meredith Hooper and *Interview with a Shark & Other Ocean Giants Too* by Andy Seed.

There are also a number of genres within the broader genre of non-fiction texts. As well as narrative non-fiction (the retelling of a real-life story or factual detail told in a story style), factual information can be presented in various different styles, which will be explored a little further in this chapter.

In the earlier stages of the primary school curriculum, particular genres for writing are not specified: in Year R, pupils learn to write simple phrases and sentences that can be read by others, and in Year 1, pupils learn to sequence sentences to form short narratives. Pupils in Years R and 1 may well compose texts which convey factual information in a narrative style (e.g., 'Yesterday, we went to the zoo' or 'This morning I planted a seed').

From Year 2, the expectation that pupils will begin to develop knowledge and skills beyond the narrative style is presented: pupils will learn to write narratives about personal experiences and those of others (real and fictional), write about real events and write for different purposes.

In Years 3 and 4, pupils will learn to use simple organisational devices, for example, headings and subheadings in non-narrative material, and to organise paragraphs around a theme.

In Years 5 and 6, non-narrative texts are not explicitly mentioned in the end-of-year expectations. However, the expectation that children will continue to build their knowledge and understanding of non-narrative texts is clearly communicated in the introduction to the Upper Key Stage 2 section:

> By the end of year 6, pupils' reading and writing should be sufficiently fluent and effortless for them to manage the general demands of the curriculum in year 7, across all subjects and not just in English, but there will continue to be a need for pupils to learn subject-specific vocabulary.
>
> They should be able to reflect their understanding of the audience for and purpose of their writing by selecting appropriate vocabulary and grammar.
>
> Teachers should prepare pupils for secondary education by ensuring that they can consciously control sentence structure in their writing and understand why sentences are constructed as they are.
>
> Pupils should understand nuances in vocabulary choice and age-appropriate, academic vocabulary. This involves consolidation, practice and discussion of language. (DfE, 2013, p. 31)

This freedom from constraints regarding specific text types that must be taught allows teachers to choose those best suited to the interests and development needs of the class. Progression in non-narrative writing will develop through the complexity of the texts that children compose as their knowledge of text types grows and deepens. This occurs through their engagement with an increasingly wide range of models which use more complex and varied language structures, and communicate more complex ideas, supporting them to write extended pieces in different styles. This enables the children to build their knowledge of:

- Text structure and layout.
- Language choices.
- How to structure, vary and extend their sentences.
- How to organise and extend their ideas.

The above points draw on the expectations presented in *Appendix 2* of *The National Curriculum in England: English Programmes of Study for Key Stage 1 and Key Stage 2*. If we are to ensure that children see writing as a meaningful experience in which language and texts are carefully shaped and crafted by each writer to communicate their knowledge and ideas in the most effective ways, we must use texts that model brilliant use of the language devices and features presented there.

As with any learning, you need to find out what the children already know prior to starting a new unit of work. This supports you to pitch the work accurately, building on their previous learning to consolidate and extend their knowledge, understanding and skills.

Non-narrative Writing

Moving beyond the writing of real and imagined stories offers children rich opportunities to engage with a wide range of texts written in different styles or for different purposes. This enables them to deepen their understanding of language and their ability to use it in different ways, supporting their development as confident and competent speakers, listeners, readers and writers. This range includes:

- Information texts which present information on one topic, for example, a book about frogs.
- Explanation texts which describe how something works, for example, the water cycle or the organs of the human body.
- Persuasive texts which aim to sell or promote a product, experience or point of view.
- Instruction texts which provide directions on how to perform a task, learn a new skill or cook a recipe.
- Balanced discussion texts which present different sides of an argument.
- Evaluative texts which give a review of a product such as a book or film, or an experience such as a visit to a theme park or the theatre.

Just as language continuously evolves, so too do the different ways in which we can produce spoken or written texts. Developments in technology have allowed us to create a range of new texts such as blogs, wikis and TikTok videos which use different combinations of the spoken and written word, sound and music, animation and movement. Therefore, genres develop over time, with an increasing number of children's books including more than one style of writing. For example, in the book *Stone Age Boy* by Satoshi Kitamura, the majority of the text is presented in a story form but includes a double-page spread of factual information. Such texts offer really exciting opportunities for children to engage with many different styles of writing and to develop their knowledge, understanding and skills as writers. Bearne and Reedy note that 'it is not just the structure of a text that determines its purpose, but also the content and the intention of the writer and the language and organisational features chosen to fit the specific purpose' (2017, p. 316).

The National Curriculum in England: English Programmes of Study for Key Stage 1 and Key Stage 2 does not specify how many or which styles of non-narrative text are explored so it is worth considering the following:

- What are your children interested in and what are they learning about in other parts of the curriculum? Using their interests and knowledge as a foundation for their writing offers them a chance to draw on what they know, typically making the writing task easier as this is supportive of cognitive load, and to further develop their knowledge through the act of writing.
- Which great models of non-narrative texts can you find for their age group? A well-chosen high-quality text enables children to see language used in authentic and meaningful ways, often inspiring them to try out new ways of writing.
- What are the most logical next steps for them in terms of their development in language and/or writing, and what experiences would support them to achieve these? Making sure that the style of writing you choose is well-matched to key teaching points offers a purposeful and motivating context for learning.
- Where is there genuine purpose and audience for any writing they do? Purpose and audience are essential elements of the writing process and are key to motivation.

Activity   Reflecting on Your Knowledge of Non-narrative Texts

Using the list at the start of this section, think about the different styles of writing and list as many examples of high-quality texts for each style as you can. Published children's books are a good source (remember to include any hybrid texts which make use of more than one style), but you could also think about other kinds of texts, for example, online texts, publications such as The Week Junior and WRD magazine which often include a wide range of styles in each edition, leaflets and so on. Are there any areas where you need to build your knowledge of a particular style or for a particular year group? How will you achieve this? There are a number of good websites which will help you here, and children, teachers and librarians are often a very good source of information.

Curriculum and Pedagogy for Non-narrative Writing

As with narrative writing, effective sequences of learning both build and expand on the knowledge of texts and language that children acquire through their reading, spoken language, and vocabulary and grammar learning. The need for a coherent sequence of learning is established in Chapter 10 and further explains in more depth a sequence of learning that enables children to:

- Read to build their knowledge of a text type.
- Understand the writing process.
- Explore the language and structure of texts.

- Generate ideas for the content and structure of their own writing.
- Draft their writing.
- Revise their writing.
- Edit and proofread their writing.
- Share their writing with an audience.

In non-narrative writing, children need to build their knowledge of the writing style associated with the purpose of the text and their knowledge of the content-what to write about. As noted by Ofsted (2022):

> Perhaps not surprisingly, research suggests that greater knowledge of the topic leads to better writing. Additionally, 'discourse knowledge' is important. This is knowledge about how to write, including knowledge about the genre of writing, linguistic and grammatical knowledge, and knowledge about how to carry out specific aspects of the writing process.

In both non-narrative writing (e.g., instructions, explanations, persuasive adverts and leaflets) and narrative non-fiction writing (e.g., historical recounts, diaries and letters), learning is often sequenced so that in their English lessons, children learn about the text type, while at the same time learning the content for the writing in one or more other areas of the curriculum. When the children have enough knowledge of what they are going to write about and enough knowledge about the genre for their writing, the two elements can be brought together so that the children compose an independent piece of writing using the content they have learned.

Again, reading and spoken language are key components of an effective learning sequence. Planning rich opportunities for children to engage fully with the text type through reading and response activities and planning rich opportunities for discussion and experimentation are key to enabling the children to compose high-quality pieces of non-narrative writing.

There is a danger when teaching non-narrative writing that too much focus on the linguistic and structural features of a typical example of any particular text type may take place at the expense of building knowledge and understanding of what makes a particular text high-quality. Ofsted (2022) note:

> Although discourse knowledge of the features of certain text types and genres of writing is important, listing the features that pupils must include in a piece of writing might lead to pupils using textual and language features without understanding why they are useful and what purposes they serve.

Durran (2019) cautions that an approach which focuses on the surface features of a text type, rather than on the extent to which it has achieved its purpose in relation to its intended audience, can work against children's development as real writers. He proposes that when reading as a writer, children explore the impact of different ingredients of the text such as the author's choice of words and sentence structures as well as his or her use of structural features. For example, in an instructional text aiming to inform young children about how to cook biscuits, the author might decide to start by engaging them with a question, such as 'Have you ever wondered how to make delicious, crumbly cookies?' Later in the text, the author might ensure the text is easy to follow by presenting one simple instruction on each line and numbering them. Thus, Bearne and Reedy suggest that

> rather than sticking to formulae, teaching non-fiction depends on providing opportunities for children to speculate, explore and investigate whilst creating different ways to help them gather and shape ideas. (2017, p. 317)

Reading to build children's knowledge of a text type

As noted earlier, it is not suggested that any text will have only one example of text type within it. Some texts move seamlessly back and forth between different styles of narrative and/or non-narrative writing or may include more than one kind of non-narrative writing. The starting point for planning a learning sequence might spring from the teacher's consideration of what text type or style of writing might engage children and provide a meaningful context in which to develop one or more aspects of their writing. Alternatively, it could spring from a high-quality text which he or she knows will stimulate the children's interest. Another possibility is to use the children's interests as a starting point, thinking of one or more writing styles that would support their progress as writers and then choose one or more high-quality examples to serve as models. Whatever the starting point, the choice of model is key.

Activity   Choosing a High-Quality Text for Non-fiction Writing

Gamble and Yates's (2013) experiences of working with teachers and pupils in one school reveals some interesting insights into pupils' views on non-fiction. They found that pupils viewed non-fiction in schools as restricted to information books used for research into specific curriculum topics. When asked to share their favourite non-fiction texts from home, the children brought in a much wider range of texts on topics of personal interest to them. This raises interesting questions about our choice of non-fiction texts, and the way that we display and use them with children to spark their curiosity and foster a sense of connection and interest. Again, it is worth reading a text a few times to really get a sense of what it has to offer children (Gamble, 2022).

(Continued)

As you re-read the text, consider the following questions: (based on Wilson & Scanlon, 2011):

- What kind of text is it? Is its purpose to 'describe, narrate, explain, instruct, give and respond to information, or argue'? (DfE, 2013).
- What is the structure of the text? Does it need to be read in order from the beginning, or can the reader dip in and out? What features of non-fiction texts does it use – for example, heading and subheadings, pictures, diagrams or illustrations, and captions? Is there a contents page, an index, or a glossary?
- How is the information conveyed? Is it through the use of a narrative style? What role do the pictures play? What kind of pictures are they? Are they illustrations or diagrams?
- How is the text laid out? Is there anything unusual or interesting about this? Is each page laid out in the same way? Does the text keep the same font all the way through?
- How is the language used? How formal is the register of the text? What tense and person are used? Is there a sense of a narrator? Are there places where the reader is addressed directly? Is there use of imaginative language such as alliteration or are words chosen for their onomatopoeic quality? Is there a use of metaphor and simile? Is there the use of rhetorical questions?
- How much technical language is used? Are technical terms explained? Will the reader understand them or do they need some background knowledge?
- How are sentences structured? Do they follow a similar format? Is there a variety of structures?
- Does the text invite the reader to think deeply or differently about a subject? Does it raise any issues to be debated?
- How is punctuation used? Is additional information demarcated by the use of brackets, dashes or commas? Are exclamation marks used for effect? Is there the use of bullet points?
- Does the text offer an opportunity for critical reflection, for example is the text purely informative or is presenting a particular viewpoint? Are all the facts believable and accurate? Has any information been missed out and if so, why?

To enable children to build their knowledge of the text type effectively, it is important that they are given sufficient time to read and reflect on the text. This is provided through high-quality book talk (see Chapter 9). In the case of non-narrative writing, the teacher may also initiate discussion on the layout of the text, and the use of any devices which aim to help the reader's understanding of the material. The teacher's role here, then, is first to provide thought-provoking texts. Secondly, the teacher needs to facilitate high-quality discussions, making use of open-ended prompts and modelling how to share our responses as readers. The teacher must also show genuine curiosity and interest in what the children have to say, supporting them to resolve any challenges, for example, if two readers have interpreted the text differently.

Understanding the writing process

There are a number of useful sources of information about different text types, such as Rachel Clarke's excellent document 'Progression in Non-fiction Texts' which presents the structural and grammatical features of different text types and can currently be downloaded free of charge from her Primary English Shed website.

In this phase of the sequence, children can move from thinking as a reader to thinking as a writer, building on their implicit knowledge of the text's style to consider it from the perspective of a writer. This enables them to build on their implicit understanding of the text, which was developed through their reading and book talk, making it

> increasingly explicit in order to develop the habit of reading with a writerly eye and a writer's curiosity, wondering, How did the author do that?...In this sense, it is reading with a view to imitating a writer but not just copying....Reading with a writer's eye can help to deepen understanding of how language has been crafted to create different effects. (Corbett, 2008, p. 2)

Again, the teacher should model the kinds of thinking required and plan carefully which elements of the text are useful for the children to reflect on.

As part of this step, the children should also experiment for themselves, trying out different ideas to see how they work from the writer's perspective. The teacher will need to model ideas first, using the think-aloud strategy to explain his or her thought processes so that children can see how an idea taken from the model text can be used by the writer in their own way. One study of teachers found that modelling the use of questions such as 'What am I trying to say? How does that sound? What do I want to say or do next? How could I say that? And What will my reader be thinking or feeling as they read this?' were particularly helpful (Bearne et al., 2011).

To support them in trying out new ideas, children could engage in some collaborative writing, for example, producing a large version of an instruction text or creating a particular part of a persuasive leaflet. This allows them to experiment together, articulating their thinking and exploring the impact of the texts, words and sentences they produce. Sharing the cognitive load, and increasing the pool of ideas and experience, can scaffold new learning effectively. If the children are exploring particular sentence structures, this will link in their grammar learning in a meaningful and authentic way. See Chapter 11 for ideas on teaching these elements from a model text.

Generating Ideas for the Content and Structure of the Children's Writing

The second part of capturing ideas enables children to generate ideas for their own writing. As noted in Chapter 12, it is helpful to think about capturing ideas as a form of planning, 'furnishing children with ideas and giving them something to write about' (Clements & Tobin, 2021, p. 210). When developing their knowledge of what to write about – the content of the non-fiction writing – children may engage with high-quality non-fiction texts or participate in first-hand experiences, such as watching short films or documentaries (available within the BBC's Class Clips resource), going on visits, having a visitor come into school, or handling artefacts. There are a number of spoken language activities which help children select and rehearse key content for their writing, such as:

- Creating an amazing fact or 'Did you know?' display.
- Playing a true or false game (they could write the questions) or making a display.
- Creating something visual such as a collage/story map/zig zag book/PowerPoint or display.
- Playing a game such as 'Just a minute' where the children have one minute to share their knowledge on a particular subject which can be challenged by listeners if they hesitate or repeat themselves.
- Using drama techniques such as freeze-framing and miming.
- Playing a game such as Babble gabble, where working in pairs, pupils have to tell each other everything they know at the same time.
- Retelling their knowledge in a tennis match style, each player saying one word at a time, or a circle, each person saying the next word.
- Planning and creating a podcast, oral news report or short video.
- Using role-play games, for example, by inviting a world expert on to a chat show for an interview.

Pupils could also use drawing strategies such as flow charts or mind maps to show what information they have learned. The teacher will need to plan carefully how the children will gather the content knowledge needed for the writing and give opportunities for purposeful collaboration and discussion which allow the children time to recall and articulate their knowledge so that it is readily available for writing at the drafting stage.

The remaining stages of the writing sequence are the drafting stage, the revision stage, the editing and proofreading stage, and the sharing stage.

A Learning Sequence Example for Year 6 Pupils Based on *What It's Like to Be a Bird*, Written by Tim Birkhead and Illustrated by Catherine Rayner

This is a non-fiction text about birds which has elements of narrative non-fiction and non-narrative information. It starts with a double-page spread written in an entirely narrative style, inviting the reader to imagine how it might feel to fly:

Close your eyes. Spread out your arms and imagine that they are the broad, majestic wings of a bird. Picture yourself soaring high above the land. The dawn breeze ruffles your feathers, lofty mountain peaks rise up to greet you, and the first beams of morning sunlight dance across your back. (p. 4)

The following double-page spreads provide a paragraph or two of narrative non-fiction which builds a vivid picture in the reader's mind before switching to a non-fiction informative style to convey facts about one of twenty different types of bird:

A rustle, a shriek and a click-click-click – we are not alone in this cave! Is a frightening monster hiding in the darkness?

The curious oilbird roosts in the pitch-black caves of Central and South America, sometimes in colonies of up to 20,000 other oilbirds. (p. 9)

The final double-page spread is written in a purely non-narrative non-fiction style, informing the reader about birds' senses.

The first double-page spread sets the tone for the book but after that, pages can be dipped in and out of as the reader wishes. A contents page helps the reader navigate the book, providing intriguing titles and the name of the bird for each double-page spread ('The Hunter who Listens *great grey owl*'). Illustrations fill both pages, seamlessly integrating words and images. As well as the main body of the text, there are two or three captions presented in italics.

Throughout the text, particular words or phrases are presented in bold or larger text to stimulate interest ('It's dinnertime', and 'ready for take off!').

The register of the text is moderately formal. The reader is often addressed directly through the questions and invitations to imagine what it might feel like to be a bird. The text is written in the present tense. Words are chosen carefully for a range of reasons including their onomatopoeic quality ('squawking' and 'Bang!'), and there are hints of alliteration ('perching and preening'). There is some use of technical language, such as fovea, but this is clearly explained. The reader will need to draw on his or her store of vocabulary (or have a dictionary to hand) for words such as wading, dowdy and funnelled.

Sentences are structured in different ways. There are a number of questions and some short statements. Dashes are used to add extra information, and there is some use of ellipsis and colons.

As suggested by the title, the text invites the reader to think about what it might feel like to be a bird. The author engages the reader through vivid descriptions of what the reader might see, hear and smell. This stimulates the reader to think differently about birds, encouraging them to view their worlds from the inside rather than looking at them from a distance as we do in everyday life. The text very much focuses on the most thrilling aspects of being a bird, allowing the writer to maintain the sense of energy and awe established at the beginning.

Lesson Plan

Here is one suggestion for a lesson plan within this sequence of learning (Table 13.1). Remember that the sequence should unfold logically for the children, so you may play around with the order of the different steps as best fits the learning.

Planning a Context for Writing

High-quality text: *What it's Like to Be a Bird* written by Tim Birkhead and illustrated by Catherine Rayner.

Purpose and audience: Compose an information text on an animal of your choice for the parallel class.

Relevant Prior Learning: Prior to the lesson, children have read *What it's Like to Be a Bird* and discussed it in small groups. Powerful verbs were explored through the use of drama techniques which invited the children to explore the different movements (e.g., swooping). They were invited to share their thoughts on the book, and to choose and write their favourite phrase on to a card for a class display.

Children have worked in pairs to choose their favourite double-page spread and written a glossary to accompany it. For homework, or in a previous lesson, the children chose an animal of their own to research, aiming to find some amazing and unusual facts about them. They have also written some fast poems about their animal through which they have generated some powerful vocabulary (see Chapter 14). The class has chosen one animal to focus on together – the teacher will use this for modelling, demonstration and scribing.

This part of the learning sequence focuses on:

- Exploring the language and structure of non-narrative writing.
- Generating ideas for the content and structure of non-narrative writing.

What will children learn?

- To select and organise ideas, facts and key points.
- To select, and use judiciously, vocabulary, grammar, form, and structural and organisational features, including rhetorical devices, to reflect audience, purpose and context, and using Standard English where appropriate.
- To make notes.

Planned next steps: Children will develop their plan into a piece of writing, following the stages of the writing process as appropriate.

What will effective learning look like?

Children will be able to:

- Explain how they have organised their plan.
- Explain where and how they have selected vocabulary carefully and expressed their ideas in a particular way.
- Demonstrate appropriate use of note form on their plans.

How will learning be assessed and what are the opportunities for effective feedback?:

- Listening in to children's discussions to gauge their understanding.
- Using feedback questions to check the children understand where they are going and to check how they are going.
- Observing children's flip chart sheets to see what they have noticed about the author's craft.
- Engaging with children's drafts, noting how effectively they have crafted their language and expressed their ideas in fluent prose.

Table 13.1 A lesson plan for teaching non-narrative writing

Today's lesson sequence/content
Specific Resources Needed:
1:00: Share the page King and Queen of the River Castle. In small groups, ask the children to look at the text closely and discuss it, focusing on: • How is the writing structured and laid out? • What styles of writing has the author used? • How has the author crafted language and what effect does this have on the reader? • How has the author used punctuation? • Which are the most powerful words and phrases? What impact do they have on the reader? • Have the children noticed anything else they would like to discuss?
1:25: Ask each group to share their thoughts while the teacher takes notes (it could be useful to have large flip chart pages with each of the five questions on to support this).
1:25: The teacher then demonstrates how to use these ideas to plan a class model text, using modelling with think-aloud, first mapping out text boxes, identifying roughly what information may be included in each, and identifying the writing style for each, for example, 'So first I am going to map out where the bits of text will go. The first part of the text starts with a narrative style. I think I'll put the first box here on the page and make a note that I need a narrative style. There are a couple of unusual facts that I know about frogs. A group of frogs is called an army and frogs drink through their skin. I might choose the first one here and get the reader to imagine that they are like a soldier, standing with their regiment'. At this point, or perhaps further into the lesson if the children need to go off and start planning, the teacher could also think about specific lines or words to be included, for example, identifying a powerful idea that can be presented in bold text with powerful use of sophisticated punctuation (like this line from the text: 'Swans have a rule: do not cross this line – enter at your peril!'), trying out some different ideas.

(Continued)

Table 13.1 A lesson plan for teaching non-narrative writing

Today's lesson sequence/content
1:35: Pupils to plan their own pages, trying out ideas from the discussion and their prior work. Teacher to circulate, observing the children's work and giving feedback to scaffold the learning. The teacher's observations can form the basis of explicit teaching points as to support the class in the drafting, revision or editing stages. The teacher might choose to share good examples with the class during this time, as this can be really useful in supporting pupils who are unsure (although it is important to give the pupils uninterrupted time for planning where possible).
1:50: Ask the children to work with a partner to share their plans. Each pupil has five minutes to do so while the other acts as a response partner. Pupils can of course amend their plans if they wish to. The teacher might choose to highlight and reinforce any key points that will support the children's writing over the next few days.

From here, pupils are likely to be ready to write, although you might wish to give some more directed time for them to play with language, for example, by asking pairs to choose one of the favourite phrases shared in their prior learning and to have a go at composing their own phrase in a similar style. As the writing process unfolds, the teacher should continue to observe and read the children's drafts, giving both individual verbal feedback and identifying key points for whole class teaching inputs. Ensure that some time is protected for the sharing of the children's final drafts at the end.

Adaptive/Responsive Teaching

Adaptations and responses are likely to be really similar to those used when teaching fiction writing as it is the content rather than the process which is different. Therefore, considerations could include:

- Support for pupils to record their ideas such as specific writing implements or paper, writing frames or sentence strips. Some children might benefit from using resources to help them separate the composition and transcription process more clearly, for example, using a talking tin or other recording device so that they can think about their ideas first and transcribe them afterwards.
- Ensuring that all pupils are ready to write at each stage of the sequence, or identifying whether some need more time to rehearse the content of their ideas which may be more challenging as they will be using factual detail which must be accurate. A graphic organiser to show the structure of the writing (e.g., the theme of each paragraph) might be helpful.
- Whether some pupils might find it hard to sustain their focus and so need extended periods of writing chunked into smaller units.
- Whether pupils can access models of writing, word banks, dictionaries and thesauri at the right time for them – some pupils may prefer to use these in the initial drafting stages while others may find them more helpful (and less disruptive to the flow of their writing) if they access them at the revision stage.

Summary

This chapter has considered how a teacher could plan the teaching of non-fiction writing. The importance of considering the place of individual lessons within a carefully planned sequence of learning which builds children's knowledge of texts, readers, language and the writing process has been considered, along with suggestions for how the teacher could provide meaningful and authentic opportunities for writing for a range of specific purposes and audiences. The importance of making connections across the English curriculum more widely and developing children's spoken language and reading skills is emphasised as key to effective practice.

Further Reading

1   For more ideas on linking writing to other areas of the curriculum, read *Inviting Writing: Teaching and Learning Writing Across the Primary Curriculum* by Adam Bushnell and David Waugh.

2   To widen your knowledge of high-quality non-fiction texts, visit the reviews section of Justimagine.co.uk and filter your search by non-fiction. You will find many reviews of high-quality non-fiction texts for the primary age range, with useful insight into some of the features you might want to draw out from the text.

3   To further develop your understanding of the conventions of non-fiction texts, visit https://primaryenglished.co.uk/blog/progression-in-non-fiction-texts.

4   Pie Corbett's *Talk for Writing Across the Curriculum* offers a wealth of suggestions for spoken language activities which are tailored to specific genres of non-fiction text. This is a very useful resource – even if your school does not follow the commercial Talk for Writing approach in full.

References

Bearne, E., Chamberlain, L., Cremin, T., & Mottram, M. (2011). *Teaching writing effectively: Reviewing practice*. UKLA.

Bearne, E., & Reedy, D. (2017). *Teaching primary English*. Routledge.

Clements, J., & Tobin, M. (2021). *Understanding and teaching primary English: Theory into practice*. SAGE.

Corbett, P. (2008) *Primary 'Writer-talk'*. The National Strategies. https://foundationyears.org.uk/wp-content/uploads/2011/10/Writer_Talk1.pdf. Accessed on October 20, 2022.

Department for Education. (2013). *The National Curriculum for England: Key stages 1 and 2 framework document*. Crown Publishing.

Durran, J. (2019) Reading as writers; writing as readers: An account of a Year 5/6 teaching sequence. https://jamesdurran.blog/2019/05/09/reading-as-writers-writing-as-readers-an-account-of-a-year-5-6-teaching-sequence/. Accessed on May 03, 2023.

Gamble, N. (2022). *Interview with Nikki Gamble. English 4–11*. United Kingdom Literacy Association and English Association.

Gamble, N., & Yates, S. (2013). *Exploring children's literature* (3rd ed.). SAGE.

Ofsted. (2022). *Research and analysis Research review series: English*. https://www.gov.uk/government/publications/curriculum-research-review-series-english/curriculum-research-review-series-english

Wilson, A., & Scanlon, J. (2011). *Language knowledge for primary teachers* (4th ed.). Routledge.

14

Planning to Teach Poetry

Chapter Objectives

This chapter will:

- Identify the key elements of a high-quality English curriculum, focusing on the use of poetry.
- Consider what effective pedagogy for teaching poetry might look like.
- Demonstrate ways in which you could plan lessons involving poems.

Introduction

Poetry is great. Some of my favourite times in the classroom were those days when we could escape from the daily timetable, either because for some reason (often a breakdown in technology!) we couldn't do our lessons in the normal way or perhaps because it was getting close to a holiday and had some spare time in which to be really creative. For me, those days were always filled with poetry – sharing them, performing them and writing them. Poetry itself is a kind of freedom I think – freedom to look at the world differently and freedom from the rules that govern sentences. It is however all about language, inviting children to play with words, to absorb and choose the most interesting and powerful, and to experiment with or experience creative sequencing and layout.

Cremin et al. (2015, p. 115) suggest that poetry is an integral part of childhood:

> Outside the classroom, children's lives are packed with poetry: they engage in a world of rich language play and experiment with and imbibe playground rhymes, songs, football chants, jingles, jokes and lyrics, often without recognising their essentially poetic nature.

This is supported by Marsh and Bishop's (2013) research into children's playground games in which the authors found that children really enjoyed verbal play.

A survey of practice in relation to the teaching of poetry in schools carried out by Ofsted in 2007 found that many primary school pupils enjoyed learning poems by heart and that they were often particularly enthusiastic about performing poems to an audience. They also found that older pupils were frequently inspired to re-read poems because of their intellectual demands.

Another piece of research into poetry carried out by Cooray et al. for the National Literacy Trust (2017) found that 46% of children and young people chose to engage with poetry in their free time, reading or listening to it, creating it and/or performing it. In addition, young people who received free school meals were significantly more likely to read and write poetry outside school than their peers.

The study also found that children and young people felt that poetry offered a good way to express themselves and share their feelings, with 76% saying it made them feel creative and 57% saying they thought it enabled them to create something special out of words. Those surveyed often described a poet as someone who is creative, funny, imaginative and intelligent.

In reflecting on his time as Children's Laureate, Rosen says

> If we look at the world of poetry and at when it works for us as readers and listeners, it will to a great extent be because it arouses feelings in us, gets us thinking, engages with ideas, gets us to look closely (or look afresh) at something…offers us possibilities, takes us into a dream world… (2011, p. 16)

Poetry is great.

Curriculum Continuity and Progression

Poetry can be found in both the reading and writing sections of *The National Curriculum in England: English Programmes of Study for Key Stage 1 and Key Stage 2* forming part of the range of reading through which we aim to develop children's pleasure, motivation, vocabulary and understanding as readers. A number of reading and writing expectations can be achieved through the inclusion of poetry but poetry is mentioned specifically as follows:

- In Year 1, pupils will listen to and discuss a wide range of poems, beginning to appreciate them and learning to recite some by heart.
- In Year 2, pupils will continue to build up a repertoire of poems learnt by heart, appreciating these and reciting some, with appropriate intonation to make the meaning clear. As well as continuing to listen to and discuss poems, they will also express their views. The range of poetry used in the Year 2 classroom should include both contemporary and classic poems.
- In Years 3 and 4, pupils will continue to listen to and discuss a wide range of poems, recognising some different forms of poetry and preparing poems to read-aloud and to perform, beginning to show an understanding through intonation, tone, volume and action.
- In Years 5 and 6, pupils will recite a wide range of poetry by heart, preparing poems to read-aloud and to perform, beginning to show an understanding through intonation, tone and volume so that the meaning is clear to an audience. They will continue to listen to, read and discuss and wide range of poems. (DfE, 2013).

All of these experiences build on children's experiences in Year R in which they will sing a range of well-known nursery rhymes and songs and perform songs, rhymes, poems (and stories) with others.

Curriculum and Pedagogy for Poetry

We might start by defining a poem. The Oxford English Dictionary defines it as 'a piece of writing in which the expression of feelings and ideas is given intensity by particular attention to diction (sometimes involving rhyme), rhythm and imagery'. There is some debate about whether songs are a form of poetry, and a number of poets have given their own definitions through poetry itself (a favourite of mine is John Hegley's 'What a poem is not').

Just as in reading and writing more widely, the most effective sequences of learning in poetry are usually built around one or more excellent models. These offer rich opportunities for children to both develop and practise using their knowledge and skills as thoughtful and reflective readers and writers.

As highlighted earlier, poems can be read (by the children themselves or through a teacher's read-aloud), performed or written; there is no need to do all these things with the same poem, but it is good to aim to achieve a balance over the course of a school year.

Activity Choosing a Poem

Both Goodwin (2011) and Lambirth (2015) note that the only good reason for choosing a poem to share in the classroom is because you like it. Just as in the rest of our teaching across the curriculum, sharing our passion for and interest in what we are teaching will really help the children to respond with enthusiasm. There are several different ways to find poems that you like. Your school or university library should have a good collection of poetry books, both by individual authors and as compilations which may or may not be themed, so spend some time browsing. There are also some great online sources such as the Centre for Literacy in Primary Education's (CLPE) National Poetry Centre which can be found at https://clpe.org.uk/poetry. This is an absolute goldmine of poems and has many fantastic video clips of poets reading their poems and pupils performing them too. In addition, there is an excellent resource for developing your knowledge of different types of poems.

Goodwin (2011) suggests that it is worth taking your time to re-read a poem that you like: 'The more you read a poem, the more you will find in it' (p. 42).

As you re-read it, you could consider the following questions:

- How does the poem make you feel?
- What does it make you think?
- Are there any parts that prompt you to build pictures in your mind?
- Which words and phrases stand out to you and why?
- Are there any connections that you make to your own life and experiences, or other texts or your knowledge of the world's places and history?

It is also worth considering how the poem is structured. Is it a free verse poem or a structured one with patterns in syllables, lines and rhymes? If it is structured, is it in a specific form such as ancient Japanese haiku (a poem with 17 syllables in total, typically spread over three lines with five syllables on the first, then seven syllables and then five syllables) or a Tanka (with a total of 31 syllables, typically spread over five lines with a five-, seven-, five-, seven- and seven-syllable pattern). Another structured form is the limerick (a humorous poem consisting of five lines with a syllable pattern of eight, eight, six, six and eight in which the first, second and fifth lines rhyme with each other, and the third and fourth rhyme with each other). You might also come across clerihews (a four-line usually humorous poem where the first two lines rhyme with the other, and the last two likewise) or couplets (pairs of lines with the same rhyme and rhythm). Cinquains are another structured form. These are five-line poems where the lines follow a two-, four-, six-, eight- and two-syllable pattern and the subject of the poem is usually the first or final line of the poem.

Some poems tell a story in poetic form, for example, narrative poems and ballads. Many have elements of wordplay, perhaps including some alliteration, where some of the words are chosen because they start with or include the same sound, or assonance, where a particular vowel sound is repeated within the poem. Words may also be chosen for their onomatopoeic qualities, meaning that the word reflects the sound it makes (such as bang or crash).

Imagery is also often a key feature of poetry, for example, the use of similes, where something is compared to another thing, metaphor, where something is described as if it is something else, or personification, where something is given human-like qualities.

Other types of poems include kennings, often attributed to Anglo-Saxon or Norse times where a two-word phrase is used to describe the noun it replaces, and calligrams and concrete poems, where an aspect of the poem's presentation reflects the subject of the poem or is presented in the shape of the subject of the poem.

List poems are also popular. These poems are, as implied, presented in the form of a list such as 'Ten Things Found in a Wizard's Pocket' by Ian McMillan.

For a more comprehensive list of many different kinds of poems and poetic devices, along with some examples, visit the excellent online resource: https://clpe.org.uk/poetry/poetic-forms-and-devices.

You can also follow a number of children's poets on social media platforms or visit their websites. They often share poems they have been working on and/or suggest ideas for poems the children might like to write.

Responding to Poems

Before responding to any poem, children need to become familiar with it. It is useful to read it, and perhaps to let them read it, several times. This might be independently, in pairs or in groups, and might be silently or aloud. You might choose to do some shared reading as a class. This allows the children to get used to how the poem sounds and to begin to make meaning from it.

Children's responses to poems might be through talk and/or other expressive means. A teacher could share questions similar to those presented in the 'Choosing a poem' box, leading a discussion between pairs or small groups of pupils or the whole class, or as prompts for pairs or small groups of pupils to manage themselves. The principles of book talk could be applied here, giving the children time and space to think deeply about the poem, discussing the bits they really liked and sharing their puzzles and questions to reach a shared understanding (see *Tell Me: Children, Reading and Talk* by Aidan Chambers for more on this approach).

Longer responses to poems might involve the creation of some artwork such as drawing or sculpture, or the creation of a musical accompaniment or representation using instruments or voices. One idea from the Centre for Literacy in Primary Education (CLPE) web resource is the creation of poetry boxes, where pupils assemble or make objects from the poem to put into a box or turn the box itself into the setting of the poem for retelling. Other responses can include some writing such as a letter or diary to or from a character, object, place or theme in the poem.

Performing the poem is also a form of response. Pupils can work individually, in pairs, or in small groups to perform the poem as a kind of readers' theatre. In this approach, the text is marked, rehearsed and performed through voice acting. They could dramatise one part of or the whole of the poem, or use a drama technique such as tableau to create a frozen scene from the poem. They might also improvise what came before or after one or more ideas in the poem.

Performing Poems

While the use of dramatisation as outlined above may be a more informal response to the poem, some poems will be chosen for more formal performances. In their review of what works well in teaching poetry in the primary classroom, the CLPE notes that because of its connection with wordplay, games, songs and rhymes, poetry:

> should be heard as well as read. If poetry is not given a voice, if it just stays on the page as a printed object, then it is not going to come alive for most children. The experience of being read to is likely to be the real foundation of children's knowledge of poetry, and is also going to be a major influence on how they write themselves. So it is important that it should be as rich, interesting and 'ear-catching' as it can be. (2018, p. 5)

There are some compilations of poems specifically designed for performance such as *Poems to Perform: A Classic Collection chosen by the Children's Laureate* compiled by Julia Donaldson, *Poems Aloud: An Anthology of Poems to Read Out Loud* compiled by Joseph Coelho, and James Carter's *Zim Zam Zoom: Zappy Poems to Read Out Loud*. The web resource https://perform-apoem.lgfl.org.uk/also has several poems which lend themselves to this. Although in general poems are designed to be read-aloud, some children's poets are particularly focused on performing them, for example, Brian Moses has shared video and audio recordings of some of his poems with rhythmic accompaniments on his website.

When preparing to perform a poem, children can consider their stance and use of expression and gesture. There is an authentic and purposeful opportunity to connect this to children's reading fluency, enabling them to practice and experience what fluent reading sounds like. The BBC's class clips video resource has some top tips for performance from the poet Joseph Coelho, and Michael Rosen has shared a video on YouTube through the Puffin Books channel (https://www.youtube.com/watch?v=RvV23xoZRkI). You could make a connection to Voice 21's Oracy Framework which aims to inspire effective communication through its focus on the physical, linguistic, cognitive, and social and emotional skills which underpin this (for more on this, see Chapter 4). To develop children's skills in a structured way, you could make use of the Reader's Theatre strategy which may involve the teacher modelling one or more of the specific aspects of reading fluency identified by Rasinski such as expression and volume, phrasing, smoothness or pace and children echoing back to practise. Pupils then work on the text in pairs or small groups before sharing their performance. This approach is outlined fully in the Education Endowment Foundation's (EEF) Improving Literacy in Key Stage 2 Guidance Report (second edition).

The performance can be as low-key as feels right. Sometimes a group may only perform for the teacher, or at the same time as one or more other groups, or to their classmates – one other group or all the other groups. Other audiences might include parents, school governors or volunteers, other classes, or the whole school. Performances might be recorded and shared – there are no rules!

Another way for children to perform poems is to use Michael Rosen's idea of a Poetry Show. The children work in small groups to choose a poem to present to the class. They have 20 minutes of rehearsal time and can choose how they want to perform it, for example, using drama, mime or adding a musical accompaniment, or they might choose different group members to perform the chorus and verse parts or different lines.

Any of the ideas suggested above in the responding to poetry or performing poetry sections could be used with many different kinds of poems, including classic poems as specified in *The National Curriculum in England: English Programmes of Study for Key Stage 1 and Key Stage 2*.

Using Classic Poems

Specific classic poems are not named in *The National Curriculum in England: English Programmes of Study for Key Stage 1 and Key Stage 2* and so the choice is left entirely to the teacher. Some popular choices are The Jumblies or The Owl and the Pussy Cat by Edward Lear for Year 2, and The Highwayman by Alfred Noyes from Year 4 onwards. A useful starting point might be the BBC's Talking Poetry resource which, along with a number of well-known contemporary poems, includes two episodes on classic poetry with some accompanying notes. This can be found at https://www.bbc.co.uk/teach/school-radio/english-ks2-classic-poetry-1-talking-poetry/zkj36v4 where actors read an assortment of classic poems by authors such as Rudyard Kipling, TS Eliot, WH Auden, Walter de la Mere and Lewis Carroll. There are also some beautifully illustrated picture book versions of some classic poems such as Alfred Noyes's *The Highwayman* or Ogden Nash's *The Tale of Custard the Dragon*, and a number of classic poetry collections which are available in bookshops and often school or university libraries too.

Some classic poems use archaic or unusual language, or rely on some particular background knowledge, so it can be useful to pre-teach unusual words or spend some time tuning into the time or place in which the poem is set so that children's comprehension is not disrupted when they meet the poem itself. Other ways to make a poem more accessible include strategies such as leading discussion or drama on a theme from the play, or using objects or pictures to develop children's background knowledge and tune them in. Music or film clips could also be used, as could related texts, for example revisiting Donaldson's *The Highway Rat* as a warm-up for Noyes's *The Highwayman*.

Children may also face challenges when a poem is presented very differently from poems they have seen before, or if a poem is not what they were expecting. In his book *What is Poetry?*, Michael Rosen explores a number of things that a poem can do, for example, capture a moment, play with words or be symbolic. Once children are familiar and confident with exploring poetry, they will hopefully be keen to try out new poems. However, in the early stages of building their confidence, it might be useful to think carefully about poems you want to share, considering what you might do to help them make sense of them. For example, if you going to introduce a poem which uses symbolism, the idea that a word or image can represent something else, you might talk about what symbolism is. You might give some examples yourself and then set up some discussions where children explore this idea, or introduce similar poems which are more straightforward.

If you want to explore the poem more formally, you can do this once the children are familiar with it through any of the above activities. You will want to explore some poems in more depth in order to develop the children's knowledge and understanding of various poetic devices such as rhythm and rhyme, metaphor, simile and personification through poems that are appropriate for their age. You might start by asking the children what they have noticed about the words and their layout; from there it is usually helpful to focus on one idea at a time, giving the children time to discuss the idea. Rosen (2016) suggests that the children can act as poem detectives, identifying what he calls secret strings that run through the poem or particular bits of it. For example, they may spot some alliteration or the use of particular words to create an image.

Reading Poetry Lesson Plan

The ideas presented so far in this chapter are fairly informal but could, of course, be developed more formally into lesson plans as needed by identifying one or two key learning objectives and adding timings, resources and ideas for formative assessment and adaptive teaching as needed. The first lesson plan included here shows how you might use a classic poem with some Year 4 children (Table 14.1).

It is based on the high-quality text: *The Spider and the Fly* written by Mary Howitt and illustrated by Tony DiTerlizzi.

Relevant Prior Learning: Prior to the lesson, the children read *The Spider and the Fly* and discussed it in small groups. They looked at the pictures and talked about how these support the meaning of the words, intensifying the suspense that the author has created through her language choices. They have responded to the poem in various ways, including writing a diary as one of the characters and doing some drama work to create a kind of conscience alley where half the children voiced the dead creatures whispering a warning to the fly, and the other half voiced the spider's attempts at persuasion. They have considered the characters of The Spider and the Fly in some depth, using the role on the wall activity.

What will children learn: (NC expectation: listen to and discuss a wide range of poems, recognise some different forms of poetry and prepare poems to read-aloud and to perform, beginning to show an understanding through intonation, tone, volume and action)

- To prepare a poem to read-aloud and perform, using intonation, tone, volume and action

Planned next steps: The children will perform their poems to the other classes in the school (each group visiting a different class).

What will effective learning look like?

Children will be able to:

- Read the poem aloud using appropriate intonation, tone, volume and action to show they understand it.

How will learning be assessed and what are the opportunities for effective feedback?:

- Listening into children's discussions and rehearsals to check that they understand what is meant by intonation, tone, volume and action and can adapt their voices appropriately
- Watching their finished performances

Table 14.1 A lesson plan for teaching poetry

Today's lesson sequence/content
SPECIFIC RESOURCES NEEDED:
Examples of poems that are read-aloud (e.g., from the CLPE web resource)
Children will need their own copy of The Spider and the Fly poem (this need not be the picture book version we have been looking at as they will just need the words of the poem for this lesson).
11.00 am: Ask the children to talk in pairs about their experiences of someone reading to them and what really makes them pay attention and listen. Generate a list of key points.
11.05 am: Introduce the children's challenge: to prepare a reading performance of The Spider and the Fly to share with another class.
11.10 am: Share a video from the CLPE resource (e.g., AF Harrold giving advice on performing a poem) and, with the class, list some ideas about what makes a good reading performance.
11.15 am: Watch a poet reading/performing their own poem – this could be the same author, e.g., AF Harrold reading 'The Flavour of Night', or could be different (NB think about what would be most useful to share with the children – in this case, it might be most helpful to choose a poem with a similar mood). Share the words: intonation, tone and voice (I have deliberately left out action as I want to work on the sound first – you might choose not to) and check that children know what they mean (this should link to their work on reading fluency). Now watch the poem again, asking the children to look out for the way the poet uses them to enhance their reading (you might prefer to repeat this for each of the three words so that the children listen out for one at a time). Note down some of their thoughts in relation to each of the three words intonation, tone and voice so that they have some success criteria to follow.

(Continued)

Table 14.1 A lesson plan for teaching poetry

Today's lesson sequence/content
11.20 am: Give the children copies of the poem which they can mark as needed. Organise them into small groups (between 3 and 5 is suggested – of course, not all groups have to be the same size) and ask them to begin to rehearse their own reading performance. This activity really draws on the Reader's Theatre idea outlined in Chapter 6. If the children are experienced with this, they will need far less direction. If not, you may wish to give them a few minutes and then pause them to talk about different ways of organising the group (e.g., they could take turns to say one or more lines, they could read all or some lines together, or they could have one main narrator voice and parts for The Spider and the Fly – any of which could be taken by two or more pupils talking in unison).
11.25–11.45 am: Circulate, listening in and giving feedback. You could pause the groups to have a quick discussion about one or more of the terms (e.g., intonation) and/or ask the children to share some good examples or choose ones you know are good. Remind the children to look at the key points list as needed.
11.45 am: Draw the children together and ask them to reflect on their performance so far. How effectively do they think they have used intonation, tone and voice up until this point? What might they work on in the next lesson to enhance their performance further?

The children will need time to prepare high-quality readings/performances and may benefit from doing this over two or three days, so it would help to be flexible in your use of time here. If you do extend this over more than one lesson, make sure that you always leave a few minutes for a plenary to draw together key points from the lesson and to look ahead to the next one. You could introduce the 'action' idea when or if you feel they are ready and that this wouldn't distract from their voices. You could place limits, for example, only allowing them to include one or two actions. Again, watching and discussing a model would be helpful to them; this could be you modelling good and bad use of action!

The children will also benefit from trying out their performances on each other before they perform them to their actual audiences. As each group will have a different audience, encourage them to share their ideas with each other so that each performance is the best it can be. Model giving clear feedback using the key points lists before asking the children to do this in their groups. You could also record each group and share this with the whole class for constructive feedback to be given (including by the performing group themselves). Make sure you give good time for the children to act on the advice given before they have to do their final performance.

When the children do perform their poems, ask the audience to give them some feedback.

Writing Poems

You will have seen that the National Curriculum's references to poetry focus on the reading of poetry, with no mention of writing it. This does not mean that we should not teach poetry writing as part of our writing curriculum though – it offers children opportunities to work intensively with the most powerful words to convey their thoughts or experiences and in my experience, many children really like the fact that they are freed from the usual conventions of writing sentences. Poetry writing also involves language play which can build children's flexibility with language, and the skills that they learn in trying out different ways of saying things and using poetic techniques such as the use of alliteration, rhythm and metaphor will support their other kinds of writing too. Therefore, when deciding on learning intentions, draw on those identified in the writing composition strand of the National Curriculum for English, and follow all the stages of the writing process so that pupils have time to plan, draft and write, evaluate, revise and edit, and then share and celebrate.

In the same way that you would approach any other piece of writing, the children need to read one or more examples of a poem or type of poem that they can use as a model for their own writing, and they will need to spend some time generating ideas for their own writing. You don't necessarily need to do these things in the same order every time; you could start by generating ideas for what to write about and then share a model of how one poem has done this, or you might start with the poem and use that as a stimulus to start gathering ideas for your own poems.

It may be that you want to create a shared experience where children begin to think about the subject of the poem in some depth. For example, you might want to link this to a particular element of cross-curricular learning, like the Great Fire of London or volcanoes, in which case, you might start by watching some film clips, looking at pictures, or reading part of a story. The subject of the poem might be something the children have experienced out of school, for example, dreams, holidays or family life, or themselves. You might want the children to observe something very closely, for example, the outside environment or an everyday object.

Language is key in poetry so spending time gathering words together is a worthwhile investment which will offer the children a bank of rich vocabulary to draw on. They can generate this as they observe or reflect on the theme of the poem, offering a good opportunity for spoken language development.

Modelling how to use your language bank to support the composition of a poem through live modelling is also a crucial step, and you will need to show them how to play about with different formats and revise your poem before you decide on a final version. Gradually releasing the responsibility to the children as you begin to share the composition task with them will support them in moving towards independence.

You could follow-up your performance of *The Spider and the Fly* by getting the children to compose their own narrative poems. You may want to give children the choice of animals so that they can use any predator/prey combination that they like, or you may perhaps want to stick more closely to the original poem by taking one of the ghostly characters that can be seen in Tony DiTerlizzi's illustrations and telling their story. If you want to continue to use the original poem as a model, the children could choose one of the characters and create a conversation with the spider (it might be helpful to do some work on alternative lines that the spider might have used to lure prey into its lair). Alternatively, you might choose a different model for the poem, for example, perhaps one which features just the poor deceased insect's voice. As with other writing, think about the indirect planning experiences that will get your poets ready to write, for example, making use of images, film clips and drama strategies such as role on the wall, improvisation and conscience alley.

You could also use *The Spider and the Fly* as a jumping-off point for writing some more structured poems, for example, you could use the fast poem structure outlined below to create poems about spiders and/or flies. Alternatively, you could write kennings. Kennings originated from Anglo-Saxon times and were originally ways of naming swords, for example 'death bringer'. Today they are used as very short poetic devices where something is named through a two-word expression that describes its qualities, for example, 'fly catcher'.

Activity   Write Your Own Poem

Fast poems

A fast poem uses powerful vocabulary to describe. It consists of four lines and may include a title in addition (mine often do). It is laid out as follows:

Line one – one word which should be a noun (you could leave out the title and just write the name of the thing the poem is about here)
Line two – two words, both adjectives
Line three – three words, all adverbs
Line four – four words, all verbs

Here's an example:
Crab

Decapod
Spiky and sandy
Quickly, sneakily and ferociously
Scuttling, snapping, creeping and gripping

You could use any starting point you like, for example, objects, observations, pictures, films, trips, hobbies, interests, emotions, etc., and make use of cross-curricular learning if you'd like to. You could also ask the children to write about experiences (e.g., nights) and memories (holidays). The quality of the vocabulary is key so think about what will help to generate this. For example, you could show some audio-visual resources, use books, engage in some drama work, or give pupils time to draw or discuss the theme of the poem first. Access to a thesaurus or resource such as *Descriptosaurus* (Alison Wilcox) might also be helpful. You will need to model each stage of the process clearly. For example, I might just start with word collection – writing as many words as I can think of to do with the theme for the poem and then making use of resources to extend my thinking. I might then classify my words in to different word classes and see whether I have some powerful vocabulary in each category. I would then select and arrange the words carefully. I might want to make use of a poetic device such as alliteration, or I might try that and then reject it if I thought it excluded some of my better words, or if I just didn't like the effect!

Now have a go at writing your own fast poem. Reflect on what supports you to do this as you go and make a note of the stages to use as a basis for your planning your own fast poem lesson.

It is worth taking your time when writing poetry if you want to produce writing of real quality. Poetry offers an excellent way to get children to observe something really closely and really think carefully about their language choices. There are all sorts of things in the classroom that the children could write about. In my first school, our behaviour system involved each class having a marble jar so that a collective reward could be given to the class. When the jar was full, the class could negotiate a reward. One year, our very first day was spent matching up each pupil with a marble, observing it really closely and writing a short poem to describe what the swirls of colour in the middle reminded them of, for example,

> Waves of pale blue and seaweed green
> Tumble, twist and fall
> Sparkling in the sun's warm light

We then used marbling inks to create patterned paper which we used for mounting our work, presented in a circular shape with the children writing the lines of their poem across the circle to reflect the way the colours were intertwined in the marble itself. We then created kennings from the children's poems and the children used the names to tell the class which marble they had put into the jar ('Sea twister is in'). Of course, I modelled the process step by step so that the children could see how to go about it themselves, and they collaborated really well, helping each other out with ideas and sharing constructive responses to each other's ideas and use of language.

When you're writing poetry, setting the scene can often be helpful. Use the interactive whiteboard to share music and images of the subject under focus. You could also find some different ways of using the classroom space, for example, by moving the children into a circle or getting them moving around the room. I once saw a really good Year 6 poetry lesson in which the teacher played atmospheric music and scenes of the sea on the whiteboard, dimmed the lights and asked the children to talk around the room imagining they were under the sea and writing the things they could see as expanded noun phrases on post-it notes. This was really effective in getting them to generate powerful language phrases to use in their writing.

Adaptive/Responsive Teaching

Considerations could include the following:

- Providing additional time for pupils to activate or build prior knowledge through first-hand experiences and discussion of audio-visual resources.
- Providing more time for children to engage with poetry in advance of the lesson so that they are comfortable with the medium (choose examples carefully as you need to know exactly what you want them to contribute to the children's experiences. For example, you might choose poems for the way that the poet has used words or poetic devices that

you want the class to use, read poems on the same theme, or read examples of poems written by you or a previous class because they match the end product you want the children to achieve).

- Getting the children to work collaboratively to generate ideas and vocabulary, and making use of resources such as thesauri. It can be helpful to build a whole class word bank using their ideas so that any pupil can draw on the words as needed.
- Making sure that each stage of the process is modelled clearly (some pupils may benefit from seeing it modelled more than once, perhaps as part of a smaller group the second time around).
- Providing alternative recording methods such as word processors and sound recording devices to reduce some of the cognitive load of writing.
- How you might make use of a wider range of poems or invest some time in looking at one or more additional poetic devices to stimulate pupils in need of stretch and challenge.

Summary

This chapter has considered how a teacher could plan the teaching of poetry, exploring ideas for ways to read, respond to and perform poetry as well as strategies to support the writing of poetry.

Further Reading

1   Visit the CLPE's resource on teaching poetry at https://clpe.org.uk/poetry. This will extend your knowledge of poetic forms, devices and terminology and introduce you to a wealth of poems by a wide range of diverse authors. There are also ideas for using poetry in the classroom.

2   Read Michael Rosen's *What Is Poetry? The Essential Guide to Reading and Writing Poems*, published by Walker Books.

3   Visit https://nationalpoetryday.co.uk/ to find out how you can take part in National Poetry Day. There are archived resources from previous years which you can also use in the classroom. These are organised by theme so are really useful for supporting cross-curricular learning.

References

CLPE. (2018). *Poetry in primary schools: What we know works.* CLPE.

Cooray, J., Fearnley, B., Femi, C., Nash, M., Sumpton, L., & Wojcik, A. (2017). *Young city poets – Evaluation report.* National Literacy Trust.

Cremin, T., Bearne, E., Dombey, H., & Reedy, D. (2015). *Teaching English creatively.* Routledge.

Department for Education. (2013). *The National Curriculum for England: Key stages 1 and 2 framework document.* Crown Publishing.

Goodwin, P. (2011). Chapter 4 actual poems, possible responses. In M. Lockwood (Ed.), *Bringing poetry alive: A guide to classroom practice* (pp. 38–51). SAGE.

Lambirth, A. (2015). Chapter 6: Commentary and practical implications: Righting the 'wrong kind of orientation'. In A. Wilson, S. Dymoke, M. Barrs, & A. Lambirth (Eds.), *Making poetry happen: Transforming the poetry classroom*. Bloomsbury Academic.

Marsh, J., & Bishop, J. (2013). *Changing play: Play, media and commercial culture from the 1950s to the present day*. Open University Press.

Rosen, M. (2011). Chapter 1: Reflections on being children's laureate and beyond. In M. Lockwood (Ed.), *Bringing poetry alive: A guide to classroom practice*. SAGE.

Rosen, M. (2016). *What is poetry?: The essential guide to reading and writing poems*. Walker Books.

15

Planning to Teach Spelling

Chapter Objectives

This chapter will:

- Identify the key elements of a high-quality spelling curriculum.
- Consider what effective pedagogy for teaching spelling might look like.
- Demonstrate one way of approaching the planning of a spelling lesson.

Introduction

Spelling sits within the transcription strand of the writing curriculum and is focused on developing children's abilities to write accurately in order that they can communicate their ideas and emotions to others. The ability to spell quickly and accurately supports a pupil's ability to write their ideas fluently, drawing on their knowledge of 'the relationship between sounds and letters (phonics) and understanding the morphology (word structure) and orthography (spelling structure) of words' (DfE, 2013, p. 5). Research tells us that a lack of proficiency in spelling has the potential to cause several challenges for young writers. Less proficient spellers tend to write compositions using only words that the author is confident they can spell accurately, thus limiting the range of vocabulary and quality of their writing (Joshi et al., 2009). Moreover, the more time and attention proficient spellers need to devote to this aspect of transcription, the greater the level of interference with the other aspects of the writing process (Graham & Santangelo, 2014). This view is supported in the Education Endowment Foundation's guide to *Improving Literacy in Key Stage 2*, which states:

> Fluent writing supports composition because pupils' cognitive resources are freed from focusing on handwriting, spelling, and sentence construction and can be redirected towards writing composition. Extensive practice, supported by effective feedback, is required to develop fluent transcription skills. (Bilton & Duff, 2021, p. 11)

There is sometimes debate about whether spelling is 'caught' (i.e. that a person is just naturally good at spelling or not) or taught (Can teachers really make a difference?). However, research tells us that well-designed teaching and learning really do make a difference (O'Sullivan & Thomas, 2007), supporting children to develop both interest and competence in steadily expanding the number of words they can spell accurately and growing their confidence and skill when attempting new words.

Curriculum Continuity and Progression

If a child has met the relevant early learning goals for the end of Year R, they will be able to write recognisable letters, most of which are correctly formed; spell words by identifying sounds in them and representing the sounds with a letter or letters; and write simple phrases and sentences that can be read by others (DfE, 2021). This will have been supported by daily phonics teaching and enhanced through meaningful and authentic provision and opportunities across the Early Years Foundation Stage curriculum.

The National Curriculum in England: English Programmes of Study for Key Stage 1 and Key Stage 2 identifies specific expectations for pupils in each year group in both the main body of the document and in *Appendix 1*. As well as daily phonics teaching which continues from Year R into Year 1 focusing on building children's knowledge of grapheme-phoneme correspondences and common exception words, learners study rules and patterns. From Year 2 onwards, the requirements listed in the English programmes of study and *Appendix 1* define the rules and patterns that children must learn, along with a statutory list of common exception words to be learned by pupils in Year 2, with further word lists for pupils in Year 3/4 and Year 5/6. These lists are described as being 'a mixture both of words pupils frequently using their writing and those which they often misspell' (DfE, 2013, p. 49). The guidance provided suggests that these words could continue to be learned incrementally by studying a few each week. This builds on effective phonics provision from Year R/Year 1 where children learned phonemic knowledge of grapheme-phoneme correspondences (GPCs) and a few tricky words each week.

Curriculum and Pedagogy

Teachers will need to plan both the content of their spelling lessons – what they will teach – and the pedagogy through which they will teach it – how they will teach. This is key to ensuring that curriculum time is used purposefully, maximising children's progress and engaging children in their learning.

Research Focus: A Pedagogy for Spelling – Five Ideas From Research

O'Sullivan and Thomas's research (2007) shows that teachers who were enthusiastic and genuinely interested in children's discoveries about words were more effective teachers of spelling. They also note that it is important that children are encouraged to focus on their own progress rather than comparing themselves with other learners as this is typically unhelpful.

Alderman and Green (2011) highlight the importance of making connections to the joy, creativity and emotional impact of words. This fits well within current thinking on the importance of developing children's vocabularies.

It is helpful to view and present spelling as an active thinking task, supporting children to approach it from a problem-solving perspective for which they need to develop cognitive strategies, giving them a clear plan of attack to use when learning a new word or attempting to write an unfamiliar word (Joshi et al., 2009).

Zutell (1996) identifies tasks which are best for learning spellings as those which give children plenty of opportunities to recall and reproduce words, identify and study the tricky parts, and consider the strategies that will help them to remember these. This reflects Mercer's (2000) view that learning is an active process which offers opportunities for cumulative and exploratory talk in which children listen to and build on each other's ideas, engaging constructively but critically in discussing words and their spellings.

Research also shows that learners need sufficient time to be able to develop and consolidate their understanding of words and patterns (Templeton & Morris, 1999), and that time will also be needed for learners to revisit and revise learning to ensure it is secure (Gagen, 2010).

Teachers often report that one of the challenges in teaching spelling is that the content defined in the National Curriculum seems to be above the level of their learners; this concern is supported by research by Morris et al. (1995) and Wallace (2006) which showed that when learners study words at an appropriate level, they make more progress than if they study words and patterns that are at their frustration level. Therefore, one of the keys to teaching spelling effectively is to focus carefully on what our learners can achieve lesson by lesson, identifying the small chunks of learning which will support the growth of knowledge and designing well-scaffolded lessons which reduce frustration where possible.

To help us identify the small chunks of learning, we need to continue to build on the concept of supporting children to make phonically plausible attempts at spelling that is established in Year R where, through their phonics learning, pupils learn one way of representing each of the 44+ phonemes so that to write the word 'please' as 'pleese' is good as the pupil has applied their knowledge of how to write the phoneme 'ee'. As pupils are taught alternative phoneme-grapheme correspondences, they will further develop their accuracy but it is important to retain this focus on supporting learners to build their knowledge of possible ways of spelling parts of words when we consider the National Curriculum Programmes of study. Some learners will be ready to look at the spelling of whole words in order to ensure that the word is accurate from start to finish, but for others, the focus will be on developing their knowledge of a new pattern or rule for just one part of the word and they may not yet be ready to focus on all other parts of the word. Therefore, increasing children's knowledge of phonically plausible patterns is our aim when planning for these learning objectives. However, when pupils are learning to reproduce the words from the specified word lists, our focus is on accurate recall of the whole word. Here, we will want our learners to attempt to spell the words, taking care not to overload them with a focus on too many words at a time.

We must consciously seek to build learners' linguistic knowledge by teaching them about words as well as how to spell words. We need to provide time for our learners to look at words and think about them, to listen to how they sound and to know how it feels to say them. Explicit teaching is key to helping them to recognise patterns and connections, as is providing extended time for them to look at, and to talk and think about words. Children's learning will also be strengthened by planning collaborative experiences in which they work together to articulate and develop their knowledge as they ask each other and themselves questions such as 'How is this word spelt?', 'How do I pronounce it?', 'What sounds can I hear?', 'What letters can I see and in what order?', 'What patterns can I recognise?', 'Does my attempt at spelling this word look right?', and 'Which strategies are most helpful when I try to learn how to spell this word?' (Westwood, 2014). These approaches will help to scaffold children's learning effectively, reducing frustration as they work with support and structure.

To develop children's proficiency in spelling, they need good teaching which is focused on:

- Developing a secure knowledge of four key sources of information about words.
- Developing knowledge of multiple ways of learning spellings (a repertoire approach).
- Regular, purposeful practice to embed and apply their knowledge.

Research Focus: Developing Children's Knowledge of Words

Bear and Templeton note that there are three layers of information in words: the alphabetic layer, the pattern layer and the meaning layer (1998, p. 223). In the alphabetic layer, children learn the direct match between phonemes and their associated graphemes. This corresponds with the teaching for Year R outlined in most systematic synthetic phonics programmes which teach the simple alphabetic code thus enabling children to begin to spell simple words such as 'dog'. Some words also have a pattern layer; children begin to learn alternative phoneme-grapheme correspondences, for example, that the long 'e' sound can be spelled as 'ee', 'ea', 'e_e' and so on. This corresponds with phonics teaching that takes place in Year 1 and teaches the complex alphabetic code. Finally, there is the meaning layer; as children move on in their spelling, they learn that words can contain different units of meaning which are signified by the use of root words, prefixes and suffixes.

Fellowes and Oakley (2010) propose that there are four key sources of knowledge which children will draw on in order to become proficient at spelling and must thus be built systematically through the study of words. These sources are: phonemic knowledge, orthographic knowledge, morphological knowledge and etymological knowledge.

Phonemic knowledge builds children's understanding of grapheme-phoneme correspondences to represent words, and, as noted above, is systematically taught in England's schools through Year R/Year 1 daily phonic lessons. This phonemic knowledge is the first source of information developed. Following on from this foundation, children need to develop three further sources of knowledge to become proficient spellers.

The second source of information children can draw on is orthographic knowledge. Many of the words children learn to spell in the early stages of learning directly match simple phonemes with graphemes. As they explore more complex words, which include one or more alternative graphemes, they will need to build their knowledge of the way words look to know that they have selected the correct one. This is developed from systematic phonics teaching in Year 1 where children begin to learn a number of alternative grapheme-phoneme correspondences and thus must begin to build their visual memory of the way words look. At this stage, phonic knowledge is no longer sufficient on its own.

The third source of knowledge is morphological knowledge. This develops children's understanding of the meaning of the word itself and any of its components, for example, root words, prefixes and suffixes. This knowledge can be helpful for a speller as they can draw their understanding of meaning. For example, if they wish to spell a word such as 'talked', using their knowledge that the root word 'talk' is a verb and the suffix 'ed' signifies that the action happened in the past can help a child to remember to spell the word talked with an 'ed' ending rather than a 't' ending which is what they might hear.

Finally developing children's etymological knowledge of words, knowing about where words come from, can also help children. For example, in *Appendix 1* of *The National Curriculum in England: English Programmes of Study for Key Stage 1 and Key Stage 2*, children in Year 3/4 are expected to learn that the 'k' sound which can be heard in words which are Greek in origin will usually be spelled 'ch' (scheme, chorus and echo).

Explicitly teaching children about the four sources of knowledge will help to provide a structure for their learning which will grow over time. Making links really clear, for example, by saying 'today we are going to learn a new prefix which will grow our morphological knowledge' will help them to see the underlying structure rather than just being presented with an endless list new of new objectives throughout their primary school years. You could support children's learning further by building a working wall display of the four sources of knowledge and associated strategies.

Activity   Building Your Knowledge of Continuity and Progression in Learning in the National Curriculum

Look at the programmes of study which are outlined in *Appendix 1* of *The National Curriculum in England: English Programmes of Study for Key Stage 1 and Key Stage 2*. Which sources of knowledge do each of these requirements help to build in order to develop children's proficiency as spellers? The second source of knowledge, orthographic knowledge, is not as clearly signposted as the other three. Where can you find opportunities to support the development of this source of knowledge through the requirements listed?

Developing Children's Use of Strategies for Spelling

As well as building children's knowledge about words, we need to develop their knowledge of different strategies for learning words; these strategies can typically be applied to any group of words and therefore could work for any of the suggested words in *Appendix 1*, including the word lists but also for children's personal spellings. Research tells us that one of the challenges of teaching spelling is that children can go into a kind of autopilot while copying out a word several times without really engaging any cognitive resources into how to reproduce the word accurately. However, by engaging them in the aim of learning a word, asking them to study and try to remember the word, then to hide and try to reproduce the word accurately before checking it, and finally asking them to evaluate the success of their chosen strategy, they are taking a much more active approach (Zutell, 1996). This supports the development of what Cordewener et al. (2016) refer to as spelling consciousness, a learner's understanding of areas of difficulty within spelling and their ability to identify and correct errors.

There are some key strategies which can help children to learn words, although different strategies may be useful for different words. The need for children to learn a range of strategies is suggested by Kwong and Varnhagen (2005) as no strategy alone will support the accurate reproduction of all words. Kraai (2011, cited in Westwood, 2014) observes that proficient spellers have a bank of ways for learning, storing, recalling and checking the spelling of words they use, but less competent spellers often have limited strategies and resort to rote learning, so it is important for us to develop children' knowledge and understanding of a range of proactive strategies for learning spelling.

Some effective strategies that are supported by research are as follows:

1   'Look, say, cover, write, check' – here, the pupil looks at the word, says it aloud, covers it, writes it and then removes the cover to check it. It is important that children do this for the whole word rather than checking after writing each letter.
2   Visual emphasis – This is based on studying how the word looks, identifying the tricky part and making this look visually different through the use of colour, size or font, for example, 'lib**r**ary'. The pupil then covers it, tries to reproduce it and checks it.
3   Auditory emphasis – The pupil studies and considers how to break down the word and articulate the parts in such a way as to emphasise the tricky bit to help recall the spelling, for example, saying it as 'lib-*r*-a-ry'.
4   Mnemonics – This is a learning technique to aid retrieval, often taking the form of a phrase, sentence or rhyme in which each letter of the word creates an image or connection that helps it to be remembered. You may already know one or more of these for spelling challenging words, for example, remembering because as 'big elephants can't always use small exits'.
5   Multi-sensory – This involves children practising their word on a surface which gives them some sort of tactile feedback, for example, sandpaper or carpet. Research shows this can be a useful strategy and might be particularly effective for children with learning difficulties (Westwood, 2014).

To help children to build awareness of, draw on and make connections to the different sources of word knowledge that we systematically expanding through our teaching, we can also use some checking questions such as 'As you try to write the word, what sounds can you hear? Does it look right? Are there different parts within the word which you know the meaning of? Where does the word originate from?' Building such questions into a routine for having a go will support learning (Westwood, 2014).

Activity   Reflecting on Your Own Strategies for Spelling

Think of three or four words that you find hard to spell. You could get a head start on any from the National Curriculum word lists that you are unsure of, use the ones I have suggested or search for words that are difficult to spell. Study each word and have a go at the strategies listed to help you to learn them. You should be able to use a search engine to find the words' origins. Once you can confidently recall each word accurately, reflect on the following questions: Which strategy was most effective for each word? Were there any other strategies that would be more useful? What else did you need to help you to learn each word? What would you need to happen next in order for you to embed these words in your long-term memory?

   Suggested words: onomatopoeia, mischievously, logorrhoea, xanthosis

Lesson Plan

Here is a suggestion for a lesson plan for a Year 3 class (Table 15.1). It focuses on one of patterns identified in *Appendix 1* of the National Curriculum. You will be able to adapt it for younger or older pupils; to do this, consider how long they can focus their attention when listening to a teacher or working with others, and how you could simplify or increase the level of challenge.

Relevant prior learning: This is the first lesson of looking at prefixes and root words. I have chosen one word from the Year 3/4 list to use as this will help the pupils build their knowledge of how to spell this, as well as their understanding of what prefixes and suffixes are and how these can be used to change the meaning of some words. In the lesson, they will need time to study and discuss the words and note how they are constructed. I also want them to have opportunities to recall the words during the session.

What will children learn:

- To break a word into parts (syllables) to spell it
- Know that 'dis' is a negative prefix and be able to spell it
- To be able to spell the word 'disappear' from the Year 3/4 word list

Planned next steps: When other prefixes outlined in *Appendix 1* are taught, make connections back to this lesson. Display the word on the wall after the lesson and encourage pupils to check their spelling when they use the word. Revisit for practice little and often.

NC reference links:

- Apply their growing knowledge of root words, prefixes... (etymology and morphology) as listed in *Appendix 1*, both to read aloud and to understand the meaning of new words they meet (reading)
- Use further prefixes and suffixes and understand how to add them

What will effective learning look like:
Children will be able to:

- Break a word into parts to spell it.
- Spell the prefix 'dis'.
- Explain what the prefix 'dis' means.
- Use phonemic and orthographic knowledge to inform the spelling of the other parts of the word.
- Be able to use the terms 'root word' and 'prefix' confidently and accurately.

How will learning be assessed:

- Observe pupils' retrieval attempts to check they can write 'dis' and 'disappear' accurately
- Listen in to pupils' discussions to check they can apply their knowledge of the meaning of the prefix 'dis' when using it with appropriate root words

- Listen in to pupils to check they are considering appropriate strategies for learning to spell new words

Table 15.1 A lesson plan for teaching spelling

Today's lesson sequence/content
SPECIFIC RESOURCES NEEDED:

Word cards (1 × large set of each)

unhappy	undo	unfair	unlock (1 × large set)
dishonest	disagree	disobey	disappear (1 × large set)

Additional word cards (three or four smaller sets for groups if needed):

dislike	disappoint	disable	disarm	disgrace
disorganised	disqualify	dissatisfied	displease	disintegrate

9.00: 2-minute verbal review – words with the prefix 'un' studied in Year 1 – unhappy, undo, unfair, unlock. Children tell a partner, then reveal the word. Check they know the meaning.

9.02: Tell children that today we are going to be learning how to spell a new prefix. Ask what the word 'prefix' means (a prefix is a group of letters that is added to a root word to change its meaning). Display all four words with the prefix 'un'. Play a quick fire game where I say 'prefix' or 'root', and children have to call out the right part of the word. Ask children to tell a partner what would happen if you took the prefix 'un' away from the words. Check they understand that this flips the meaning of the words so that they now have the opposite meaning.

9.05: Explain that today we are going to learn a new prefix 'dis'. Like 'un', 'dis' a negative prefix. It means not or none. When we add 'dis' to the beginning of a word, it takes the opposite meaning.

Show the four key words for today. Ask pairs to read and talk about each word to check they know the meaning. Display four definitions which are numbered. Shuffle the four 'dis' word cards and reveal one. Ask children to show (using fingers or writing the number) which definition it fits. Prompt children to explain their reasoning, if appropriate, or model this for them.

9.08: Ask each pair to work together to check they can spell the prefix 'dis'. Mix up the un and dis root word cards and play a quickfire game 'opposites' where I show a root word and the children have to write the prefix that will turn that word into its opposite.

9.10: Using the word 'disagree', model how to study the word and identify its straightforward/tricky parts, considering appropriate strategies for learning it, for example, splitting it up into prefix and root word, writing one at a time, using over-articulation to emphasise the 'ee' sound at the end, using visual emphasis to highlight the 'g and double 'e' (making those parts bigger or in colour), or considering a mnemonic such as 'disagree, one g, two ees'. Ask children to talk to their partner about which strategy they think would work best for them and why. Choose a couple of children to explain their thinking and reinforce the use of the strategies as appropriate.

9.12: Get each pair to join with another pair. Focus on the word 'disappear' as that is on the Year 3/4 word list. Ask them to talk about the sequence of letters in the word and think about which part/s might be tricky to spell. Ask the groups if they can think of a way (strategy) to help each group member to remember the spelling. Ask groups to practise recalling the word (e.g., they could take turns saying and show the word to the others and then hide it so that the others practise written recall). Groups could go on to try this with the other 'dis' words too.

9.20: Plenary–Ask pupils to review today's learning by pairing up with someone they haven't yet worked with today. They should be able to spell the prefix 'dis' and explains what it means – ask them to check with each other, and should be able to explain the terms 'root word' and 'prefix'. Ask them to share which strategy(ies) they found most helpful in learning to spell the word disappear. How often do they think they would need to practise it to make sure it sticks?

You'll see that the plan shown above is for quite a short lesson. Moats (2005) advises that an investment of 15-minute spelling instruction a day is needed for children to establish a firm knowledge base which can be reduced as they become more proficient. Of course, as in the case of all learning, some learning objectives may work better as parts of longer lessons, while others will fit much shorter spans of time, so here, the length of the lesson is matched to the planned learning, aiming for a balance between achieving the intended objectives and a good pace to keep the lesson focused and purposeful.

For the above lesson plan, you will see not only that the learning objective has been taken straight from the National Curriculum but also that the word 'disappear' from the Year 3/4 word list is included as it fitted well here. You might be thinking that learning to spell 'dis' is perhaps too straightforward for Year 3 pupils. However, you are likely to have learners from a range of starting points and so for those with low prior attainment in spelling, focusing clearly on something achievable makes much more sense than expecting that they will be able to spell all the example words accurately in full. Learners with high prior attainment may well be able to proceed beyond this objective and so there are resources ready which can easily be integrated into the lesson if formative assessment shows this to be the case. This will enable those pupils to apply their knowledge of 'dis' to a range of words, thus deepening their knowledge and the range of vocabulary on which they can draw in their writing. They can also be given the challenge of learning to spell as many of the words as possible in full.

Introduction to the Lesson

Effective phonics teaching always starts with a review of prior learning in order to build automaticity; spelling is no different. Children will need to revisit learning frequently in order to consolidate their knowledge and understanding so developing efficient routines which allow children to recall previous learning is essential. In this lesson, the teacher reviews learning from the Year 1 curriculum as this is related to what is about to come.

The Main Lesson

Teacher modelling is a key strategy for teaching spelling. Learners will become increasingly skilled at studying words, noticing their tricky bits, drawing on sources of knowledge, and trying out and evaluating different strategies, when this is modelled and explained aloud frequently by the teacher. It is important to model strategies for learning to spell a new word and for having a go at a word when writing independently so make sure you take opportunities to model these processes outside spelling lessons, for example, when you are teaching writing. What you choose to model will be informed by the children's prior learning – take care not to overload them.

The lesson could be extended. This could involve looking at more words, engaging the children in one of the longer learning opportunities explained below, or involve an engaging application task which encourages learners to see the connection between spelling and authentic writing. For example, the lesson could move on to share the opening of *Mr Happy* from the *Mr Men* and *Little Miss* series of books by Roger Hargreaves. Using the opening of *Mr Happy* as a model, the teacher could show the children how to write a short story opening about an invented character called Mr Unhappy. The children could then work collaboratively to make up their own characters using the prefix dis, for example, Mr Dishonest or Little Miss Disobedient. This would give children a number of opportunities to reproduce the prefix while reinforcing the meaning in an engaging context.

Other Ways to Develop the Children's Learning

There are other spelling activities that also support children's construction of knowledge about words. The use of spelling investigations, word hunts, word studies and word sorts give opportunities for children to explore patterns in more depth. This kind of learning might start with a longer lesson on the first day with shorter sessions which build on it later in the week or could be spread over several days.

Word Hunts

In a word hunt, children create list of words that fit a particular pattern, for example, how many words can you find that end in 'ly'? How many words can you find with the 'igh' sound in? To do this, they might think of words that they know or find in books. They could do this individually, in small groups, or as a whole class. Remember that the teacher needs to show great enthusiasm for and interest in all the words the children find.

Word Sorts

Using either a list that has been gathered through a word hunt, or a list provide by the teacher, the children can examine the words to see whether there are any ways to sort them. The real aim here is to get them to look closely at words and take ownership of building knowledge, for example, discovering through their observations that when making the plural form of a word, you need to change the 'y' to an 'i' before adding an 'es' ending. There are many different types of word sort, for example, closed sorts where you give a pattern or rule and ask the children to sort the words accordingly, or open sorts where children investigate the words to see if they can generate some rules or patterns for themselves. Word sorts can be repeated to build familiarity; this may be particularly useful for children who need more time to develop their understanding, again through shorter sessions on a number of days rather than a longer one just once. Pupils can also work in different groups and pairings to complete word sorts, giving them the opportunity to collaborate with a range of peers.

Collaborative Spelling Test

This activity is outlined in detail in Tony Martin's excellent *Talk for Spelling* minibook. It involves children working in mixed ability pairs to have a go at spelling words given by the teacher. Once the pair has made their attempt, they join with another pair to compare their thinking. After this has taken place, each group chooses one member who can visit another group and check the spelling of one or two words, memorising any changes they want to make when they return to their home group. The home group then discusses the spellings and agrees their final attempts before the teacher reveals the answers. This activity really encourages children to explain their thinking, discuss possible combinations of letters and draw on their knowledge and strategies in a collaborative way. It may be a particularly useful activity for learning words from the word lists, and Martin advises that the teacher uses it to assess the children's understanding.

Evaluating Spelling Activities

You may well have come across other activities which propose to give children practice at spelling. Although they may engage children, a number of these don't really have sufficient focus on the goal of developing children's knowledge about words, or using and evaluating strategies which practise whole word recall to justify giving up precious curriculum time, so consider carefully whether they are really worth investing in.

Developing Routines

Developing routines can really help to ensure that spelling time is used efficiently. Routines for practising and reinforcing spellings can be established by providing a wall display or mat which shows the key question prompts listed earlier in this chapter so that children can very quickly find what they need and practise weekly focus words, word list words, personal spellings or previous spellings regularly.

Using Resources

Resources to help spelling can include building working wall displays which help them to remember new learning, while the provision of word mats for children to refer to in independent writing will help them to remember to apply their knowledge. Another useful resource is a 'have a go' pad which children can use to try out a word three times in different ways before deciding to use the one that looks right (this is really helpful in reinforcing the importance of studying how a word looks). The use of word cards, both blank and pre-written, to aid sorting is worth considering, as is the use of personal word books or word cards where children record words that they are learning to spell. Key spellings such as days of the week and common exception words can be useful but make sure that the children know how to use them and can navigate them with ease so that they don't become wallpaper. Having attractive dictionaries – preferably of different sorts such as the Ace Spelling dictionary and the Barrington Stoke School Dictionary which may be helpful to some pupils – will support independence. Some good apps which say the word aloud are also available.

Plenary

The plenary asks the children to check their learning against the lesson objectives. It also asks children to reflect on the effectiveness of the strategies they employed and to take ownership of the learning process thus promoting metacognition. Listening to these conversations will give the teacher useful feedback on the impact of the lesson.

Adaptive/Responsive Teaching

Some possible ways in which you could adapt the learning for those needing additional scaffolding or stretch and challenge are:

*   Identify possible misconceptions – children might think you can add 'dis' as a prefix to any word to change its meaning.
*   Focus on particular children to check they are keeping up.
*   Make sure all children can see the board clearly and are joining in fully when asked.
*   Have additional word cards ready for pupils who need more challenge.
*   Make sure groups are collaborating effectively with all members involved.

Providing Feedback

Remember to keep the learning objective in the forefront of your mind when giving children feedback. When teaching patterns and rules, as outlined in *Appendix 1*, feedback should focus initially on the accurate recall of the pattern, for example, if you are teaching 'ence' endings, the pupils will have their best go at a word such as 'audience', but your focus is initially on the accuracy of the 'ence' ending to support progress in expanding knowledge of plausible endings and reproducing these accurately, before considering other parts of the word. When studying whole word recall of words from the National Curriculum word lists, your feedback can usefully identify which letters are accurate. Letting the learner know which parts they have recalled accurately and therefore which parts to focus on next. Similarly in personal spelling work, whole word accuracy is the goal and so again, this feedback can be focused on which parts are right and which to focus on next. Encouraging children to have a go at spelling words they find challenging is really important so recognising where they have had success will help to keep their motivation high.

Feedback can also focus on the child's use of strategies, for example, 'I can see you used the visual emphasis strategy to practise recalling the word 'league' accurately and here you have spelled the word correctly so it was a good strategy to choose for this word' or 'that was a good discussion on the different strategies you could use to learn to spell 'extreme'. Try some out and see which strategy seemed most helpful to you with this word.' Of course this will be preceded by observations of learners at work where you can assess each child's level of confidence and accuracy, the range of strategies tried, and the level of success achieved. You could also consider the use of conferencing (O'Sullivan & Thomas, 2007) which allows children to work one to one with the teacher to talk about their spelling, and identify successes and areas for development.

Assessing Children's Written Work

Recent updates to their Improving Literacy in Key Stage 1 (Bilton & Tillotson, 2021) and Key Stage 2 (Bilton & Duff, 2021) guidance highlight the value of assessing the kinds of errors that children have made in their written work, identifying errors which have arisen through misconceptions in phonemic knowledge, where the child has not made a phonically plausible attempt at a phoneme, orthographic knowledge, where the error is phonically plausible but not correct, or morphological knowledge, where the error is phonically plausible but shows that the child has not understood the unit of meaning, for example, by adding a 't' to the end of a verb such as trap to spell it as it sounds rather than adding the morphological 'ed' ending to show that the action occurred in the past. Information gathered through such analytical assessments should be used to inform future teaching.

Applying Learning Beyond the Spelling Lesson

Bilton and Duff (2021) note that developing automaticity in transcription requires extensive practice, explicit instruction and encouragement, reducing demands on working memory and thus supporting composition. To achieve this, learners need regular, dedicated time within the curriculum to build their knowledge of words and to develop efficient use of a range of strategies that support them in recalling words accurately. In connection with the ideas presented earlier in this book, it is also important that children are given authentic and purposeful writing experiences with real audiences with whom they wish to communicate so that they can recognise the need for spelling to be accurate and practise this skill. Learning will be most effectively supported when teachers also recognise opportunities for learners to apply their knowledge and skills. For example, when drafting compositions, children will need to use strategies for making their best attempt at the spelling of a word without letting an undue focus on accuracy at this stage disrupt the flow of composition. However, the process of drafting and revising a piece of writing must include dedicated time for revisiting and checking spellings at the editing stage. Taking opportunities to model the application of word knowledge and spelling strategies when demonstrating writing, and taking particular care to make connections to recently learned patterns and rules or words from the word lists, is also key to success in developing children's spelling.

Summary

This chapter has considered what research tells us about how to teach spelling effectively. The importance of continuing to build children's phonemic, orthographic, morphological and etymological knowledge is discussed along with the need to teach a range of strategies through which they can study and discuss words in order to provide meaningful and memorable learning experiences. The importance of making connections within the spelling curriculum and reinforcing application through shared writing is established.

Further Reading

1   To find out more about different ways to develop your use of word sorts, read this article: Fresch, M. J., & Wheaton, A. (1997). Sort, search and discover: Spelling in the child-centered classroom. *The Reading Teacher*, 51, 20–31.
2   To find out more about the idea of presenting spelling as a thinking activity and how to promote independence in learning, read this article: Joshi, R., Treiman, R., Carreker, S., & Moats, L. (2009). How words cast their spell: Spelling is an integral part of learning the language, not a matter of memorization. *American Educator*, 32(4), 6–43.
3   To find out more about how you can underpin your spelling curriculum with purposeful, collaborative talk, read *Talk for Spelling* by Tony Martin, published by the UKLA.

References

Alderman, G. L., & Green, S. K. (2011). Fostering lifelong spellers through meaningful experiences. *The Reading Teacher*, 64(8), 599–605.

Bear, D., & Templeton, S. (1998). Explorations in developmental spelling: Foundations for learning and teaching phonics, spelling and vocabulary. *The Reading Teacher*, 52(3), 222–242.

Bilton, C., & Duff, A. (2021). *Improving literacy in Key Stage 2 guidance report* (2nd ed.). Education Endowment Foundation. https://educationendowmentfoundation.org.uk/education-evidence/guidance-reports/literacy-ks2. Accessed on August 31, 2022.

Bilton, C., & Tillotson, S. (2021) *Improving literacy in Key Stage 1 guidance report* (2nd ed.). Education Endowment Foundation. https://educationendowmentfoundation.org.uk/education-evidence/guidance-reports/literacy-ks-1. Accessed on August 31, 2022.

Cordewener, K. A. H., Verhoeven, L., & Bosman, A. M. T. (2016). Improving spelling performance and spelling consciousness. *The Journal of Experimental Education*, 84(1), 48–74.

Department for Education. (2013). *The National Curriculum in England: English programmes of study: Key stages 1 and 2* National curriculum in England.

Department for Education. (2021). *Statutory framework for the early years foundation stage Setting the standards for learning, development and care for children from birth to five.*

Fellowes, J., & Oakley, G. (2010). *Language, literacy and early childhood education.* Oxford University Press.

Gagen, M. (2010). Effective spelling instruction. http://www.righttrackreading.com/howto-spell.html. Accessed on September 20, 2018.

Graham, S., & Santangelo, T. (2014). Does spelling instruction make students better spellers, readers, and writers? A meta-analytic review. *Reading and Writing, 27*(9), 1703–1743.

Hargreaves, R. (1997). *Mr Happy.* Penguin Putnam Inc.

Joshi, R., Treiman, R., Carreker, S., & Moats, L. (2009). How words cast their spell: Spelling is an integral part of learning the language, not a matter of memorization. *American Educator, 32*(4), 6–43.

Kwong, T. E., & Varnhagen, C. K. (2005). Strategy development and learning to spell new words: Generalization of a process. *Developmental Psychology, 41*(1), 148–159.

Martin, T. (2014). *Talk for spelling.* UKLA.

Mercer, N. (2000). *Words and minds: How we use language to think together.* Routledge.

Moats, L. C. (2005). How spelling supports reading. Winter issue 2005/06. *American Educator,* 12–43.

Morris, D., Blanton, L., Blanton, W., & Perney, J. (1995). Spelling instruction and achievement in six classrooms. *The Elementary School Journal, 96,* 145–162.

O'Sullivan, O., & Thomas, A. (2007). *Understanding spelling.* Routledge.

Templeton, S., & Morris, S. (1999). Questions teachers ask about spelling. *Reading Research Quarterly, 35*(1), 102–112.

Wallace, R. (2006). Characteristics of effective spelling instruction. *Reading Horizons, 46*(4), 268–278.

Westwood, P. (2014). *Teaching spelling: Exploring commonsense strategies and best practices.* Routledge.

Zutell, J. (1996). The directed spelling thinking activity (DSTA): Providing an effective balance in word study instruction. *The Reading Teacher, 50*(2), 98–108.

16

Planning to Teach Handwriting

Chapter Objectives

This chapter will:

- Identify the key elements of a high-quality handwriting curriculum.
- Consider what effective pedagogy for teaching handwriting might look like.
- Demonstrate one way of approaching the planning of a handwriting lesson.

Introduction

The other aspect of the Writing: Transcription strand is handwriting. As with spelling, this is focused on developing children's abilities to write accurately in order that they can communicate their ideas and emotions to others with 'fluent, legible and eventually speedy handwriting' (DfE, 2013, p. 5).

Curriculum Continuity and Progression

If a child has met the relevant early learning goals for the end of Year R, they will have developed their gross motor skills demonstrating strength, balance and coordination when playing, as well as refining their fine motor skills so that they can hold a pencil effectively in preparation for fluent writing – using the tripod grip in almost all cases. They should also be able to use a range of small tools, including scissors, paint brushes and cutlery, and begin to show accuracy and care when drawing. In writing, they will be able to write recognisable letters, most of which are correctly formed (DfE, 2021a).

The National Curriculum in England: English Programmes of Study for Key Stage 1 and Key Stage 2 identifies specific expectations for pupils in each year group in the main body of the document. In Year 1, pupils need to develop the physical skills needed for handwriting. This starts with teaching children to sit correctly at a table, hold a pencil comfortably and begin to form letters in the correct direction by starting and finishing in the right place. Children should also be taught the concept of letter families so that they understand that groups of letters are formed in similar ways; teachers should ensure children practise these. In Year 2, pupils should be able to form letters correctly thus establishing good habits from the beginning. Specific objectives focus on ensuring that the letters formed are of the right size in relation to each other. Word spaces should also reflect the size of the letters. Children should be taught to join some letters as soon as they can form them securely with the correct orientation, using diagonal and horizontal strokes.

In Year 3/4, joined handwriting is expected as the norm; pupils should be able to perform this skill at a speed that allows them to keep up with what they want to say in their writing. Again pupils should be taught to use diagonal and horizontal strokes to join some letters and to increase the legibility, consistency and quality of their handwriting. In Year 5/6, pupils should be taught to write fluently, legibly and with increasing speed, developing a personal style which allows them choice over which letters to join and the writing implement that is best suited to the task. By the end of Year 6, pupils should be able to write down their ideas quickly.

Activity   Thinking About Letters

Think about the letters in the alphabet. If you were going to divide them into families, how might you group them? What basic shapes do you think each group makes use of? Which family would you teach the children first and why?

Curriculum and Pedagogy

Guidance from the Department for Education states that 'handwriting requires frequent and discrete, direct teaching' (2013, p. 14) and that 'left-handed pupils should receive specific teaching to meet their needs'.

Studies have shown some interesting links between the development of handwriting and the development of other aspects of English and cognition. A study by Longcamp et al. (2005) showed that learning letter formation through handwriting greatly supports children's knowledge and understanding of letter representation, strengthening their ability to recognise letters visually. This is reflected in guidance on phonics teaching which highlights the importance of children learning to write words as they learn to read them, thus learning the words inside out (DfE, 2021b). A study of older learners conducted by Mueller and Oppenheimer (2014) found that when learning notes were handwritten rather than typed, the students' comprehension of the lesson material was stronger.

Research tells us that challenges in producing fluent, neat and legible handwriting are sometimes attributed to laziness or lack of interest (Berninger et al., 2009) and that in some cases, teachers have focused on presentation rather than content when judging the quality of a child's writing (Amundson & Weil, 2001; Connelly et al., 2005).

As children get older, they will need to develop the ability to write much more quickly while still keeping their writing legible. This will be key in meeting the National Curriculum's aim that

> by the end of Year 6, pupils' reading and writing should be sufficiently fluent and effortless for them to manage the general demands of the curriculum in Year 7, across all subjects and not just in English. (DfE, 2013, p. 31)

Hoy et al. (2011) found that while increased practice was effective in improving legibility, extended levels of practice were needed to combine legibility with speed in order to produce fluent handwriting (McCarney et al., 2013).

Guidance from the Department for Education highlights the physical nature of handwriting; pupils need to develop both larger, gross motor skills and smaller, fine motor skills. Woodfield (2004) suggests that there are three stages of motor skill development: first learners must attempt the skill, then they develop it through repetition, and finally, they consolidate it so that it is internalised and ingrained in muscle memory. In relation to handwriting, gross motor skills largely support effective posture, ensuring that core muscles in the body's trunk, shoulders and neck are sufficiently strong and stable enough to keep the head straight and to allow control of the arms which support the fine motor skills that direct the smaller muscles in the hands and fingers to execute the precise straight and curved line movements needed for letter formation.

As the child moves through these stages, less conscious cognitive effort is required and automaticity is achieved. As well as having a solid fine and gross motor base, there are many other skills involved in handwriting. In addition to motor skills, pupils also need to develop a number of visual skills such as visual perceptual and processing skills, and hand-eye and bilateral coordination skills which allow them to coordinate both sides of the body to maintain effective posture and ability to hold the paper while moving the pencil. Children develop these motor groups through physical activity including play and through activities such as picking things up, threading and cutting.

Effective posture can be supported by ensuring pupils are well-balanced on their chairs with both feet comfortably placed on the floor. Tables and chairs should be of the right height in relation to the child and each other. As well as correct posture, pupils must also be taught to grasp or grip the writing implement, typically a pencil in the early stages, correctly. This is essential for allowing the child to keep the wrist steady while they learn to use their fine motor skills to produce first lines and strokes, the patterns that make up letter forms, and then increasingly letter-like shapes. When the wrist is steady, the hand should be free to make writing movements. Without the correct pencil grip, children may find it hard to form letters correctly and/or to sustain writing without getting tired.

When learning to handwrite, children need to:

- Memorise and reproduce different letter shapes.
- Learn to connect these shapes with one or more phonemes which are used to make words.
- Develop and demonstrate the gross and fine motor skills necessary to hold a pen or pencil and control it to produce the lines and curves that make up the letter shapes.

Therefore, in addition to physical motor skills, some researchers have argued that orthographic (the part of language study that relates to letters and spelling) and memory processes are more important to handwriting (Berninger & Graham, 1998). Pupils have also been shown to benefit from practising orthographic–motor integration. This 'refers to the way in which orthographic knowledge is integrated with the motor demands of handwriting in order to produce letters and words' (Christensen, 2005, p. 441). This study demonstrated that a majority of pupils, who engaged in a carefully sequenced handwriting programme for twenty minutes daily over an eight-week period, generated not only improved handwriting but also longer and higher-quality texts compared to a control group. The programme provided sequenced practice in writing letters, words and sentences.

Research Focus: Teaching Handwriting – Three Ideas From Research

A number of research studies have shown that girls are generally better at handwriting than boys, and tend to write faster (see Medwell & Wray, 2007).

Research conducted by the United Kingdom Literacy Association and Primary National Strategy found that the aspects most often cited by the boys as a reason for disliking writing were technical (including handwriting and spelling) (UKLA, 2004).

As in the case of the other aspect of transcription – spelling – research indicates that if children have to devote large amounts of working memory to the ability to produce legible handwriting, they may have little working memory capacity left for higher-level processes such as the generation of ideas, vocabulary selection and the various stages of the writing process (Gathercole et al., 2004). While children can be encouraged to make their best attempt at spelling a word and then proceed with their composition, returning to check spellings at a later stage, handwriting cannot be sequenced in this way – it is necessary for all stages of the writing process (Christiansen, 2005). The solution is to build children's automaticity, the ability to carry out a process swiftly, accurately and without the need for conscious attention (La Berge & Samuels, 1974), so that they can free up cognitive space to focus on the other aspects of writing down their ideas.

Browne (1993, p. 81) outlines specific guidance for pupils who are left-handed. As well as ensuring that they are not sitting to the right of a right-hand pupil (so that their arms bump potentially restricting movement), seating them so that the light falls over their right shoulder can reduce shadow. Teaching left-handed children to hold the pen or pencil at least 3 cm from its point allows children to see what they write and prevents smudging. This distance can be indicated by wrapping a small elastic band around the pencil or making a pen mark which can be removed when they are ready, or you could use a pencil grip, masking or bandage tape (check whether children have any allergies) which could also make the pencil's surface less slippery. When copying, it is also helpful to ensure that the child can see whatever they are copying clearly so materials may need to be positioned to the right or written on the right side of the paper. Slanting the paper to the right (rather than square on to the child) is also helpful and letter formation should be demonstrated with your left hand (e.g. through skywriting in the air).

Document Summary: Bold Beginnings

In 2017, Her Majesty's Inspectors (HMI) visited and observed practice from 41 primary schools who had been awarded a 'good' or outstanding judgement from Ofsted in relation to the quality of their Early Years Foundation Stage (EYFS) provision and the school's overall effectiveness. The findings generated were published by Ofsted in *Bold Beginnings: The Reception Curriculum in a Sample of Good and Outstanding Primary Schools* and has informed subsequent guidance, for example, in *The Reading Framework* (DfE, 2023). Some key findings in relation to handwriting were:

The Head teachers at the schools involved in the study identified the importance of securing consistent accurate letter formation, forming letters in the right direction and starting and ending in the right place, before pupils were taught to join their letters. As a result, nearly all of them did not teach cursive (joined handwriting) or pre-cursive (forming letters with a lead-in stroke) script in Year R because they believed it slowed down children's handwriting while their muscles were still developing. A number of the Head teachers also believed that whiteboard pens were too chunky for the children's hands to grip correctly and that a mini-whiteboard surface was too slippery to allow children to develop sufficient control, advocating instead that effective handwriting practice should make use of pencils and paper.

Modelling

To teach handwriting well, you will need to be an excellent role model as far as your own handwriting goes. Your letter formation should be clear and even, and your words should be easy to read. You won't necessarily talk about this every time you model any writing at all as you won't want the children to become too focused on producing perfect handwriting at the expense of using great words and ideas, but you must always model good practice yourself and might sometimes notice out loud when you have written a word particularly well. Initial teacher education students do sometimes feel quite daunted by the idea of developing their hand-writing for a new primary school audience when they have reasonably been used to producing it mainly for themselves up until now. However, in practice, it is fairly easy to do (although might need an investment of time). Make sure that you are a good role model both when writing on the board and when writing in children's books.

Activity   Assessing Your Own Handwriting

Take some paper and a pen or pencil. Think of any sentence to write and have a go. What do you notice about your own body posture, pencil grip and the way you like to position the paper? Which letters do you join? Which letters do you leave to stand alone? Why? Are you a good model for the children? What might you work on?

Now think about the resources – does anything change if you use different-sized pens/pencils and write on different surfaces? How might this make things easier or more challenging for your learners? How does this knowledge change the provision you would make in your classroom?

Choosing a Learning Objective

In Year R, handwriting practice may focus on teaching patterns that will support letter formation at a later point, for example, focusing on patterns which build on the three basic letter shapes:

- l, for example, the long ladder.
- c, for example, the curly caterpillar.
- r, for example, the one-armed robot. (DfE, 2009, p. 2).

Children's initial practice in handwriting is likely to be integrated with their phonics teaching, learning to write each letter in turn as they are introduced to the sound it represents. In discrete sessions, children may practise one letter or number, or may begin to practise letters in families. Handwriting families typically group letters with similar formation together, although schools may well include different letters in different groups depending on whether they follow a particular handwriting scheme or other guidance. For example, guidance published in 2009 by the Department for Education identifies four main movement groups as follows:

- Down and off in another direction, exemplified by the letter l (long ladder): letters i, j, l, t, u (v, w with rounded bases)
- Down and retrace upwards, exemplified by the letter r (one-armed robot): letters b, h, k, m, n, p, r; and numbers 2, 3, 5, which follow a clockwise direction
- Anti-clockwise round, exemplified by the letter c (curly caterpillar): letters c, a, d, e, g, o, q, f, s; and numbers: 0, 6, 8, 9
- Zigzag letters: v, w, x, z; and numbers: 1, 4, 7 (DfE, 2009, p. 5).

Multi-sensory approaches can be supportive for pupils who are not yet secure in letter formation. Suggested activities to support this include getting learners to trace over letters made from tactile materials such as carpet or sandpaper or in trays of sand or jelly so they can feel the shape, painting big letter shapes, and completing letters made of dots (Medwell et al., 2014).

Prior to planning and teaching your own lessons, you will, of course, need to find out what the school's approach is; your class teacher will be able to give you a good idea of how many letters within the group to practise, how long to spend on your own use of modelling with think aloud, and how to plan and pace children's practice time.

As children move into Year 2, you may begin to model the use of joins between some letters. Again, find out about the school's approach to this as some may teach diagonal joins before horizontal ones, and, as identified in the National Curriculum, children will not necessarily be taught to join all letters, particularly those that end with the pen or pencil position to the left such as s, j, b, y and g. In Year 2, the idea of considering the relative size of letters is introduced, indicating that there may be an increased focus on practising words. From Year 3 onwards, the focus is on legible, consistent and high-quality handwriting in which letters are even in height and width, and ascenders (lines that go upwards such as in the letters l, t and b) and descenders (lines that go down below the line as in the letters p, j and y) parallel. As these objectives are quite broad, you may wish to break them down into smaller chunks, for example, 'to be able to write ascenders of the same height' unless you are focusing on developing children's ability to apply all their handwriting knowledge within a note-taking task, for example.

Lesson Plan

Here is one suggestion for what a lesson plan might look like for a Year 2 class (Table 16.1). It focuses on one of patterns identified in *Appendix 1* of the National Curriculum. You will be able to adapt it for younger or older pupils; to do this, consider how long they can focus their attention when listening to a teacher or working with others, and how you could simplify or increase the level of challenge.

Relevant prior learning: Pupils have learned letter formation for all letters. The majority are secure in this. A few are still developing their accuracy.

What will children learn: To be able to form letters of the correct size in relation to each other

Planned next steps: Practise this skill to develop consistency and automaticity. Move on to consolidating this skill while using spacing between words that reflects the size of the letters.

What will effective learning look like (this may be phrased as success criteria depending on the school):

- Hold the correct posture.
- Maintain good pencil grip.
- Form each letter accurately.
- Letters are well-sized in relation to each other.

How will learning be assessed:

- Observation of pupils.
- Review of their work after the lesson.

Table 16.1 A lesson plan for teaching handwriting

Today's lesson sequence/content
1:00: Ask children to recall their knowledge of which are the six tail letters (y, j, p, f, g, q) by telling a partner. Check and write them up so children can see them, modelling clear and accurate formation. Ask children to revisit the formation of these letters by writing on their partner's back or the carpet with a finger, or skywriting in the air (they could say the script aloud/in their heads to remind themselves of the formation if they want to).
1:05: Ask children to recall their knowledge of the six tall letters (t, d, h, k, l, b) by telling a partner. Check and write them up so children can see them, modelling clear and accurate formation. Ask children to revisit the formation of these letters by writing on their partner's back or the carpet with a finger, or skywriting in the air (they could say the script aloud/in their heads to remind themselves of the formation if they want to).
1:10: Introduce today's learning by sharing the lesson objective and make the connection to how forming our letters so they are the right height when they're next to each other will help the reader to read our writing so they can understand quickly what we want them to know.
1:12: Model with think-aloud, say the whole sentence, repeat it, count the number of words then model writing each word, thinking aloud about the height of each letter before writing and checking back each word to note where I did well and if there's anything I'll try even harder to achieve with the next word. Practice sentence: I like to eat cheese.
Model once more, this time using a second line to guide the height of the halfway/body letters (a, e, o, c etc.).
1:15: Independent practice – children to write the sentence five times.
1:25: Plenary – ask the children to look back at their work and tell a partner: how well they did and what they will try to do even better next time.

Introduction to the Lesson

In this introduction, the link is made to the children's prior learning. An alternative opening could have been to share some handwriting already completed and ask children to work with a partner to compare it against the learning objective(s) and/or success criteria and give feedback, asking them to explain its strengths and what would improve it further. This could have enabled them to articulate the process, reinforcing their understanding of the success criteria. This could also be a good opening for the next lesson (or a future one which focuses on the same skill) as a way for them to practise recalling their knowledge and for the teacher to assess what they have remembered. An element of fun could have been included by making the author of the opening piece of handwriting a character known to the children (some classrooms have one or more such characters whose full identity remains a mystery as they only visit the classroom when everyone has gone home and communicate with the children in writing, or in the shape of a lovable cuddly toy or puppet, or even an adult in costume, who routinely asks for advice from the children to help him or her learn new knowledge and skills) where the letters are not consistent in height and are therefore tricky to read.

The Main Lesson

The sentence used in this lesson has been kept fairly simple as this is the first time of practising this skill, freeing up more cognitive space for a focus on handwriting. It is also fairly short so that children can write the whole sentence a few times, reviewing their work after each attempt and seeing if they can improve the letter heights on their next go After they have tried the sentence a few times, they could think of their own food instead of cheese.

You could have started with individual words rather than a sentence, or modelled writing a keyword a few times, getting the children to have a go, and then moving to a short phrase or whole sentence if they seemed ready.

The practice sentence could link to any class initiative or routine such as 'sentence of the week' or dictated sentences used in phonics recently. It could use any recently learned common exception words to reinforce learning. It could also link to any genre of writing the children are currently studying, for example, if they are doing some work on information texts they could use a sentence which reinforces the style such as 'Polar bears are wild animals and they move slowly'.

Using Resources

Pupils can choose the paper they would like to use from the following: standard lines, wide lines and second lines marked (standard and/or wide depending on the needs of the children).

Have pencil grips for those who need them and illustrated prompt cards with posture/grip reminders which the children can collect independently or be guided to use.

Plenary

In this plenary, the children review their work. You could instead pick up key points from their practice, for example, 'I saw that quite a few of you found it tricky when you had a short letter straight after a tall letter as in the word 'cheese'. Talk to your partner to see if you can think of any ways that would help us to get this right next time' (you could these to the working wall display).

Adaptive/Responsive Teaching

Some possible ways in which you could adapt the learning for those needing additional scaffolding or stretch and challenge are:

- Remodel the process of letter formation while maintaining a consistent height for those who need it.
- Ensure that children can clearly see anything they are copying – it may to be too challenging for them to switch between looking at the board and looking at their work so you may want to provide a desk copy so children can see it more easily, and some children might need individual words written into their books or onto their paper so they can copy directly below the model.
- Prompt children to make use of different resources (e.g., standard or wide-lined paper).
- Ask children to work in pairs, taking turns to write one word while the other watches and gives advice.
- Build an adult-led focus group for more structured guided work (e.g., guiding the whole group to write one word at a time, then leading a guided check).
- Focus either the teacher or teaching assistant on giving instant feedback to target pupils and intervening as necessary; the other adult can monitor and assess the rest of the class.
- Pupils could practise writing other sentences, either linked to classwork or composing their own.

Providing Feedback

As highlighted in this chapter, feedback is likely to focus on posture, grip, letter formation, understanding of the similarities between letter formation if teaching families, letter size in relation to the others, and the extent to which diagonal and horizontal joins are used correctly and to which ascenders and descenders are parallel.

Where Am I Going?

You will have primarily pre-empted this through your lesson introduction where you shared the objectives and modelled what success will look like in terms of both product/task (what will a good piece look like?) and process (what will you need to do to get there perhaps in the form of success criteria), but you may see opportunities where giving children positive feedback to remind children of the lesson objective(s) would be helpful to them, for example, 'Remember to check the learning objective/success criteria from time to time to check you're on the right track' will help children to develop their metacognitive monitoring skills.

How Am I Going?

Remind yourself of the success criteria and give feedback in relation to this. Handwriting can be a sensitive issue and we don't of course want to be overly negative when a child is trying to coordinate so many skills at once. Bryce-Clegg (2013) suggests that it is really important that we celebrate children's first achievements, but also enthuse them about trying out 'different' (rather than right or wrong) ways. As you observe children, check their posture and grip. You will also want to check letter formation and possibly letter size and speed of production depending on the objectives. Highlight what the child is doing well – as well as supporting motivation, this will help them to see which aspects of their writing are well under control so that they can release some focus to direct towards the next steps, and remember to be specific in your use of praise, for example, 'Well done Joe, you have formed all your 't's and 'l's correctly there, remembering to start at the top and go straight down'. If the approach your school uses makes use of scripts you can repeat those to reinforce them.

Where to Next?

Make sure you are clear and don't overload the learners' working memories. Again, you can reinforce their use of scripts by reminding them of any steps they are missing. Once more, this might be in the form of a reminder ('Remember to keep your feet flat on the floor'), a question (Can you make all your ascenders parallel from this point?) or a hint (Try holding the pencil a little further away from the point but keep that hand position/grip).

Assessing Children's Written Work

Of course this will be of limited value for younger pupils as you will not be able to observe their posture, grip or letter formation in action. It may be useful to review if you gave a child verbal feedback in the lesson and can therefore see to what extent the child experienced success as a result. For older pupils, you can get an overview of whether each child was able to maintain quality when practising speed or note taking for example, and may be able to identify pupils at risk of falling behind depending on how much writing they managed to produce where this was the goal. You may also assess written work as a way of gathering useful information for future teaching or to inform whether a specific intervention is needed.

Application of Learning

As already considered, modelling is key. You will be presenting the children with lots of examples of your handwriting through your modelled, scribed or shared writing, and when providing any written feedback to your pupils. Make sure that you are a good role model both when writing on the board and when writing in children's books.

When thinking about the children's application of learning, you could remind children that they could have a go at trying to make all their letters the right height in relation to each other when they are completing other writing, but think carefully about how you will judge when this is achievable and won't distract them from other writing goals, particularly composition. Review their handwriting at regular intervals – when they are secure with this skill, transfer to writing in general should become more automatic.

Summary

Throughout this chapter, the effective teaching of handwriting has been explored, and key aspects of a meaningful and high-quality curriculum for teaching handwriting, starting with an integrated approach though the teaching of phonics and building on this through the primary age phase, are proposed. The importance of making connections to the wider English curriculum is established.

Further Reading

To find out more about principles of effective practice:

1   Visit the website of the National Handwriting Association https://nha-handwriting.org.uk/
2   This article on handwriting is written by an occupational therapist who offers an interesting insight into posture and grip. There is also a link to some useful videos on teaching handwriting: https://www.tes.com/magazine/archive/how-teach-handwriting-comprehensive-guide
3   This easy-to-read book explores practice for younger pupils, looking at how to develop children's enthusiasm and readiness to become young writers: Bryce-Clegg (2013) Getting Them Ready To Write, published by Bloomsbury Publishing PLC.

References

Amundson, S. J., & Weil, M. (2001). Prewriting and handwriting skills. In J. Case-Smith, A. S. Allen, & P. Nuse Pratt (Eds.), *Occupational therapy for children* (pp. 545–566). C. V. Mosby.

Berninger, V. W., Abbott, R. D., Augsburger, A., & Garcia, N. (2009). Comparison of pen and keyboard transcription modes in children with and without learning disabilities. *Learning Disability Quarterly, 32*, 123–141.

Berninger, V. W., & Graham, S. (1998). Language by hand: A synthesis of a decade of research on handwriting. *Handwriting Review, 12,* 11–25.

Browne, A. (1993) *Developing language and literacy 3–8.* SAGE.

Bryce-Clegg, A. (2013) *Getting them ready to write.* Bloomsbury Publishing.

Christensen, C. A. (2005). The role of orthographic-motor integration in the production of creative and well-structured written text for students in secondary school. *Educational Psychology, 25*(5), 441–453.

Connelly, V., Dockrell, J. E., & Barnett, J. (2005). The slow handwriting of undergraduate students constrains overall performance in exam essays. *Educational Psychology, 25,* 99–107.

Department for Education. (2013). *The National Curriculum in England: English programmes of study: Key stages 1 and 2 National curriculum in England.* Crown Copyright.

Department for Education. (2021a). *Statutory framework for the early years foundation stage Setting the standards for learning, development and care for children from birth to five.* Crown Copyright.

Department for Education. (2021b). *The reading Framework: Teaching the foundations of literacy.* Crown Copyright.

DfE. (2009). *The National Strategies-Early Years – Gateway to writing- developing handwriting.* https://www.foundationyeasrs.org.uk/wp-content/uploads/2011/11/Gateway-to-WritingDeveloping-handwriting.pdf. Accessed on August 31, 2022.

Gathercole, S. E., Pickering, S. J., Knight, C., & Stegmann, Z. (2004). Working memory skills and educational attainment: Evidence from national curriculum assessments at 7 and 14 years of age. *Applied Cognitive Psychology, 18,* 1–16.

Hoy, M. M. P., Egan, M. Y., & Feder, K. P. (2011). A systematic review of interventions to improve handwriting. *Canadian Journal of Occupational Therapy, 78,* 13–25.

La Berge, D., & Samuels, S. J. (1974). Toward a theory of automatic information processing. *Cognitive Psychology, 6,* 283–323.

Longcamp, M., Zerbato-Poudou, M., & Velay, J. (2005). The influence of writing practice on letter recognition in preschool children: A comparison between handwriting and typing. *Acta Psychologica, 119*(1), 67–79.

McCarney, D., Peters, L., Jackson, S., Thomas, M., & Kirby, A. (2013). Does poor handwriting conceal literacy potential in primary school children? *International Journal of Disability, Development and Education, 60*(2), 105–118.

Medwell, J., & Wray, D. (2007) Handwriting: What do we know and what do we need to know? *Literacy, 41*(1), 10–15.

Medwell, J., Wray, D., Minns, H., Griffiths, V., & Coates, E. (2014). *Primary English teaching theory and practice* (7th ed.). SAGE.

Mueller, P. A., & Oppenheimer, D. M. (2014). The pen is mightier than the keyboard: Advantages of longhand over laptop note taking. *Psychological Science, 25*(6), 1159–1168.

Ofsted. (2017). *Bold beginnings: The Reception curriculum in a sample of good and outstanding primary schools.* Crown Copyright.

United Kingdom Literacy Association/Primary National Strategy. (2004). *Raising boys' achievements in writing.* UKLA.

Woodfield, L. (2004). *Physical development in the early years.* Bloomsbury Publishing.

INDEX